John le Carré

John le Carré

Peter Lewis

Frederick Ungar Publishing Co.
New York

Grateful acknowledgment is made for permission to reprint lines from "September 1, 1939." Copyright © 1940 by W.H. Auden. From *The English Auden: Poems, Essays & Dramatic Writings 1927–1939* by W.H. Auden, edited by Edward Mendelson. Reprinted by permission of Random House, Inc. and Faber and Faber Ltd.

Printed in the United States of America
Designed by Ted Bernstein

Library of Congress Cataloging in Publication Data
Lewis, Peter Elfed.
John le Carré.

Bibliography: p.
Includes index.
1. Le Carré, John 1931– —Criticism and interpretation. I. Title.
PR6062.E33Z75 1985 823′.914 84-24038
ISBN 0-8044-2243-5
ISBN 0-8044-6184-8 (pbk.)

For Maggie
who aided and abetted

Like war, spying is a dirty business. Shed of its alleged glory, a soldier's job is to kill. Peel away the claptrap of espionage and the spy's job is to betray trust. The only justification a soldier or a spy can have is the moral worth of the cause he represents.

—William Hood, *Mole* (1982)

Contents

The Roots of the Square 1
An Introduction

1

A Far from Saintly George: 14
Call for the Dead (1961)

2

An Exercise in Class 40
A Murder of Quality (1962)

3

Blind Man's Double Bluff 59
The Spy Who Came in from the Cold (1963)

4

Peter Pan's Last Victim 78
The Looking Glass War (1965)

5

Pursuing the Pursuer 96
A Small Town in Germany (1968)

6

To Catch a Mole 111
Tinker, Tailor, Soldier, Spy (1974)

7

The Spy Who Went into the Heat 138
The Honourable Schoolboy (1977)

8

Ahab Chasing His Big White Whale 164
Smiley's People (1980)

9

A Country Not Ours to Give 181
The Little Drummer Girl (1983)

10

Notes 213
Bibliography 219
Index 223

John le Carré

1

The Roots of the Square: An Introduction

In a sense, John le Carré was born in 1961 with the publication of his first novel, *Call for the Dead.* At that time the man behind the nom de plume, David John Moore Cornwell, was a member of the diplomatic staff of the British Embassy in Bonn, apparently engaged on gathering intelligence, and the Foreign Office expected people in his position to use pseudonyms for any published work. Since *Call for the Dead* is about a British counterintelligence investigation involving East Germany, this requirement might be considered not unreasonable in his case. The account le Carré once gave of how he acquired his pen name has been repeated so often by journalists that it has been accepted as the truth; but as any student of his work should know, "truth" is slippery and elusive, and he, like any artist questioned about his own secret world, is likely to resort to disinformation. Interviewed by James Cameron after the publication of *Tinker, Tailor, Soldier, Spy* in 1974, he said, "I got 'John le Carré' from a London shop-front I once passed on a bus,"[1] but attempts to trace such a shop have proved fruitless. When *Time* did a cover story on le Carré to coincide with the publication of *The Honourable Schoolboy* in 1977, he admitted that his previous explanation was "perhaps . . . a lie I've come to believe."[2] He was more forthright in an interview he gave to Miriam Gross in 1980 when *Smiley's People*, the third novel in *The Quest for Karla* trilogy, was published: "I've told so many lies about where I got the name from, but I really don't remember."[3] A writer who is as sensitive to language as le Carré and who clearly takes pains to name his characters appropriately would hardly have adopted a name in the seemingly casual way he suggested to Cameron. Even if le Carré did come across the name somewhere, he must have pondered it deeply before committing himself to it, as he must also have done in the case of his principal series character, George Smiley, who is now as firmly established in the British national consciousness as Sherlock Holmes, and who may well be sent letters to 9 Bywater Street, Chelsea, just as letters continue to arrive for Holmes at 221B Baker Street.

For a man with little to smile about, Smiley's surname is distinctly ironic, but his first name carries opposing connotations. George is the name of the dragon-slaying patron saint of England and also of the two kings (George V and VI) who were heads of state when Britain emerged victorious from World Wars I and II respectively. Since Smiley was born in the first decade of the twentieth century, most of his life at the time of le Carré's first novel had been spent during their reigns. His name is therefore subtly ambiguous, corresponding to the divided nature of a man possessing heroic qualities even though he does not correspond at all to the conventional conception of a heroic adventurer. Some other examples of imaginatively assigned names are Maston, Smiley's insufferable superior in *Call for the Dead*, carrying reverberations of both "master" and "mastodon"; Mendel, with connotations of "mending," appropriate for the reliable policeman introduced in the same novel; Lacon, one of Smiley's superiors in *The Quest for Karla*, suggesting both "laconic" and "con man"; Turner, a British intelligence officer in *A Small Town in Germany* (1968) renowned for his interrogation techniques and therefore likely to "turn" or convert foreign agents into double agents; and Westerby, a conspicuously Western agent in the Far East in *The Honourable Schoolboy*.

Faced with choosing a name for himself, David Cornwell consulted his first publisher, Victor Gollancz, who "was all for a couple of strong monosyllables like 'Chuck Smith' "[4]; but as le Carré told Byron Rogers in 1982 he "reacted against that," preferring "a posh name."[5] The presence of "le" undoubtedly adds dignity to his pen name, which sounds as though it might belong to a descendant of the medieval Anglo-Norman aristocracy. As one of the best-known authors in the world today, le Carré has more than succeeded in doing what he told Miriam Gross he hoped his nom de plume might do for a young novelist: "I thought that to break up a name and give it a slightly foreign look would have the effect of printing it on people's memories."[6] There is therefore considerable irony, of which he, as an excellent linguist, must have been fully aware, in that the English equivalent of the name is John the Square, with all the connotations of old-fashioned fuddy-duddiness that the word now evokes. Indeed the anglicized form seems like a comic parallel to John the Baptist. Anyone interested in the wide range of meanings and associations of "*carré*" in French should consult the long entry in the *Grand Dictionnaire Encyclopédique Larousse*, but it is worth noting here that the phrase "*une tête carrée*" (literally, a square head) can mean both a level-headed man and—almost the opposite—a stubborn man. For a writer who excels in depicting moral ambiguities, it is appropriate that his chosen name should itself convey contradictory overtones. The name "Carré" even has connections with spying. During World War II a key French member of the predominantly Polish spy network Interallie, which functioned with considerable success in France in 1940 and 1941 until betrayed to the Germans, was Mathilde Carré, who agreed to collaborate with her captors and became a double agent before being trapped by British Intelligence. In the later part of the nineteenth century the extraordinary British spy Thomas Beach, who successfully penetrated the Fenian Brotherhood of Irish republicans in the USA and monitored its activities for over twenty years, used the French name Henri le Caron.

Because this book is essentially a critical appreciation of le Carré's novels, not a literary biography, only a brief outline of his life is necessary. Much of what is known about this retiring man, who shuns rather than courts the limelight despite his world-wide celebrity, has emerged in interviews he has given over the years, the most important of which are listed in the Bibliography. But even here a word of caution is in order. Interviews published in the form of question and answer, as most of the major British ones have been, are more trustworthy than those written up by journalists with quotations from le Carré embedded in them. When *The Honourable Schoolboy* was published, *The Sunday Times* featured a short piece by Philip Oakes based on an interview with le Carré,[7] for which the paper subsequently had to issue an apology admitting misrepresentation. Exactly five years later Nicholas Wapshott's "Profile" of the author for *The Times*[8] provoked a forceful rebuke from Graham Greene in a letter to the paper, in which he corrected what he saw as Wapshott's complete distortion of the relationship between the two novelists and concluded: "I feel sorry for Mr le Carré as I often feel sorry for myself when I have been unwise enough to give an interview to a journalist."[9]

Le Carré was born on 19 October 1931 in the coastal town of Poole in Dorset, not far from the heart of Thomas Hardy country. His childhood, about which he has probably revealed most in his interview with Miriam Gross, might euphemistically be described as disturbed. When he was very young his father Ronnie served a prison sentence for fraud, and not long afterwards his mother Olive deserted her family, leaving her two sons in the care of their father. Le Carré was out of his teens before he saw her again. Whatever else it was, life with Ronnie cannot have been dull. Le Carré has described his father as "magical," "a colourful and curious personality," "a fantasist," "a Micawber character who always managed to spend twice as much as he earned—or twice as much as he obtained," and as a result the two brothers found themselves "living in the style of millionaire paupers."[10] What is particularly relevant to le Carré's future career as a writer of spy fiction is that at an early age he inhabited a world in which secrecy, deception, and conspiracy were unexceptional, and on several occasions he has used espionage as a metaphor to describe aspects of his childhood. For example, in a television program about him that coincided with the publication of *The Little Drummer Girl* in 1983, le Carré told his interviewer Melvyn Bragg: "I, from very early, lived a secret life, an inward life, became extremely secretive, and began to think that I was, so to speak, born into occupied territory, because the catastrophes in our family were so great and there were so many things that I couldn't reveal that I seemed to go about in disguise."[11]

Ronnie's flamboyant life-style was in reaction to his lower-middle-class and Nonconformist background, and he was determined to turn his sons into "fake gentry" by sending them to a socially prestigious public school; to achieve this, notes le Carré, "he was prepared to steal if necessary; and I'm afraid he did."[12] Ronnie was, in effect, infiltrating his sons into the social level he himself aspired to, and the end justified the means. Le Carré and his older brother Tony consequently "arrived in educated middle-class society feeling almost like spies, knowing that we had no social hinterland, that we had a great deal to conceal and a lot of pretending to do."[13] Something of le Carré's own experience as a schoolboy probably went into his creation of Bill Roach, the lonely outsider at Thursgood's preparatory school in *Tinker, Tailor, Soldier, Spy*; the former British spy who teaches there, Jim Prideaux, recognizes that Roach has the makings of a good agent and actually employs him as a schoolboy spy. The financial difficulties experienced by Charlie's father in *The Little Drummer Girl*, which she melodramatically inflates into a crime for which he is imprisoned, may again be an echo of le Carré's childhood, although Ronnie's problems were of an altogether different magnitude.

In preparation for a public school education le Carré attended St. Andrew's Preparatory School in the Thames Valley town of Pangbourne, and then went to Sherborne School in Dorset. His brother attended a different but nearby school, Radley. Le Carré refused to imbibe the prevailing public school ethos and "defected from Sherborne at the age of 16" before taking his university entrance examinations. Instead he went, like "a political refugee," to Switzerland where he studied at the University of Berne for a year, mastering the German language. This was the beginning of what he calls "my whole German connection,"[14] and he took the opportunity to see for himself the ruins of Hitler's Third Reich by traveling through postwar Germany before its reconstruction. In one way or another, Germany plays a part in a majority of his novels, including four of the first five.

When he was called up for military service, his command of German made him an obvious choice for special duties in the chaotic aftermath of World War II, and he served with the British Army of occupation in Austria as an intelligence officer, spending most of his time interrogating some of the many displaced persons living in refugee camps. To resort to the parlance of popular journalism, a spy was born. After national service le Carré was accepted by Lincoln College to read Modern Languages at Oxford in 1952, and although he had to withdraw for a year in order to earn money by teaching, he graduated in 1956 with first-class honors. It was during his Oxford period that le Carré married for the first time, his bride, Alison Ann Veronica Sharp, being the daughter of a high-ranking officer in the Royal Air Force. It has often been pointed out that one of her names is shared by George Smiley's wife, Ann, but the resemblance stops there. George Smiley himself is partly modeled on le Carré's tutor at Lincoln College and a former Chaplain at Sherborne School, Rev. Vivian Green, described by le Carré as "my mentor at Oxford . . . whom I admired very much."[15]

Like another highly successful English novelist of his generation, John Fowles, le Carré studied European rather than English literature at the university, and if Fowles has been strongly influenced by French writers, le Carré sees himself as owing a literary debt to German writers. Questioned by Miriam Gross about the writers who mean most to him, le Carré replied that he had been "enormously influenced by Greene," was "passionate about Conrad," and loved "the big French storytellers," especially Balzac, but that "the strongest literary influence was all that German literature that I devoured either compulsorily or voluntarily."[16] In an interview with Michael Barber in 1978 le Carré said that

> having a largely German-oriented education has made me very responsive to 19th century German literature. The predominant form of the lately-emerging novel in Germany then was what they called *Bildungsroman*, a novel of education, in which a single character was taken through a variety of rooms, as you might say, a variety of encounters and experiences, and brought out at the other end changed and generally a morally-reformed figure. If that didn't happen there was an apocalypse of some kind and he was destroyed. And I think one could say that to a great extent that form is something I've clung to in my own novels. Generally speaking, they are finally about one person.[17]

It is precisely in these terms that le Carré described his treatment of Jerry Westerby, "the honourable schoolboy" in the novel of that name, when the book was published, likening it to his handling of Leamas, "the spy" in *The Spy Who Came in from the Cold* (1963), both characters moving "through a series of experiences until they arrive at their apotheosis."[18] Whereas *Bildungsroman* usually implies the education of a young person, le Carré employs it more loosely to apply to characters in different age groups, both Leamas and Westerby being middle-aged. The pattern le Carré draws attention to is obvious enough in the case of Charlie in *The Little Drummer Girl*, but it also has relevance to Avery in *The Looking Glass War* (1965), Turner in *A Small Town in Germany*, Cassidy in *The Naive and Sentimental Lover* (1971), and even to the much older Smiley in both *Call for the Dead* and *The Quest for Karla* trilogy.

After Oxford, le Carré was recruited not by British Intelligence but by probably the most famous of all English public schools, Eton College, where he taught German for two years. When asked whether he thought public schools should be abolished, le Carré said: "I wish devoutly that we could get rid of public schools, and what I've seen of them only entrenches that wish."[19] His direct experience of the public school system, first as a pupil at Sherborne and then as a tutor at Eton, clearly convinced him of its social undesirability, an attitude that finds expression in fictional form in his second novel, *A Murder of Quality* (1962), with its devastatingly satirical presentation of an imaginary public school, Carne. Le Carré may have disliked Eton, but he nevertheless found it "absolutely fascinating":

> I had never had any experience of the British ruling class before and it probably coloured my later writing more than any other experience.

> People who rail against the English upper classes don't know how awful they really are—the way they talk, the way they function. Their prejudices are absolutely stunning.
>
> At the time that I was there we had, I think, 12 or 13 Old Etonians in the Cabinet. I was there during the Suez crisis, and I remember we got up a letter from young masters, which we sent to *The Times*, saying that we wished to dissociate ourselves from the actions of Old Etonians in the Cabinet.[20]

The way in which this experience colored his writing is most conspicuous in *A Murder of Quality*, but combined with his subsequent experiences of British Intelligence, the Foreign Office, and diplomatic life, it does seem to manifest itself in the other four novels in which Smiley is a major character—the treatment of Maston in *Call for the Dead*, for example, or of Roddy Martindale in *Tinker, Tailor, Soldier, Spy*, or of Oliver Lacon throughout the trilogy—and even more strongly in *The Looking Glass War* and *A Small Town in Germany*.

Le Carré left Eton in 1958 and, according to James Cameron, "had a shot at freelance illustrating"[21] before joining the Foreign Service. He was, for example, responsible for the drawings in Maxwell Knight's book *Talking Birds* (1961). However, in a *Newsweek* special report published at the same time as *The Little Drummer Girl*, Alexis Gelber and Edward Behr claimed that reliable sources had finally confirmed the long-held though invariably denied suspicion that le Carré had himself been a "spy" and that on leaving Eton and before entering the Foreign Service he worked for the Security Service (MI5) under none other than Maxwell Knight.[22] According to the *Newsweek* investigators, le Carré's career in the Foreign Service from 1960 to 1964, first as a second secretary at the Embassy in Bonn and subsequently as a consul in Hamburg, was devoted to work for the Secret Intelligence Service (SIS or MI6). Le Carré has always been admired for the convincing realism with which he creates the world of intelligence in his novels, with all its boring, humdrum routine, and from the first he has given the impression that he was writing to some extent from the inside. His eventual admission, which he made in his television interview with Melvyn Bragg shortly after the *Newsweek* report, consequently came as no surprise: "I wasn't Mata Hari and I wasn't Himmler's aunt, but it would be stupid of me to pretend that I was not, like Somerset Maugham, Graham Greene, and lots of other writers, for a time engaged in that work. . . . I have always tried to deny it and keep away from the subject, and I intend to go on doing so."[23] Although *Newsweek* has taken the credit for "blowing" le Carré's cover, the Moscow *Literary Gazette* identified him as a former intelligence agent over seventeen years earlier in 1965, but this attracted little attention in the West and was in any case easily dismissed as a smear on a novelist considered to be a literary Cold War warrior in the Soviet Union.

Le Carré did not begin writing seriously until he was nearly thirty, and completed his first three novels while employed by the Foreign Office. This, no doubt, helps to explain why they are his shortest books. The runaway sales of his third novel, *The Spy Who Came in from the Cold*, gave him the financial security to abandon his diplomatic career and become a full-time writer, something he has pursued with considerable success for the last twenty years. Le Carré's first marriage ended in divorce in 1971, but in the following year he married Valerie Jane Eustace, an editor at Hodder and Stoughton, his British publishers during the 1970s and 1980s. From his two marriages le Carré has four sons. Apart from his occasional travels to carry out research for his novels, he divides his time between his London home in Hampstead, his rural retreat on the southwest tip of England near Penzance in Cornwall, and his mountain chalet in Switzerland. Virtually all his creative energy as a writer has gone into his ten novels, although he has published a couple of short stories and tried his hand at television drama. He has also written a long essay about the most notorious Soviet "mole" to have operated inside British Intelligence, Harold "Kim" Philby; an appreciation of one of the most renowned of living British photographers, Don McCullin, included in a book of McCullin's work with the Conradian title *Hearts of Darkness* (1980); and newspaper feature articles about the Palestinian problem, in which he became particularly interested while writing *The Little Drummer Girl*.

The critical problem posed by le Carré's fiction is exemplified by two recent reference books. He rightly receives a substantial entry in *Who's Who in Spy Fiction* (1977), compiled by Donald McCormick, but he is not among the 106 novelists considered worthy of inclusion in *British Novelists Since 1960* (1983), Volume 14 of the sumptuous, American-produced *Dictionary of Literary Biography*. Similarly, le Carré features prominently in two fairly recent historical surveys of spy fiction, Julian Symons's "A Short History of the Spy Story"[24] and Michael Gilbert's "The Spy in Fact and Fiction,"[25] but is conspicuous by his absence from comparable surveys of the postwar English novel. This difference in treatment corresponds to the distinction frequently made between popular or entertainment fiction and serious or art fiction, a distinction that would have puzzled many major novelists of the eighteenth and nineteenth centuries, who managed to be popular and serious, entertaining and artistic. A regrettable consequence of the achievements of the great modernist novelists in the first half of the twentieth century has been an intellectual suspicion of traditional fictional methods and storytelling and a tendency to exalt technical innovation, poetic experimentation, and any novelistic aspiration to the condition of music. Tired of the conventional novel, we have had, in France, not only the *nouveau roman* but the *nouveau nouveau roman*, while in the English-speaking world the postmodernist novel seems to be giving way to the postpostmodernist one. This is bound to leave a novelist like le Carré, who upholds a nineteenth-century and therefore old-fashioned conception of narrative art while also exploiting the potential of a popular genre, well and truly out in the cold as far as the academic world is concerned.

It will readily be admitted that he is excellent of his kind, the best of all possible spy novelists, the highest of highbrows in his field, the purveyor of intriguing entertainment for the thinking man, but in all such judgments there is an implicit condemnation—he is not a "real" novelist in the way that, for example, William Golding and John Fowles are. There is an interesting difference between le Carré and Graham Greene in this respect. Greene has written a number of novels involving spies, humorously in *Our Man in Havana* (1958) but usually seriously as in *The Confidential Agent* (1939) and *The Human Factor* (1978), yet because these books do not predominate in his oeuvre he is accepted as a novelist; academic respectability has been accorded to Greene even though a number of his novels, especially in the 1930s, were aimed at a popular readership. Of le Carré's oeuvre, however, only *The Naive and Sentimental Lover* is considered "straight" because the other nine make use of espionage, detection, or crime, so that he is stamped as that lesser breed, a thriller writer or spy novelist. Furthermore it is Donald McCormick's contention in his introduction to *Who's Who in Spy Fiction* that, whereas detective fiction has "come to be accepted as a branch of literature," spy fiction has not and "has been much more the subject of sneers and derision."[26] It is true that "some of the best-known and most prolific writers of this genre have given the spy story a bad name,"[27] as McCormick claims, but it is also true that, in the recent past, academic literary criticism in the English-speaking world, under the impact of Marxist and structuralist literary theory, has taken a more positive interest in popular genres than in the days when moralistic criticism was dominant and popular genres were ignored except for the occasional grunt of indignant dismissal.

Ralph Harper's pioneering existentialist study, *The World of the Thriller* (1969), is a landmark, and important studies since then include Joan Rockwell's "Normative Attitudes of Spies in Fiction" in *Mass Culture Revisited* (edited by Bernard Rosenberg and David Manning White, 1971), John G. Cawelti's *Adventure, Mystery, and Romance: Formula Stories as Art and Popular Culture* (1976), Bruce Merry's *Anatomy of the Spy Thriller* (1977), Jerry Palmer's *Thrillers: Genesis and Structure of a Popular Genre* (1978), and Stephen Knight's *Form and Ideology in Crime Fiction* (1980). Nevertheless there is a tendency in some of this recent theorizing to impose new or reinforce old categories, which can be illuminating but also procrustean. It is salutary to remember that Graham Greene labeled *Brighton Rock* (1938), one of his grimmest and most intensely "Catholic" novels, an "Entertainment," presumably because it employs thriller conventions, even though these are so radically transformed as to be almost unrecognizable. The human mind needs classifications but, as in the case of Greene's description, classifications can be falsifications.

The term "spy fiction," like "detective novel" or "mystery," suggests a type of novel that is inherently restricted by certain formulas and stereotypes peculiar to itself, and in many cases this is self-evidently true, but not all novels dealing with either espionage or crime can be designated in this way. No one has ever called *Crime and Punishment* a mere crime novel or Conrad's *The Secret Agent* and *Under Western Eyes* mere spy stories. What is of concern here is a spectrum or continuum of possibilities rather than fixed categories. At one end are the crudest blood-and-thunder adventures of secret agents, and at the other great novels of the ironic sophistication of *The Secret Agent*. Le Carré is not of Conrad's stature, but he is well towards Conrad's end of the spectrum, and is certainly much closer to Conrad than to John Buchan and Ian Fleming. When interviewed for *Time* in 1977, le Carré said: "When I brought back, but did not invent, the realistic spy story, it was misinterpreted as a great new wave."[28] Even though le Carré did not invent the realistic spy story—if we exclude Conrad, that distinction probably belongs to Somerset Maugham in his Ashenden stories, which have influenced le Carré—he was being overmodest in what he said. It is often urged that le Carré was bringing back the qualities of Eric Ambler's work of the 1930s, but as Julian Symons noted in 1974 even le Carré's first novel "represented a distinct turn in the spy story, offering something quite different from the easy sophistication of Eric Ambler" let alone "the Superman thrills of Ian Fleming's James Bond." Even Ambler, argues

Symons, "had made the spy story adventurous, cheerful, rather a lark," and he suggests that le Carré's genuine "newness was perhaps the reason why the book was turned down by more than one publisher. At least, it is the face-saving explanation for the publishers concerned."[29]

It could be maintained that in writing about espionage le Carré was dealing with what he knew, just as in writing about the Far East and service at sea in his early work Conrad was not indulging in exotic and romantic adventures but drawing on first-hand experience. But there is a much more important point about the metaphorical significance of the intelligence world, which le Carré himself expressed eloquently to Michael Barber in 1978:

> We have learnt in recent years to translate almost all of political life in terms of conspiracy. And the spy novel, as never before really, has come into its own. There is such cynicism about the orthodox forms of government as they are offered to the public that we believe almost nothing at its face value. Now, somehow or other the politicians try to convey to us that this suspicion is misplaced. But we know better than that. And until we have a better relationship between private performance and the public truth, as was demonstrated with Watergate, we as the public are absolutely right to remain suspicious and contemptuous, even, of the secrecy and the misinformation which is the digest of our news. So I think that the spy novel encapsulates this public wariness about political behaviour and about the set-up, the fix of society. And I think also, in entertainment terms, it makes a kind of fable about forces we do believe in the West are stacked against us.[30]

Furthermore the metaphorical significance is as applicable to private life as to public life. When Melvyn Bragg suggested to le Carré in a television interview about *Tinker, Tailor, Soldier, Spy* in 1976 that "political doubt is a metaphor of the whole book because every relationship is necessarily insincere," le Carré replied:

> It's necessarily insincere. Every relationship, I think, is fraught with a nerve-wracking tension. That, to be truthful, is how I see life. . . . In short, we have to be enormously cautious with our commitments—yes. I think all of us live partly in a clandestine situation. In relation to our bosses, our families, our wives, our children, we frequently affect attitudes to which we subscribe perhaps intellectually, but not emotionally. We hardly know ourselves—nine-tenths of ourselves are below the level of the water.[31]

It is partly in these terms that le Carré explains the enormous appeal his novels have had. What is inescapable in his work is the indissolubility of the private and the public, the personal and the political, a point neatly presented in his New Testament reference during some remarks to James Cameron in 1974: "Very few people aren't interested in deceit—intelligence work, espionage. It's the contemporary arena of the cold war. People have always been fascinated by the anatomy of betrayal. Judas is a very memorable character."[32] The novel that prompted this interview, *Tinker, Tailor, Soldier, Spy*, which is about Smiley's quest for a "mole," contains a joke alluding to Judas as the archetypal double agent: "Jesus Christ only had twelve, you know, and one of them was a double."[33] In effect le Carré is interpreting the Crucifixion, which is central to Christian theology and, symbolically, to Christian civilization, as the result of an act of betrayal by a trusted friend who proves to be a mole, selling intelligence for personal gain. Perhaps what le Carré is doing in his spy fiction is reactivating in contemporary terms a crucial element of the Passion.

Le Carré has gathered armfuls of reviews, but examinations of his fiction as a whole or even of individual novels in depth are virtually nonexistent. Without wishing to inflict flocks of predatory graduate students on le Carré, one might question some of the assumptions buried in the collective unconscious of an academic literary establishment that ignores le Carré so assiduously but that has turned another very successful English novelist of his generation, John Fowles, into a major research industry, especially in the USA. Andrew Rutherford's essay "The Spy as Hero: Le Carré and the Cold War," a chapter in *The Literature of War: Five Studies in Heroic Virtue* (1978), was the first sustained treatment by a British academic of le Carré as an important literary figure meriting comparison with such established writers as Evelyn Waugh and inclusion in a work of literary scholarship. For Rutherford, who devotes part of his essay to an illuminating analysis of the psychological satisfactions offered by spy thrillers, le Carré "provides us with exciting, disturbing, therapeutic fantasies of action and intrigue; but in his best work he also engages with political, moral and psychological complexities, demonstrating the capacity of entertainment art to transcend its own self-imposed limitations."[34] Since Rutherford, a few Americans have followed suit, including John Halperin, for whom "John le Carré is the only writer of espionage 'thrillers' today who is also a writer of literature,"[35] and especially David Monaghan.[36] In the rest of this book one chapter is devoted to each of le Carré's novels with the exception of *The Naive and Sentimental Lover*. The almost unanimous verdict is that this novel is the weakest of his ten, and it is the only one that falls competely outside the formulaic models of spy and mystery writing to which le Carré has devoted himself, but it is discussed briefly in the chapter on *Tinker, Tailor, Soldier, Spy*. What might be thought to be a disproportionate amount of space is allocated to le Carré's first two novels, which have been so overshadowed by the novels since *The Spy Who Came in from the Cold* that they are often regarded as mere prentice work. This is far from the case, and they are therefore more in need of recognition than any of his subsequent work.[37]

2

A Far from Saintly George: *Call for the Dead* (1961)

Introducing George Smiley

George Smiley, a central figure in five of le Carré's ten novels and a significant presence in two of the others, has become to his creator what Sherlock Holmes is to Conan Doyle, Hercule Poirot to Agatha Christie, Lord Peter Wimsey to Dorothy Sayers, and Philip Marlowe to Raymond Chandler. Today, nearly a quarter of a century after Smiley made his entry in *Call for the Dead*, we have become so accustomed to him and to le Carré's idiom that it is easy to overlook how original that début was. In his book about the development of crime fiction, *Bloody Murder* (1972), the doyen of English writers on the subject, Julian Symons, rightly described *Call for the Dead* as "unjustly neglected,"[1] and two years later championed it strongly as "an extraordinarily assured first novel, and altogether a brilliant performance,"[2] in a long, lukewarm review of *Tinker, Tailor, Soldier, Spy*. Before the publication of *The Honourable Schoolboy*, the well-known English crime writer Michael Gilbert claimed that, of le Carré's "two superlative books in this field,"[3] *Call for the Dead* was marginally better than *The Spy Who Came in from the Cold*.

When le Carré published his first book, such distinguished "Golden Age" exponents of the classical detective novel as Agatha Christie and Margery Allingham were still writing, and even though that particular mode was long past its peak, its potential was not completely exhausted. In *Call for the Dead* le Carré makes use of the underlying formula of the classical detective story, but by building on it a realistic novel about espionage in the context of contemporary European politics rather than an intriguing murder case of the traditional type, he revitalizes and transfigures it in such a way that he produces a substantially different kind of fiction. Le Carré is not the first writer to combine the story of detection with that of espionage, since during World War II several writers of classical detective fiction made their series characters serve king and country in various ways, but such manifestations of timely patriotism, essentially romantic in conception, have very little in common with le Carré's realism. By employing this particular formula rather than an adventure or thriller one for a novel concerned with espionage, he also achieves an equally innovatory transformation, indeed radical inversion, of the routine spy story in the tradition running from William Le Queux through John Buchan and "Sapper" to Ian Fleming.

Le Carré does not describe the adventures of the spy as hero, but the process by which the spy is identified and tracked down as though a criminal. The point of view is not that of the spy but of the spy catcher. Le Carré was therefore departing in almost every way from the exceedingly popular and much imitated mode that Ian Fleming had established for stories about secret agents at the time. By the late 1950s Fleming, who had launched his James Bond books with *Casino Royale* in 1953 and who was producing a best seller virtually every year, was undoubtedly the thriller writer most in vogue in England. The Bond novels are essentially reactivations of the legend of Saint George and the Dragon in terms of Cold War politics with a generous sprinkling of violence, derring-do, and eroticism. The glamorous and sophisticated superman is decked out with all the trappings and savoir faire expected of a hero by a society intent on consuming conspicuously after the long gray period of wartime and postwar austerity. More or less single-handedly (he needs the other one to toy with any female who strays within reach) he defeats his own and his country's enemies, thus ensuring the continued existence of Western democracy. At a time of great public anxiety about the possibility of a third world war, Bond's existence, even though fictional, provided an emotional reassurance that the dragon of Soviet imperialism could be held in check. The widespread appeal of Fleming's novels obviously rested on their ability to satisfy the imaginative needs of very different people in different ways. At one level these absurdly extravagant romances, far removed from realism despite all the contemporary detail and associations, projected an image of male fantasy in Bond himself, the self-sufficient, resourceful, and irresistible hero. For British readers during a time of national uncertainty when the country was dismantling its huge Empire and looking for a new postimperial role, Bond embodied the patriotic belief that Britain could still be Great.

Le Carré has never disguised his dislike of James Bond, and *Call for the Dead* can partly be seen as a fictional reply to Fleming, with the middle-aged Smiley conceived as a realistic antidote to Fleming's romance hero, whom le Carré has described as "the ideal defector" and "the ultimate prostitute."[4] Questioned about *The Spy Who Came in from the Cold* during a television interview with Michael Dean in 1974, le Carré rejected the suggestion that he consciously intended writing anti-Bond novels in the early 1960s:

> That was nonsense. I'm not nearly clever enough to have done that at the time, and I wrote about the things that I knew of, the tensions in Berlin which I witnessed: institutional behaviour, British nostalgia for power, perhaps, and I imported from my experience of the Foreign Service a great deal of the way paper is moved around and the dinginess of decisions, sometimes.[5]

Le Carré is right to insist that his novels exist on their own terms, not in terms of burlesquing something else, but it is impossible to believe that, as a writer, he was not affected by the Bond cult. Writing in 1966 le Carré defined the opposite approaches of Fleming and himself to the world of espionage, arguing that "Bond on his magic carpet takes us away from moral doubt, banishes perplexity with action, morality with duty."[6] A literary analogy of the relationship between Fleming and le Carré might be that between Richardson's *Pamela* and Fielding's *Joseph Andrews*, rather than that between Richardson's novel and Fielding's parodic skit, *Shamela*.

An immediately striking feature of *Call for the Dead* is that le Carré delays opening the main narrative until chapter 2. According to most guides to fiction writing, especially thrillers and detective stories, this is an elementary mistake, since what the author should be doing is arousing interest in events or creating mystery and suspense by launching straight into the action. Le Carré, on the other hand, seems to be deliberately drawing attention to his departure from the accepted formula as he holds back the story line in favor of a leisurely introduction, which provides more than its title, "A Brief History of George Smiley," suggests. He not only presents his protagonist in some depth in this biographical sketch, which is relevant to all the

Smiley novels, but also establishes the realistic ambience in which Smiley functions. This stylish and consciously literary chapter could easily lead into a different kind of novel, a straight or even satirical treatment of the upper echelons of the British Civil Service, notably its intelligence branch, without a mystery element at all. At times le Carré's writing recalls Evelyn Waugh in its detached, witty poise, yet despite touches of humor the presentation of Smiley is basically sympathetic. In particular, Smiley is all too vulnerably human rather than superhuman.

Described by his wife in the first paragraph of *Call for the Dead* as "breathtakingly ordinary," the chubby, bespectacled, ill-dressed Smiley could hardly be more different from the womanizing Bond:

> Short, fat and of a quiet disposition, he appeared to spend a lot of money on really bad clothes, which hung about his squat frame like a skin on a shrunken toad. Sawley, in fact, declared at the wedding that "Sercomb was mated to a bullfrog in a sou'wester." And Smiley, unaware of this description, had waddled down the aisle in search of the kiss that would turn him into a Prince.[7]

This approximates to Dickensian grotesque and certainly suggests the caricature of burlesque, a satirical inversion of the archetypal romantic hero—tall, lean, muscular, manly, debonair, and certainly not a squat waddler. The allusion to the fairy tale about the princess and the frog is an ironic extension of the "toad" simile, since in the nonmagical world of the novel no glamorous transformation of ugly frog into handsome prince is possible. In chapter 5 the same simile is further developed during a flashback concerning Smiley and his titled, aristocratic wife, Lady Ann Sercomb, when she calls him "toad" no fewer than five times over dinner, but here the apparent insult is used as an affectionate nickname in the private language of man and wife. A transformation of a kind has taken place, corresponding to the emergence of Smiley, who might seem no more than an antitype from the initial description, as the nearest thing to a hero in le Carré's complex, unromantic, even tragic world. Another nickname Smiley acquires because of his appearance is "Mole" (p. 7), a word not applied to him in later novels where it assumes a completely different significance.

Considering that Ann plays no part whatsoever in the main narrative and has been divorced from Smiley for many years before the events described in the novel take place, she features fairly prominently. Ann is named in the first sentence of the book, even before Smiley himself, and the novel ends with his flying to Zurich to see this one woman in his monogamous life, after receiving a letter in which she states her desire to return to him—"an offer which no gentleman could accept" (p. 118). Smiley is haunted by memories of his former wife and their short married life together at the end of World War II before she deserted him, leaving him in possession of a broken world. If Ann brought personal and social glamor into the breathtaking ordinariness of Smiley's life, her departure stripped him of these attributes, as le Carré points out in an unusually elaborate and extended metaphor: "And so Smiley, without school, parents, regiment or trade, without wealth or poverty, travelled without labels in the guard's van of the social express, and soon became lost luggage, destined, when the divorce had come and gone, to remain unclaimed on the dusty shelf of yesterday's news" (p. 2). The repetition of "without" emphasizes that, on his own, Smiley has nothing of sufficient snob appeal—the right school, distinguished parents, and so on—to recommend him to high society as one of the elite. The final image is used elsewhere to portray Smiley as a man destined to be an also-ran, at least in the eyes of the world: "Smiley was no material for promotion and it dawned on him gradually that he had entered middle age without ever being young, and that he was—in the nicest possible way—on the shelf" (p. 6).

In chapter 14 le Carré reveals that Smiley's emotional wound was so deep after Ann's desertion that "he had begun by rigorously excluding all trace of her" (p. 113). Subsequently he has come to terms with her rejection of him, and his retention of one of their wedding presents, a beautiful piece of Dresden china, symbolizes this hard-won acceptance of loss. At times he imagines how Ann would respond to situations in which he finds himself. Yet the past and the sense of what-might-have-been hang heavily on Smiley: "It was Ann who had robbed him of his peace, Ann who had once made the present so important and taught him the habit of reality, and when she went there was nothing" (p. 33). This is why he cannot finally reject the "offer which no gentleman could accept" and goes to Zurich even though he knows exactly what Ann is capable of and can hear her voice behind her letter: "I have wearied my lover, my lover has wearied me, let me shatter your world again: my own bores me. I want to come back to you . . . I want, I want . . . " (p. 119). In yearning for Ann, Smiley is nostalgically clinging to England's as well as his own past; yet as a feckless aristocrat Ann embodies the upper class in its anachronistic decadence, without a role and devoted to private pleasure, no longer fulfilling its traditional function as a ruling elite that embraced public duty and responsibility. Significantly, the Smileys have no children. The novel ends in a downbeat way for several reasons, not with the triumphant sense of conspiracy thwarted, order restored, and mission accomplished usual in spy fiction, and the final image of Smiley on what seems likely to be a painful visit to his ex-wife is of a sad, desperate cuckold engaged on "the pathetic quest for love." The abrupt shift of viewpoint in the closing paragraph, so that Smiley is interpreted by a young man on the plane, produces a sour irony, which intensifies le Carré's reversal of routine, upbeat endings: "He knew the type well—the tired executive out for a bit of fun. He found it rather disgusting" (p. 148). Outside the context of his professional world, Smiley seems a human and social failure.

Smiley has worked abroad as a spy and now operates in London for a British intelligence organization called "the Department" in this novel, referred to as "the Service" in *A Murder of Quality*, and thereafter in le Carré's fiction known as "the Circus," ostensibly because its offices are in Cambridge Circus in the center of the city, although the word obviously carries other connotations; the location itself contains an ironic in-joke, Cambridge University in the 1930s having been a successful recruiting ground for a number of future Soviet double agents including Kim Philby. Several actual intelligence organizations have acquired familiar names, used mainly by insiders: the CIA, for example, is "the company," and MI6, "the firm." In keeping with le Carré's systematic deglamorizing of orthodox spy fiction, Smiley is the opposite of a swashbuckling adventurer. One of le Carré's points is that in the real world, unlike that of fictional romance, inconspicuous, drab, cautious nobodies make vastly superior spies to swashbuckling adventurers, who would not last long. Spying is, after all, a lonely, undramatic, unexciting, routine job for the most part, best left to the unassuming and self-effacing. Smiley himself had no aspirations to become involved in espionage. At heart he is a donnish intellectual who would feel most at home in the Senior Common Room of one of England's ancient seats of learning. Yet it was through these that he was recruited for what one of his appointing committee "blushingly described as the Secret Service" (p. 3).

After leaving his "unimpressive school" for his "unimpressive Oxford College" (p. 2), Smiley's ambition was to obtain a fellowship at his alma mater and devote his life to scholarship, principally concerned with the fairly esoteric subject of seventeenth-century German literature. Indeed at the end of the war Smiley left intelligence work to devote himself to his beloved field of academic research in Oxford as well as to his wife, before being recalled in 1947. Reminders of

Smiley's command of German and expertise in German literature are scattered througout the novel: "A German would call him *flott* thought Smiley" (p. 13); "He saw her as a wheedling *Backfisch*" (p. 32); major figures such as Brecht, Georg, Goethe, Herder, Hesse, and Kleist are mentioned or even cited. And it is Smiley's knowledge of German and Germany, combined with his retiring and unexhibitionistic personal qualities, that led him in 1928, at the suggestion of his tutor, to face a panel of the Overseas Committee for Academic Research without having the faintest idea of what this euphemism masked. Bizarre as this description of how Smiley was recruited as a secret agent may seem, it does accord with the public school and Oxbridge old-boy system for selecting potential spies current between the two world wars, with tutors at the two old English universities keeping a lookout for suitable undergraduates who could then be passed on to their friends in the appropriate departments of the Civil Service.

Having been offered a post as intelligence officer without having requested it or even considered it, Smiley found himself in a world that provided him with various satisfactions, none of which had to do with adventure, action, mayhem, sex, or any of the standard ingredients of spy thrillers, especially Ian Fleming's. Instead of being surrounded by James Bonds, Smiley was pleased to find himself in the company of "colleagues equally obscure in character and origin," and what appealed to him most was the frequent opportunity to flex his intellectual, not his physical, muscles—to undertake "academic excursions into the mystery of human behaviour, disciplined by the practical application of his own deductions" (p. 2). In outlining Smiley's career as a spy in Germany, first as an academic there during the 1930s and then under the guise of an agent for a Swiss arms manufacturer during the early and middle years of the war, le Carré emphasizes the isolation, the almost intolerable strain, the dehumanizing aspects of the job: there is a notable absence of technical wizardry, fast cars, hard drink, and luscious girls. Smiley had his "deep love of England" to sustain him but, as a highly self-conscious character, was only too well aware of the essential falsity of his life, of how his necessary reliance on the cold intellectuality that enabled him "to observe humanity with clinical objectivity" was stifling his potential for feeling: "Always withdrawn, he now found himself shrinking from the temptations of friendship and human loyalty; he guarded himself warily from spontaneous reaction" (p. 4). There is also a contradiction between Smiley as a university teacher in Germany concerned with truth and beauty (significantly he teaches Keats) and as an "international mercenary of his trade," necessarily living a lie. The gulf is between the world of art, philosophy, and permanent values, to which Smiley as a scholar is committed, and the world of social and political reality in which he has to operate, with all its duplicity, intrigue, and moral ugliness. He cannot be other than a divided character, a man of integrity functioning in a world that undermines integrity.

If nostalgia for a lost world is an important element in Smiley's life, it is not only because of his memories of Ann. He also recalls with great affection the prewar and wartime style of his profession, at least in its characteristically English form. He remembers the days when "you took your orders over a glass of port" in Magdalen College, Oxford, and also "the inspired amateurism of a handful of highly qualified, underpaid men" (p. 6). He is "homesick for the dilapidated terrace house in Knightsbridge where it had all begun " (p. 7). The curious club Smiley belongs to, which is described in chapter 11, "The Unrespectable Club," confirms this image of Smiley as one of the inspired amateurs of the old school as opposed to the slick, Establishment yes-men who have taken over. His club is "unrespectable," not because it is notorious as a den of drunkenness and debauchery, but because it has no social status, no snob appeal. Top people, those "who adorn the pages of 'Who's Who,' " belong to more fashionable clubs. Smiley's is for outsiders within the Establishment like himself, and its total lack of pretentiousness and modishness accords with his own character. Even more singularly, it is a club without a future; it looks back to the past:

> Naturally enough, most of the members were approximate contemporaries of Smiley at Oxford. It had always been agreed that the club was to serve one generation only, that it would grow old and die with its members. The war had taken its toll of Jebedee and others, but no one had ever suggested they should elect new members. (p. 84)

Smiley's moral and intellectual conservatism is made most explicit near the end of the novel in an important passage contrasting his own individualistic philosophy of life with that of his wartime collaborator Dieter Frey, a dedicated socialist now working for the Soviet bloc: Smiley

> hated the Press as he hated advertising and television, he hated mass-media, the relentless persuasion of the twentieth century. Everything he admired or loved had been the product of intense individualism. That was why he hated Dieter now, hated what he stood for more strongly than ever before; it was the fabulous impertinence of renouncing the individual in favour of the mass. When had mass philosophies ever brought benefit or wisdom? Dieter cared nothing for human life:

> dreamed only of armies of faceless men bound by their lowest common denominators; he wanted to shape the world as if it were a tree, cutting off what did not fit the regular image. (p. 130)

The strength of Smiley's convictions is not surprising for someone who has lived in Germany during almost the whole of Hitler's Third Reich and experienced at first hand all the horrific abuses of power perpetrated by the Nazis in the name of a mass philosophy that presented itself as a form of socialism.

With his strong roots in the past, Smiley might have been more at home had he remained in Matthew Arnold's "sweet City with her dreaming spires" ("Thyrsis") pursuing recondite German poetry after the war instead of doing his duty by returning to government service when asked to do so. The reason for Smiley's return to intelligence work—"the revelations of a young Russian cypher-clerk in Ottawa had created a new demand for men of Smiley's experience" (p. 6)—is interesting because it indicates how le Carré locates his fictional world in relation to the real world, maintaining a much closer connection than is usual in novels involving spies. The Russian here referred to was in actuality Igor Gouzenko, who defected to the West in September 1945 and whose "revelations" included information about the Soviet penetration of British intelligence organizations, the extent of which is still being made public at the present time. Later in the novel, references to Klaus Fuchs and Donald Maclean, two of the most notorious British subjects who were working for the Soviet Union, achieve the same purpose of sustaining credibility.

Yet the recalled Smiley is out of place in the new-style world of intelligence, which has been transformed into just another Whitehall bureacracy by its current controller, a professional civil servant rather than an inspired amateur: Smiley's boss and bête noire, Maston. The presentation of Maston is consistently satirical, and though the novel is written in the third person the viewpoint is plainly that of Smiley himself. The impeccable Maston, "with his expensive clothes and his knighthood, his distinguished grey hair and silver coloured ties" (pp. 6–7), is the perfect "off the peg" (p. 13) civil servant with a genius for the affectation, toadyism, and deviousness so much appreciated in the corridors of power, especially by government ministers. Known to Smiley and his friends as "the Head Eunuch" (p. 7) and to the police as "Marlene Dietrich" (p. 27), Maston is the archetypal bureaucrat who can "reduce any colour to grey" (p. 7) and for whom reality consists of paperwork: "Paper was fact, Ministers were fact, Home Secretaries were hard fact" (p. 40). This might seem like crude caricature, but what redeems the portrait of Maston from this is a grudging recognition, perhaps even admiration, of what a superb and unfaltering performance he maintains at all times: "My God, thought Smiley; you really do work round the clock. A twenty-four-hour cabaret, you are—'We Never Closed' " (p. 16).[8] The appropriateness of the irony here is obvious to anyone who recognizes that this slogan, also the title of chapter 2, was that used by the Windmill Theatre near Piccadilly Circus, which remained open during the bombing of London in World War II, when many theaters were dark, and provided lavish girly shows much appreciated by servicemen on leave. The implication is that Maston maintains a Civil Service equivalent of the glossy façade and flashy superficiality of a performance in a burlesque theater. In the new dispensation of Maston's empire, the nostalgic Smiley is no longer at ease. At the end of the novel Smiley turns down the offer of promotion, preferring to go his own way and leave Maston to "his arid paper and his shiny politicians" (p. 148). Taking the Smiley novels as a whole, his departure from the Circus in *Call for the Dead* is, of course, only temporary, but throughout the series he continues to have an uneasy and ambiguous relationship with the organization, part-outsider and part-insider.

It is almost inevitable that reviewers and journalists should have speculated about the relationship between Smiley and le Carré himself. How much of le Carré has gone into his series character? There are obvious resemblances: in terms of class, both have indeterminate origins; both were educated at public school and Oxford; both are German specialists; both have belonged to British Intelligence. But the question is like asking how much of T. S. Eliot went into J. Alfred Prufrock. Both Eliot and le Carré were young men when they created these middle-aged characters so that there is an immediate distance between creator and creation. Le Carré told Miriam Gross that he "wanted somebody who was part of the seamless transition—as it looked to someone of my generation—from the hot war to the cold war," which meant a member of "the generation of the traitors."[9] Writing about the poets of the 1930s Robin Skelton identified people born betwen 1904 and 1916 (this includes Smiley) as forming a distinct generation,[10] and according to le Carré this age group "felt particularly strongly that one must commit oneself one way or another, that there is no middle way." Smiley, he continues, "committed himself to the Establishment cause—although I don't think it's enough for him.

He has a sense of decency but he's not sure where to invest it."[11] Le Carré too committed himself to the Establishment cause, however much he disliked aspects of the Establishment.

It is in his political stance that Smiley most closely represents le Carré's own position. While admitting to Miriam Gross that he always votes "Socialist—with misgivings,"[12] he made it clear that he believes, "reluctantly, that we must combat Communism. Very decisively"; and turning to Smiley he said:

> His engagement against Communism is really an intellectual one. I think he stands where I stand: he feels that to pit yourself against any 'ism' is to strike a posture which is itself ideological, and therefore offensive in terms of practical decency. In practice almost any political ideology invites you to set aside your humanitarian instincts.[13]

A number of le Carré's political statements endorse Smiley's commitment to defend the values he upholds by means of his secret work. In his 1976 interview with Melvyn Bragg, le Carré justified the need for intelligence operatives because they are the people who "actually combine thought with deeds" and are therefore "the infantry of our ideology."[14] In 1978 he told Michael Barber that "whether it's age or maturity" he found himself "committed more and more to the looser forms of Western democracy at any price. And I've become more and more disenchanted about the possibility of understanding with the Soviet Union as it's constructed at the moment."[15] Over four years later he defended the activities of intelligence organizations to the *Newsweek* reporters: "It's bad enough to have an inefficient secret service, but to have none at all would be disastrous. . . . The dishonesty of politicians puts a premium on intelligence gathering."[16] The moral problem of how far you can go to preserve a society without destroying the very values you are trying to defend pervades le Carré's fiction.

The Fennan Case

With its pattern of mystification and detection, the main narrative of *Call for the Dead*, which is presumably set in 1961 although le Carré nowhere states this,[17] accords in some respects with the formula of the classical detective story, but also differs from it. The novel moves steadily towards the solution of a problem, but the problem is not the conventional one of exposing the murderer. There are murders in the novel, but the identity of the killers is not the point at issue since there is no doubt about who they are well before the end. The process of inquiry does lead to the identification of a spy, but even this seems secondary to the investigator's (Smiley's) need to find an explanation for the chain of events he finds himself involved in, unwittingly in the first instance. This last point is important because it distinguishes Smiley's status in the novel from that of the classical detective or the hard-boiled private eye. The classical detective almost always enters the mystery or conspiracy as an outsider, armed with his honed powers of ratiocination as well as his intuition, and remains detached from the situation. The private eye of hard-boiled American fiction relies less on reason than the more gentlemanly detectives of English crime fiction and usually becomes embroiled in the situation he investigates so that clear-sighted objectivity is often impossible, but initially he is brought into that situation as an outsider. Smiley may share Sherlock Holmes's and Hercule Poirot's passion for logic and deduction, but like Philip Marlowe he finds himself a participant, even a victim, as well as an observer. Yet unlike Marlowe, Smiley turns out to be the unconscious instigator of the complex series of events that the novel charts. It is in Smiley's own past as a spy and in the tormented history of Europe during the previous thirty years that the answers lie. Le Carré produces some decidedly original variations on the fictional formulas underlying *Call for the Dead.*

The plot opens with the time-honored device of a death that appears to be suicide. The dead man is a senior civil servant at the Foreign Office, Samuel Fennan, who has just been investigated by Smiley as a security risk after the receipt of an anonymous letter accusing him of being a member of the Communist Party while a student at Oxford during the 1930s. During the investigation Fennan has admitted this, but Smiley has found nothing to suggest lingering Communist sympathies and has not only completely cleared Fennan but unofficially told him as much. Fennan's apparent suicide on the day following their interview consequently comes as a shock to Smiley, especially as an alleged suicide note presents a completely contrary interpretation of what happened between them. According to the note, Fennan believes himself to be suspected of treachery so that his entire career is in ruins. For Maston "it's a clear case of suicide" (p. 13), but Smiley is rightly perplexed by the anomaly between what he knows took place and what the note indicates.

Later in the novel (chapter 8), when he is recovering from the nearly fatal attack on him in Adam Scarr's yard by the East German agent Mundt, Smiley recalls his interview with Fennan in some detail, and in doing so ponders on the social, political, and economic context in which men of their age matured. As a German Jew who came to England in the 1930s to escape Nazi anti-Semitism, Fennan, like so many of his contemporaries at Oxford and Cambridge, was almost bound to become involved in left-wing politics. With the rise of Fascism and the apparent disintegration of capitalist democracy, Communism (then viewed through rose-tinted spectacles by many young intellectuals) seemed to offer the only hope for the future and became a secular form of religion. Some gave their lives for their new faith and ideals, including the gifted young Cambridge poet mentioned by le Carré, John Cornford, who was killed at the age of twenty-one while fighting against Franco in the Spanish Civil War. Fennan has told Smiley a story only too typical of the period involving an encounter between altruistic middle-class Oxford students and Welsh miners on a hunger march, representatives of the working class the intelligentsia were siding with but also knew nothing about. The result was mutual incomprehension.

Fennan's account of his eventual rejection of the Communist Party and of Marxism is not one of sudden renunciation leading to hostility. It is, rather, a process of growing up to accept the contradictoriness, complexity, and sheer untidiness of human experience: first of all by acknowledging "the disproportion between the dream and reality" and abandoning the naive hopes of instant paradise that the young intelligentsia thought revolution would bring; later, after succumbing to "the intellectual purity of Marxism . . . which exacted total sacrifice to an unassailable formula" (p. 64), by turning his back on such a systematic philosophy, which he had once found inspiring. Yet le Carré emphasizes that Fennan, in parting company with Communism, was not dismissing it out of hand as a worthless bauble that deceived him for a while. The metaphor le Carré prefers is that used by Saint Paul in the First Epistle to the Corinthians: "when I became a man, I put away childish things." Fennan has "sadly" put away the intellectual idealism of his undergraduate years "as a treasure he had outgrown and must leave at Oxford with the days of his youth." He can afford to recall it with pleasure, not contempt, because he has long since ceased to be captivated by it. Le Carré's sympathetic portrayal of Fennan's early commitment to Marxism, endorsed by Smiley's warm response to this ex-Communist now working with highly confidential material at a senior level in the Civil Service of his adopted country, is noteworthy because it indicates a level of maturity all too rare in fiction dealing with espionage. The standard spy thriller employs the simplistic scheme of right-wing goodies against left-wing baddies, concluding with all the reds under the bed dead. Morally and politically le Carré is operating at the level of good mainstream fiction. Furthermore his inclusion of what might be considered all this "background material," which does not advance the plot, is indicative of his interest in his characters as historical agents, not as individuals operating in a vacuum or ciphers in a formula.

Chapter 3, "Elsa Fennan," containing Smiley's first interview with Fennan's widow, is another good example of how le Carré expands his fictional world beyond the confines of any formula of mystery or spy writing. The witty, sardonic description of the part of the Home Counties where the Fennans live, for example, is irrelevant to the plot but helps to fix the action in an immediately recognizable social context and adds to the intermittent satire of aspects of England throughout the novel. Criticism of England and the English pervades le Carré's oeuvre, and can be surprisingly bitter for an author often regarded as quintessentially English. Merridale Lane is middle-class suburbia aspiring to old-worlde, upper-class status. Le Carré's ironic use of verbs is particularly effective: trees are "cajoled," houses (known as "character dwellings") "crouch" behind them, rusticity is "enhanced" by wooden owls that "keep guard" as well as by "crumbling dwarfs indefatigably poised over goldfish ponds." In a particularly acidic piece of irony at the expense of English conservatism, le Carré notes that the logic of the residents' pursuit of "weathered antiquity" as a guarantee of true social standing demands that "even the beams on the garage may boast of beetle and woodworm" (p. 17). High reputation is to be measured in terms of rot, decay, and corruption. In chapter 4, "Coffee at the Fountain," the account of Miss Adam's neighboring Fountain Café, which "was all Tudor and horse brasses and local honey at sixpence more than anywhere else," continues le Carré's assault on the sham and the pretentious in middle-class England:

> Miss Adam herself dispensed the nastiest coffee south of Manchester and spoke of her customers as "My Friends." Miss Adam did not do business with friends, but simply robbed them, which somehow added to the illusion of genteel amateurism which Miss Adam was so anxious to preserve. (p. 26)

It is sometimes said that hypocrisy is the foundation stone on which much of English public and private life securely rests, and le Carré is most adept at nosing out the hypocrisy and falsity concealed behind bourgeois gentility. Significantly, Smiley feels that a cosmopolitan Jewish intellectual like Fennan, who is "Hampstead and *au-pair* foreign girls" (p. 18)—Hampstead is a district of north London popular with the well-to-do intelligentsia—does not belong in this epitome of middle England.

The interview itself, which is echoed later in the novel by a second confrontation between Smiley and Elsa, raises issues that are to become much more prominent in the denouement, as well as developing the subject of European politics touched on in the brief account of Smiley's career in Germany during the rise of Nazism. As a German Jewess who has survived, Elsa embodies some of the suffering of the European Jews: "It was a worn face, racked and ravaged long ago, the face of a child grown old on starving and exhaustion, the eternal refugee face, the prison-camp face, thought Smiley" (p. 19). Variants of this description appear elsewhere, emphasizing Elsa's position as victim. Faced with this woman, whose life gives the impression of being a catalogue of pain and oppression, Smiley feels positively guilty since it appears that he has precipitated her husband's violent death. Her mention of "loyalty" in connection with Fennan causes Smiley to question himself about the meaning and validity of such an easily spoken word ("Loyalty to whom, to what"), and one line of defence he contemplates ("I was only doing my duty") strikes him as absurdly inadequate because it begs the crucial question: "Duty to *whom* for God's sake?" (p. 20). The chronic ambivalence of words such as "loyalty" and "duty" in the context of twentieth-century European history becomes a most important issue.

It is extremely ironic after chapter 2, which describes Smiley's hostility to Maston because of his closed, bureaucratic mind, that Elsa should now accuse Smiley in turn of possessing just such an inhuman mind:

> The mind becomes separated from the body; it thinks without reality, rules a paper kingdom and devises without emotion the ruin of its paper victims. But sometimes the division between your world and ours is incomplete; the files grow heads and arms and legs, and that's a terrible moment, isn't it? The names have families as well as records, and human motives to explain the sad little dossiers and their make-believe sins. . . . It's like the State and the People. The State is a dream too, a symbol of nothing at all, an emptiness, a mind without a body, a game played with clouds in the sky. But States make war, don't they, and imprison people? To dream in doctrines—how tidy! . . . you have no place among real people. You dropped a bomb from the sky: don't come down here and look at the blood, or hear the scream. (p. 21)

Whether or not her attack on him is justified, it has the effect of undermining Smiley to some extent in the reader's eyes, coming as it does immediately after the chapter in which Smiley's standards have been used to undermine Maston. Le Carré is establishing a world of relative not absolute values, far removed from the moral and human simplicities of James Bond's black-and-white world of heroes and villains. In the next chapter (4), Smiley does in effect acknowledge the validity of her charge when he sets out for London, "back to the unreality of containing a human tragedy in a three-page report" (p. 30).

Nevertheless Smiley remains puzzled by two things when he leaves Elsa. There is the contradiction between his knowledge that Fennan had nothing to worry about and Elsa's account of his distraught state after his interview with Smiley. Secondly, there is the telephone call to Fennan's house that Smiley takes, believing it to be from his office, only to discover that is is from the local exchange in response to a request. As Police Inspector Mendel soon establishes, Fennan himself asked for the morning call shortly before his death so that it is truly a call for the dead. This and other oddities seriously undermine the suicide theory, which Smiley sums up ironically:

> Fennan decides to commit suicide. He asks the exchange to ring him at 8.30. He makes himself some cocoa and puts it in the drawing-room. He goes upstairs and types his last letter. He comes down again to shoot himself, leaving the cocoa undrunk. It all hangs together nicely. (p. 29)

In spite of Elsa's obvious lies when he returns briefly to ask her about the call, Smiley cannot see her as a possible murderer, because "there was no aggression in her, no will but the will to preserve" (p. 34). At the same time he is aware of how untrustworthy his own intuitions could be. A passage from Hesse, ending "Each is alone," comes to his mind, and he is forced to admit to himself that "we know nothing of one another, nothing. . . . However closely we live together, at whatever time of day or night we sound the deepest thoughts in one another, we know nothing." This is reminiscent of Conrad, the unsurpassed portrayer of the essential isolation of all human beings, and an important influence on le Carré.

Smiley and Mendel, who retires from the police early in the novel, work closely together outside the normal channels of investigation, but Mendel is not playing Dr. Watson to Smiley's Sherlock Holmes. Because the case, with its blend of violent crime and espionage, requires both police and counterintelligence methods, the practical Mendel is a necessary ally of the intellectual Smiley. It is Mendel who carries out much of the footwork, necessary interviewing, and tailing, for which he is much better suited than Smiley, whose main weapons are logic and imagination. After Smiley discovers a stranger in his house at the end of chapter 5, subsequently identified as Mundt, it is

Mendel who tracks down Mundt's car to Adam Scarr's garage in Battersea, a rundown area of London south of the Thames. Before Scarr is found dead in the river, apparently having drowned accidentally while drunk, although Mendel and Smiley see his murder as part of the pattern of violence commencing with Fennan's death, this extraordinary figure, with his orotund, circumlocutory, and metaphoric style of speech, is threatened by Mendel in chapter 7 into disclosing Mundt's telephone number. This leads Mendel to the office of the East German Steel Mission in the north London district of Belsize Park, only to learn that it was evacuated on the day of Fennan's murder. Mendel's other main contribution to the case during Smiley's convalescence in hospital in the central part of the novel is to investigate Elsa Fennan's fortnightly visits to the Weybridge Repertory Theatre. Le Carré's depiction in chapter 10, "The Virgin's Story," of such Weybridge thespians as the histrionic, bitchy Ludo Oriel and the "Virgin" herself, Elizabeth Pidgeon, with her affected patter and fondness for mindless hyperbole, verges on caricature and adds to the social satire in the novel; but the Virgin is not unobservant and is able to provide Mendel with invaluable information about Elsa's regular meetings with Mundt at the theater, and about both his failure to arrive and Elsa's departure in panic on the night of Fennan's death.

Le Carré's characterization of Mendel, who appears briefly in a couple of subsequent Smiley novels, is less searching than that of Smiley, but the policeman (ex-policeman for most of the novel) emerges as a rounded figure; he is too complex to fall into any of the stereotypes of policemen prevalent in crime fiction, whether paternal or mean, nice or nasty. The initial description of him as "a thin, weasel-faced gentleman who spoke very rapidly out of the corner of his mouth" (p. 24) is not attractive, but his concern for Smiley after the latter has been viciously attacked is genuine and deeply felt. Mendel's ensuing interrogation of the appropriately named petty criminal Adam Scarr, who has evidently been fabricating a tissue of lies, reveals his capacity for ruthless intimidation and toughness. On the other hand the house that the unmarried Mendel has purchased for his retirement reveals him in a very different light: in its kitchen Smiley "was amused to notice the extreme tidiness, the almost feminine neatness of everything about him" (p. 42). Mendel's old-maidishness is evident in other things: the way he drives "with a kind of school ma'amish pedantry" and his fondness for Smiley's car because of "the fussy way it had been maintained" (p. 75). The two men have a natural affinity even though

Mendel lacks the subtlety and sophistication of Smiley and is capable of outbursts of prejudice such as this diatribe:

> Krauts. Huns. Jerries. Bloody Germans. Wouldn't give you sixpence for the lot of them. Carnivorous ruddy sheep. Kicking Jews about again. Us all over. Knock 'em down, set 'em up. Forgive and forget. *Why* bloody well forget, I'd like to know? Why forget theft, murder and rape just because millions committed it? (p. 47)

Smiley, who knows Germany intimately, would never speak so crudely and xenophobically, but he can understand such attitudes to the new, revived Germany with its economic miracle, especially when they come from Elsa Fennan who suffered under the Third Reich.

More than once in the novel Smiley decides that his involvement in the Fennan case has come to an end, only to find that the case suddenly involves him again, the first occasion being in chapter 5. Though armed with various pieces of circumstantial evidence suggesting foul play, Smiley, after returning from his interview with Elsa Fennan, fails to shake Maston's total conviction that Fennan took his own life, the most convenient explanation for officialdom since it threatens no further upsets. Smiley's strong suspicion that Fennan has been murdered is immediately vindicated, however, when he finds in his mail a letter from Fennan written the previous day—the day of his death—in which he makes an urgent request to meet Smiley again. Smiley's response, paradoxically, is not to pursue the case but to relinquish it. Tired of dealing with the impossible Maston, Smiley writes him a letter of resignation, affixing to it Fennan's letter, then leaves Cambridge Circus, apparently no longer bothered about Fennan's death. The irony is that no sooner has Smiley taken his decision than the problem that "no longer existed" (p. 40) for him reasserts its existence very dramatically. Smiley drops the case, only to find that the case has not dropped him. Arriving home, Smiley correctly intuits that the unknown intruder he sees (Mundt) is waiting inside to kill him since he is obviously not a burglar. Smiley, the pursuer manqué of Fennan's murderer, now finds himself the pursued, a position confirmed at the end of the next chapter (6) when he is brutally attacked with a piece of lead pipe and left for dead.

Condemned to a hospital bed while Mendel takes to the road, Smiley can make only intellectual contributions, but his powers of deduction are hard at work. Convinced "that Fennan had left something important unsaid" (p. 65) at the time of their interview, Smiley assembles everything he knows in the hope that logic will make connections between separate pieces of information and so provide a breakthrough. Smiley now feels sure that his meeting with Fennan must have caused grave concern to someone who knew both of them and saw them together, leading to Fennan's murder and the attack on himself, but beyond this there is uncertainty and confusion. Nevertheless, with the help of a colleague, Peter Guillam, who is a fund of information about the spying techniques of the German Democratic Republic, Smiley establishes that the East German Steel Mission must have been a cover for an intelligence mission relating to Fennan in some way. Guillam's close collaboration with Smiley is repeated in some of le Carré's later novels.

With Smiley's departure from the hospital, the narrative takes an unexpected move forward by paradoxically moving back in time. Over dinner at his unfashionable club in chapter 11, Smiley reminisces at length to Mendel and Guillam about his life in prewar and wartime Germany, but especially about a young Jewish student, Dieter Frey, who, despite being deformed, cut a dashingly romantic figure at his university. As a committed socialist Dieter revealed to Smiley his hostility to Nazi Germany in no uncertain terms, and Smiley assumed that this firebrand student was destined for a concentration camp. To Smiley's surprise he subsequently learned that Dieter has not only evaded Nazi persecution but has been recruited by British Intelligence, so that the two men worked hand-in-glove during Smiley's wartime operations in Germany. Despite his hotheaded streak Dieter proved to be "a magnificent agent" (p. 90), and by being able to provide plenty of information about troop and munition transports helped the Allied war effort considerably. Smiley later recalls "memories of dangers shared, of mutual trust when each had held in his hand the life of the other" (p. 124).

In terms of plot the reason for Smiley's extended exposition is that the Head of the East German Steel Mission in London is none other than Dieter Frey. A figure from Smiley's past has invaded his present. Yet le Carré lingers over Smiley's account for two reasons: to create an essentially favorable and sympathetic picture of Dieter, who is referred to by his first name throughout the novel, suggesting a closer relationship to Smiley than the use of "Frey" would indicate; and to amplify his treatment of the political and human contradictions of modern Europe. Dieter can be seen as both friend and foe. Yet when, as Smiley's wartime agent, he was an ally, he was also a traitor to his own country, even though treachery against the Third Reich may have been morally admirable. And now that he is working for the Soviet bloc and is therefore an opponent on the other side, he also happens to be serving his country and working for the socialism that inspired his hostility to Hitler. At the end of the novel Smiley suggests that Dieter's commitment to East Germany may be a way of exorcizing his guilt for his wartime treason. The world le Carré presents here, through Smiley's recollections of recent European history, is one of tortuous ambiguity and relativism where loyalty can be disloyalty and duty a crime.

Ambiguity is central in the crucial chapter (12) in which Smiley confronts Elsa for the second time, "Dream for Sale." With the evidence suggesting that Fennan was a spy and Elsa his courier, Smiley now goes on the offensive in an attempt to break her down and force a confirmatory confession from her. At first it seems that he has achieved this most successfully. In retrospect it is clear that Elsa has not been tricked into revealing all, and has in fact tricked Smiley into accepting his own hypothetical interpretation of the case, if only for awhile. What she has to say is an ambiguous mixture of truth and deception: she explains how she and her husband first met Dieter, that Mundt (whom she calls Freitag) killed Fennan as a suspected double agent after Dieter had seen Smiley with her husband, and that she typed the "suicide" letter. At the same time she acts the part of a pathetic victim in a deliberately misleading way, yet can do this so convincingly only because in one sense she is a pathetic victim of history, in the form of the Nazi era:

> "Look at me," she said; "What dream did they leave me? I dreamed of long golden hair and they shaved my head, I dreamed of a beautiful body and they broke it with hunger. I have seen what human beings are, how could I believe in a formula for human beings?" (p. 95)

She claims to be a woman without illusions, ideals, or dreams; her only devotion was to her husband, whom she accuses of being a political dreamer, a would-be architect of a new world, and therefore an easy target for Dieter.

By the end of the book, when Smiley finally reveals that Elsa, not her husband, is the Communist spy, it is clear that she has been engaged in an extraordinarily complex piece of role-playing throughout this interview, in which the genuine and the hypocritical are blended. In order to protect herself from Smiley, she has to condemn her real self. This explains why she emerges as such a complex character as opposed to a stereotype. She criticizes her husband for a political idealism that is actually hers, not his, something Smiley realizes only later, but she also provides a motivation that he can sympathize with:

> It was not a pretty sight for us, the new Germany. Old names had come back, names that had frightened us as children. The dreadful, plump pride returned, you could see it even in the photographs in the papers, they marched with the old rhythm. (pp. 99–100)

For many people at the time, especially Jews, the reemergence of (West) Germany as an economically powerful and newly militarized nation was disturbing, only fifteen years after the defeat of the Third Reich and the revelations about the Holocaust. The fear that the old Germany is being reborn behind the façade of the new—the premise on which le Carré's fifth novel, *A Small Town in Germany*, is constructed—is the prime motivation for Elsa's espionage. Her final outburst, with which the interview ends, epitomizes her contradictoriness. It is both an appeal for sympathy and a contemptuous rejection of any sympathy that may be proffered; it is the histrionic climax of a consummate performance for Smiley's benefit, but it simultaneously conveys an essential truth about her:

> Go away and kill Freitag and Dieter, keep the game alive, Mr. Smiley. But don't think I'm on *your* side, d'you hear? Because I'm the wandering Jewess, the no-man's land, the battlefield for your toy soldiers. You can kick me and trample on me, see, but never, never touch me, never tell me you're sorry, d'you hear? (p. 101)

With Elsa's "confession" the case appears to be closed. The irony of the moment when she tells Smiley about Dieter's enormous admiration for him because of his genius for deception is obvious only on rereading: it is then clear that she herself is actually in the process of deceiving the arch-deceiver. At this point Smiley sees himself as having been expertly deceived by Fennan. Nevertheless Smiley, with his passion for intellectual order, is still uneasy about a number of points, including the fact that Elsa has not been murdered or attacked by Mundt, while everyone else implicated has been in an attempt to leave no traces behind. Earlier in the novel the grimly ironical thought passes through Mendel's head that "it doesn't say much for her that she hasn't been murdered" (p. 76). It is while rethinking the case through from the beginning in his characteristically painstaking and logical manner that Smiley receives some information from Guillam that eventually leads him to rejuggle the jigsaw pieces so as to complete the picture. At first, however, Guillam's revelation that Fennan's diary contains Dieter's name and telephone number (a piece of lunacy for a spy) and that Fennan has been taking home unclassified material from his office when he had access to top-secret files simply adds to Smiley's sense of mystification: "Nothing made sense, nothing" (p. 110). Even so, the chapter (13) containing Smiley's mental contortions to accommodate all the information he now possesses, "The Inefficiency of Samuel Fennan," ends with the words, "It was all over" (p. 111), words that might also have accompanied his resignation much earlier in the novel.

Once again it is far from over. Gazing at one of his wedding presents, a piece of Dresden china, Smiley recalls his favorite German city, thinks of Elsa Fennan who comes from Dresden, and then, in an almost visionary moment, suddenly sees the solution that accounts for everything in the Fennan case, a solution he feels he would have seen before had he relied entirely on "the power of his mind" and not "been the fool of his own sentiment" (p. 115). Until this point le Carré has allowed the reader to follow Smiley's thought processes fairly closely so that we have seen events and people mainly from his viewpoint. Now le Carré deliberately holds back the solution Smiley has arrived at until the penultimate chapter, almost entirely devoted to the detailed report he prepares for Maston. This does not mean, however, that le Carré is indulging in that nefarious practice of some crime writers of withholding a crucial piece of evidence so as to spring a last-chapter surprise on the reader. All the information is before us: what Smiley has done is to reinterpret the facts so that they do make sense, do form a tidy pattern.

After the fairly leisurely unfolding of the narrative up to now, with several chapters devoted mainly to exposition (1: "A Brief History of George Smiley"), speculation (8: "Reflections in a Hospital Ward"), and explanation (11: "The Unrespectable Club"), the action suddenly advances with considerable pace to its denouement. This is essential if le Carré is to avoid the charge of unnecessarily keeping his readers in suspense once the process of detection is over. At the same time le Carré sustains his readers' interest by mystifying them about Smiley's behavior now that he has solved the mystery surrounding Fennan. From the time that Smiley sends a postcard to Elsa, an action not explained until later, the interest is no longer in the process of detection but of revelation and pursuit. In setting up his trap to catch the foreign agents, Smiley becomes the instigator of the action.

It is only in this closing stage of the novel that Dieter makes his entry, summoned back to London by Elsa who has been tricked by Smiley's firsthand knowledge of Dieter's methods. Le Carré's description of Dieter at the theater in the west London district of Hammersmith where he meets Elsa does seem exaggerated considering the low-key realism of the novel as a whole. He appears to have walked into Smiley's world from the pages of Romantic literature, a point that le Carré himself makes, thus preempting any possible allegation of melodrama:

> He was a man apart, a man you remember, a man who strikes a chord deep in your experience, a man with the gift of universal familiarity: to Guillam he was a living component of all our romantic dreams, he stood at the mast with Conrad, sought the lost Greece with Byron and with Goethe visited the shades of classical and mediaeval hells. (p. 122)

The mention of Goethe combined with the fact that the play being performed is by Marlowe (though *Edward II*, not *Dr. Faustus*) brings to mind the Faustian overreacher, which is precisely how Smiley sees his former colleague:

> He was the same improbable romantic with the magic of a charlatan; the same unforgettable figure which had struggled over the ruins of Germany, implacable of purpose, satanic in fulfilment, dark and swift like the Gods of the North. Smiley had lied to them that night in his club; Dieter *was* out of proportion, his cunning, his conceit, his strength and his dream—all were larger than life, undiminished by the moderating influence of experience. He was a man who thought and acted in absolute terms, without patience or compromise. (p. 124)

To emphasize that this is Smiley's view rather than the author's or the only possible one, le Carré is careful to include a very different perspective, that of the nonliterary, down-to-earth Mendel, who sees Dieter's slipping away from the theater as "the stealthy act of a common criminal" (p. 127). For Mendel, a criminal is a criminal is a criminal, and he makes no distinctions, not even crude ones. Dieter differs from those he usually deals with only in being German.

There is a Dickensian quality in the final tracking down of Dieter at night in London. This is partly because of the thick fog permeating everything, as it does in *Bleak House*, and also because of the proximity of the Thames and of the way "the foul black river" (p. 133) claims human life, as it does in *Our Mutual Friend*. The only meeting between Smiley and Dieter in the novel takes the form of a tussle on Battersea Bridge, during which Dieter refrains from killing Smiley as he could have done and falls to his own death in the "filthy water" and "stenching blackness" (p. 134) of the Thames. Smiley's response at what might be called the defeat of the enemy is not one of relief and triumph but of anguish and grief. In formulaic thrillers, such climactic moments are almost invariably rendered as victories at both the personal and public levels. Le Carré, on the other hand, stresses Smiley's guilt and remorse, partly because of his own responsibility for Dieter's death, but more particularly because the ruthless Dieter, remembering their former closeness and mutual dependence, finds it impossible to shoot Smiley, whereas the liberal humanitarian Smiley behaves as though there had never been anything between them. In passing judgment on himself—" 'O God,' said Smiley aloud, 'who was then the gentleman' " (p. 137)—he gives an ingenious twist to the famous distich, "When Adam delved, and Eve span,/Who was then a gentleman?", which provided the radical priest John Ball with the text of his great sermon preached at Blackheath during Wat Tyler's Peasant Revolt in 1381. Incidentally, Smiley could, but does not, acknowledge some responsibility for Dieter's killing of Elsa at the theater when he suspects that she has lured him into a trap. It is actually Smiley who has created a situation in which this born victim of a woman is caught between the "mighty opposites" of Dieter and himself.

What makes the short final chapter, "Between Two Worlds," so effective is that it reverses the normal formulaic situation in which the hero and his sidekicks celebrate their victory over their defeated opponents. Over dinner at the unrespectable club with Mendel and Guillam once again, Smiley offers an explanation of both Elsa and Dieter that also acts as a tribute. Now that they are safely dead, this might be no more than a perfunctory gesture of magnanimity, but Smiley's sympathetic appraisal of their motives comes close to being an exoneration. What emerges most clearly is the conflict between ideals and reality, the way in which reality can falsify dreams so that Dieter became "one of those world-builders who seem to do nothing but destroy" (p. 147). This paradox of what might be called destructive creativity is given further expression in Smiley's comment: "They dreamed of peace and freedom. Now they're murderers and spies." Yet it is self-evidently not wrong to dream of peace and freedom, to want "to help build one society which could live without conflict" (the motive Smiley ascribes to Elsa) even though, the world being what it is, attempts to actualize a new utopian order seem doomed to fail. The fault lies not in Elsa and Dieter, who are almost tragic characters, but in a fallen and divided world that cannot be redeemed by human effort. The novel ends on a note of conservative pessimism. It is symbolically significant that the Fennan case opens at night, when Smiley is summoned to Cambridge Circus, and ends at night with Dieter's death: it is also appropriate that Smiley flies to Zurich in the final paragraphs by "the midnight plane" (p. 148). The main actions of the five novels le Carré wrote in the 1960s all open and close after dark in the evening or night.

In *Thrillers* Jerry Palmer distinguishes between the "positive thrillers" of writers such as Ian Fleming and Mickey Spillane, in which "we are to be left with the feeling that the evil incarnated in the conspiracy has been expunged from the world, and that order, sweetness and light have been restored," and the "negative thrillers" of writers such as Dashiell Hammett and Raymond Chandler, in which "we feel that the same thing will happen all over again very shortly, that one particular piece of evil has been scotched, but not that evil in general has been extirpated."[18] Though too clear-cut the distinction is useful, but *Call for the Dead* falls into neither category even though it has affinities with the "negative thriller." In le Carré's novel the final impression is not "that one particular piece of evil has been scotched." For one thing the character who comes closest to being the conventional villain, Mundt, escapes to East Germany. In a James Bond or even a Philip Marlowe novel he would almost certainly end up dead. Furthermore good and evil become so relativistic in the ideological uncertainty and political confusion of *Call for the Dead* that it is hardly possible to use such moral absolutes at all. Even Chandler's world is much less ethically indeterminate than le Carré's. The spies, Elsa and Dieter, are altogether more sympathetic than Maston, the unpleasant embodiment of the British Establishment Smiley is nominally defending, even though his heart is not in it.

Compared with some of le Carré's longer and more thickly textured novels, *Call for the Dead* may give the impression that the underlying skeleton of the plot is not adequately covered and that the bare bones stick through the epidermis. Yet compared with much crime and spy fiction, *Call for the Dead* is remarkable for its political range, its human breadth, and its moral subtlety. Le Carré handles his unusual amalgam of crime detection and espionage within an intricate plot with considerable adroitness, although there are weaknesses in structure and style. Some readers will feel that the exposition of information can sometimes be too static, as in Smiley's long disquisition about Dieter in "The Unrespectable Club," which might have been presented more dramatically by means of a flashback. Others may find that there is an excessive amount of recapitulation as Smiley goes over the case in his mind. Others may think that the plot hinges too much on chance and coincidence: that everything depends on Dieter accidentally seeing Smiley with Fennan, whom he rightly suspects of being on the verge of denouncing Elsa as a spy; and that Dieter should suddenly reappear in this way in Smiley's life after seventeen years. There are occasional lapses of style too when le Carré's usual firm control of language gives way to cliché unredeemed by irony—"the inscrutable purpose of the universe" (p. 148). But whatever its limitations *Call for the Dead* must be regarded as an extraordinary literary début by a writer seeking to revitalize radically the conventions of crime and spy fiction instead of succumbing to them. Above all it is le Carré's creation of the fascinating and complex character of Smiley, scholar and spy, man of sensitivity and scruples in an insensitive and unscrupulous world, that makes the novel so memorable. It is therefore ironic that when Sidney Lumet filmed the novel in 1966, in the wake of Martin Ritt's 1965 screen version of *The Spy Who Came in from the Cold*, Hollywood politics resulted in Smiley being renamed Dobbs and substantially changed from le Carré's conception to suit James Mason's elegant style of acting; le Carré explains that "Paramount by now had a lien on the character of Smiley and would not release him."[19] The movie itself was renamed *The Deadly Affair* because, in le Carré's words, "some paragon in Columbia smelt Dracula in the original title," and Penguin reprinted its paperback edition under that title in 1966.

3

An Exercise in Class: *A Murder of Quality* (1962)

To call *A Murder of Quality* a sequel to *Call for the Dead* might suggest a closer similarity between the two books than in fact exists, but in several respects le Carré's second novel is a sequel to his first. The central figure is Smiley, whose viewpoint the reader again shares for much of the novel although as in *Call for the Dead* the use of a third-person narrative allows le Carré to describe events in a few chapters without Smiley's presence. Chronologically the Rode case in *A Murder of Quality* follows fairly closely on the Fennan case in *Call for the Dead*, with Smiley, having resigned from his post in the earlier book, no longer employed in intelligence work. Instead he is devoting his time to "a little private research on seventeenth-century Germany,"[1] as he explains to Inspector Rigby, the policeman with whom he cooperates. As here, there are numerous reminders of the previous novel, including such fleeting ones as the single mention of Mendel as a man who can be relied on and the passing reference to "an unnamed building in Knightsbridge" (p. 12), which is established in *Call for the Dead* as the focus of Smiley's nostalgia for a bygone phase of both his own life and British Intelligence.

References to Smiley's marriage are, however, far less frequent in *A Murder of Quality* than in its predecessor, and le Carré says nothing about the outcome of Smiley's journey to Switzerland to see Ann at the end of *Call for the Dead*. What does bring their former relationship to the surface is the location of most of the action in the fictional West Country town of Carne, where Lady Ann Sercomb's aristocratic family has its ancestral seat, Sawley Castle. The presence and influence of the Sawleys in the district is evident in several ways; for example, the hotel where Smiley stays is the Sawley Arms. The marriage of Ann, who is Lord Sawley's cousin, to someone considered "quite unsuitable" (p. 85) lingers in the folk memory of Carne as one of its juiciest pieces of gossip fifteen years after the wedding itself. In the circumstances, Smiley finally leaves Carne with relief even though his fears that revisiting it will be emotionally painful prove to be groundless, since nothing "of the place where his wife had spent her childhood" (p. 132) reminds him of her.

Le Carré's presentation of Smiley in *A Murder of Quality* is extremely consistent with that in the previous novel. The anti-heroic likening of Smiley to a frog is repeated in *A Murder of Quality* when Rigby, having asked about Smiley and been told, "Looks like a frog, dresses like a bookie," verifies this description for himself on their initial meeting: "Well, he looked like a frog, right enough. Short and stubby, round spectacles with thick lenses that made his eyes big. And his clothes *were* odd. Expensive, mind, you could see that. But his jacket seemed to drape where there wasn't any room for drape" (p. 26). Miss Brimley, one of Smiley's wartime colleagues in the Secret Service, remembers him for his sartorial inelegance, his diffidence, and his appearance as "the very prototype of an unsuccessful middle-aged bachelor in a sedentary occupation" (p. 16). Significantly, at the time she knew him Smiley was still young, not middle-aged; but as *Call for the Dead* makes clear, he is a man who seems to have passed from youth to middle age without any intervening phase. Smiley's response to the sensational reporting of Stella Rode's murder in the popular press as opposed to the sober accounts in two "quality" newspapers—"With an expression of distaste, Smiley screwed up all the newspapers except the *Guardian* and *The Times* and tossed them onto the luggage rack" (p. 24)—is entirely in keeping with the intellectual fastidiousness he displays in *Call for the Dead*.

Although *A Murder of Quality* is not about espionage, le Carré mentions Smiley's long career in intelligence work as a way of defining the kind of man he is, establishing again the contradictory aspects of this complex outsider so fully delineated in the previous book, such as the strange blend of intellectual integrity and his ability to make ends justify means by practicing various kinds of deception:

> A stringent critic of his own motives, he had discovered after long observation that he tended to be less a creature of intellect than his tastes and habits might suggest; once in the war he had been described by his superiors as possessing the cunning of Satan and the conscience of a virgin, which seemed to him not wholly unjust. (p. 73)

Smiley's "virginal satanism" or "satanic virginity" is abundantly evident in the three Smiley novels of the 1970s constituting *The Quest for Karla*, and only by playing down Smiley's paradoxical nature can Abraham Rothberg claim that le Carré "wishes us to consider George Smiley the epitome of the best England has to offer" and that Smiley is "Le Carré's paragon of English decency."[2] On a number of occasions in *A Murder of Quality* Smiley has recourse to deceit in order to facilitate some of the necessary interviews, and he performs his part impeccably. At the same time he acknowledges that in the case of Rode "it was a cheap trick to play on a man who had suddenly lost his wife" (p. 73).

Smiley's empirical methods of investigation, working with painstaking care from observation to deduction as he gleans information from a series of social contacts and interviews, are again obvious and reveal Smiley as "a creature of intellect":

> It had been one of Smiley's cardinal principles in research, whether among the incunabula of an obscure poet or the laboriously gathered fragments of intelligence, not to proceed beyond the evidence. A fact, once logically arrived at, should not be extended beyond its natural significance. (p. 92)

The way in which he solves the baffling problem of how the murderer disposed of his blood-stained clothes and the rubber boots he must have been wearing when he brutally battered Stella Rode to death with a piece of coaxial cable at her own home is an excellent example of Smiley's ability to yoke together apparently unconnected pieces of information so as to make a vital discovery. On this occasion Smiley cannot himself confirm his conclusion about the parcel he suspects of containing the evidence, and has to send Miss Brimley in London on what might be a wild-goose chase to verify his hypothesis. Much the same alertness to the possible significance of what might be thought unimportant, and the same intellectual subtlety in deciphering that significance, is evident in Smiley's deductions about the contents of the small brief case that Rode left at Fielding's house on the night of his wife's murder and had to return for. There would seem to be no possible link between the examination papers in the case (and therefore Tim Perkins's examination performance) and Stella Rode's murder, but after Perkins's seemingly accidental death Smiley deduces the connection. By doing so, he confirms that Perkins's death was not accidental, and the identity of the murderer is then obvious. Twice in *Call for the Dead* Smiley resorts to pencil and paper in an attempt to pin the evidence down and arrange it in a systematic way so as to arrive at a solution, and in *A Murder of Quality* he does something similar when he lists all the suspects and their possible motives in an effort to clarify this "most obscure problem of all" (p. 92).

Yet here Smiley is entering the world of the unknowable, and there are several passages in *A Murder of Quality* that recall Smiley's Conradian scepticism in *Call for the Dead* about the possibility of arriving at any certainty when dealing with human nature. Asked to offer an explanation of why the prime suspect, Rode, should have committed murder, Smiley replies: "I don't believe that we can ever entirely know what makes anyone do anything" (p. 130). Elsewhere, the eminently rational Smiley acknowledges to himself the limitations of reason when dealing with people and the absurdity of trying to attain absolute truth:

> Making his way through the Carne streets, he reflected for the hundredth time on the obscurity of motive in human action: there is no true thing on earth. There is no constant, no dependable point, not even in the purest logic or the most obscure mysticism; least of all in the motives of men when they are moved to act violently. (p. 113)

Smiley's acceptance of the principle of uncertainty in human affairs helps to explain the apparent paradox that this would-be "creature of intellect" is also a man of intuition and instinct. In *Call for the Dead* there are times when Smiley apprehends something important by non-rational or only partly rational means, notably that almost visionary moment in "The Dresden Group" when he finally solves the Fennan case by making an imaginative leap on the basis of what his logical processes have presented to him. In *A Murder of Quality* le Carré explains Smiley's heightened responsiveness to other people in terms of his career as a spy, since in order to succeed and even survive he has had to cultivate an almost extrasensory awareness:

> But this fear, this servility, this dependence, had developed in Smiley a perception for the colour of human beings: a swift, feminine sensitivity to their characters and motives. He knew mankind as a huntsman knows his cover, as a fox the wood. For a spy must hunt while he is hunted, and the crowd is his estate. He could collect their gestures and their words, record the interplay of glance and movement, as a huntsman can record the twisted bracken and the broken twig, or as a fox detects the signs of danger. (pp. 77–78)

Where *A Murder of Quality* differs significantly from *Call for the Dead* is in the context where Smiley operates. Le Carré's second novel is not concerned with intelligence work at all and conforms in many ways to the classical detective story, being primarily a murder investigation in a closed community with Smiley functioning as a private detective in collaboration with the police, rather like Lord Peter Wimsey. The murderer also turns out to be "the least likely person," a device often used by the masters of the classical detective novel. *A Murder of Quality* is consequently less strikingly original than its predecessor, although le Carré rings enough unusual changes on the orthodox formula to produce a thoroughly individual novel, and one foreshadowing two later novels about investigations in closed communities, *A Small Town in Germany* and *Tinker, Tailor, Soldier, Spy*, neither of which, however, is a murder mystery. The only connection with the world of espionage concerns the wartime association between Smiley and Ailsa Brimley, now editor of a Nonconformist weekly, *Christian Voice*. It is after receiving a disturbing letter from Stella Rode that Brim (as she is affectionately known) turns to Smiley for help even though she has not seen him for many years. In her letter Mrs. Rode, the wife of a teacher at Carne School, accuses her husband of planning to kill her and makes a desperate plea for assistance. No sooner is Smiley summoned by Brim than he telephones one of the masters at Carne School, Terence Fielding, the brother of one of Smiley's most distinguished wartime colleagues, to discover that Stella has been murdered, strangely enough after she and her husband had had dinner with Fielding himself. Smiley suddenly finds himself drawn into a situation that, out of loyalty to Brim, he feels he has to pursue further on her behalf.

After the relatively panoramic range of social and political reference in *Call for the Dead*, *A Murder of Quality* is bound to seem narrow in focus, ostensibly being limited to a small number of characters in a provincial town containing a boys' public school. Nevertheless le Carré succeeds in giving both the town and the school emblematic status so that they become representative microcosms of English society at large, metaphors of the condition of England. Furthermore, by placing Carne near the heart of Hardy's Wessex, le Carré introduces into his novel some distant echoes of Hardy, one of whose great achievements was to transform the regional into the universal. The description of Pylle in chapter 7 locates this village not only in a landscape but also in a timescape of ancient history and even legend (Roman and Arthurian Britain), much as Hardy stresses the historically remote aspects of the environment in which his characters move. In Hardy there is often a sense of the past being contained in the present, and for the villagers in *A Murder of Quality* even the distant past is tangibly close. Mundy, the local policeman, "managed to imply that the Black Death was a fairly recent disaster in those parts, if not actually within living memory" (p. 64). Although regarded locally as a witch, the village idiot Mad Janie, one of the main suspects in the case, is very much a product of the most close-knit, inbred, and incestuous communities of rural Wessex. One of the problems presented by the case is that Mad Janie is the only eyewitness and her evidence—"there's not many seen the Devil fly, Mister. But Janie seed 'im, Janie seed 'im. Silver wings like fishes 'e done 'ad, Janie saw" (p. 59)—sounds like gibberish, although it makes sense when Smiley eventually decodes it as her description of the gray-haired killer wearing a transparent plastic raincoat.

With the sentence, "Gloom and the cold" (p. 2), at the opening of the fourth paragraph of *A Murder of Quality*, le Carré establishes the bleak, wintry conditions in which the action takes place even though Easter is approaching, and there are descriptions throughout the novel of freezing weather, snow-covered landscapes, icy roads, long nights, and prevailing darkness. This short sentence sums up the external scene, but by immediately linking the weather with his evocation of Carne School le Carré suggests that the gloom and coldness are attributes of the school itself: "the cloud of gloom was as firmly settled as ever over the grey towers of Carne." In a brief and curiously worded foreword to the novel, omitted from the American paperback, le Carré warns the reader against interpreting Carne School as a "deliberate image" of one of the "dozen great schools" it might be thought to represent, such as Eton (where le Carré taught), Harrow, Rugby, or especially his own school, Sherborne, since he locates Carne in the vicinity of the north Dorset town of Sherborne.[3] He nevertheless presents Carne School as the fictional equivalent of a major English public school—an exclusive, single-sex, fee-paying, boarding school for the wealthy elite of England's hierarchical society or "the Quality," to use an old-fashioned term that le Carré puns on in the title. The murder is "of quality" in the sense that it is a sophisticated crime, but it also involves "the Quality." Furthermore there is a suggestion that "quality" itself, meaning excellence or high standards, is paradoxically being murdered by a type of school that prides itself on preserving standards, but that thrives on dead tradition and exists to perpetuate snobbishness and social division. When Brim receives Stella's letter from Carne School, the letterhead is sufficient to remind her of the often repeated words of her employer, Lord Landsbury, in defense of privilege: "The value of intelligence depends on its breeding. . . . We are not democratic. We close the door on intelligence without parentage" (pp. 13–14). Although Fielding asserts to Smiley, "The very name Carne means quality" (p. 123), le Carré radically questions this conception of "quality" throughout the novel.

Apart from Smiley's process of detection, much of the interest of *A Murder of Quality* lies in le Carré's brilliant evocation of the school itself, with all its backward-looking pretentiousness, and of the members of its staff whom Smiley thinks of as possible suspects. Indeed, although le Carré skillfully sustains the suspense of the murder investigation by periodic advances to a solution, he employs the formula of classical detective fiction as a vehicle for exploring Carne itself and what it represents. Le Carré thereby achieves a synthesis of the crime novel with the novel of social satire, and it is the latter aspect that is most in need of elucidation. The cultivation of superiority is located even within the language the school uses to describe itself. What would be called the Easter Term in the maintained or state system of education (equivalent to public schools in the USA) is known as the Lent Half because, as le Carré observes with acerbic irony, "terms are not elegant things" (p. 1). The day is measured less in hours and minutes than by the canonical hours employed by the Church to mark the seven divine offices of each day: matins, prime, terce, sext, nones, vespers, and compline. This extraordinary usage also indicates that Carne School is at the extreme Anglo-Catholic (consequently most exclusive and elitist) end of the religious spectrum constituting the Anglican Community. Even the Latin motto le Carré invents for the school, *Regem defendere diem videre* (p. 13), suggests pompous affectation. It sounds most impressive but does not make much sense—"To defend the king (and) to see the day." In treating both the institution and its staff, le Carré obviously employs caricature; but as satirists have known since the time of Aristophanes, the distortion of caricature can be a way of exposing the truth, of clarifying what is masked behind appearances. As an artistic mode realism can be only skin-deep, so in probing a world in which pretense and hypocrisy are endemic le Carré's methods of irony and caricature are more appropriate than orthodox realism.

Significantly, the novel opens with Carne School rather than Smiley and le Carré's succinct description is characterized by pungent irony:

> The greatness of Carne School has been ascribed by common consent to Edward VI, whose educational zeal is ascribed by history to the Duke of Somerset. But Carne prefers the respectability of the monarch to the questionable politics of his adviser, drawing strength from the conviction that Great Schools, like Tudor Kings, were ordained in Heaven. (p. 1)

Le Carré immediately undermines the school's widely acknowledged "greatness" by suggesting that even the accepted account of its sixteenth-century endowment is myth rather than history, a lie (or at best a half-truth) being preferred to the truth to ensure the most respectable ancestry with God very much on its side. In the very first paragraph le Carré makes the connection between respectability and hypocrisy. By a clever use of personification—"Carne had straightened its collar, scrubbed its rustic hands and face and presented itself shining to the courts of the twentieth century"—le Carré wittily describes how this "Dorset bumpkin" of a school had become "London's darling" and ingratiated itself with parents at the top end of the social scale, including royalty (the young prince) as well as aristocrats (young Sawley). Nevertheless it is not its modernity but its antique qualities that explain its success: "Carne had parchments in Latin, seals in wax, and Lammas Land behind the Abbey. Carne had property, cloisters and woodworm, a whipping block and a line in the Doomsday Book—then what more did it need to instruct the sons of the rich?" What matters is tradition and history, a past that can be traced back to the land survey carried out in 1086 by William I and known as the Domesday or Doomsday Book. As in the description of Merridale Lane in *Call for the Dead*, the presence of woodworm seems to confer prestige, although le Carré is again employing this metonym for decay ironically to subvert the notion of value based simply on age. The trappings of the Middle Ages, whether "cloisters" or "a whipping block," hardly guarantee an excellent education, but for the parents who send their boys to Carne they represent something more important: conservatism and tradition.

Smiley's whole experience of Carne is like that of a time traveler going back a century or two. Seeing the battlements of the school at a distance, he interprets them as actual defensive structures, "keeping the new world out and the old world secure," something confirmed by his sense of the boys grouped "in the leisured attitudes of eighteenth-century England" (p. 78). In this environment it is to be expected that the curate at the D'Arcys' sherry party should embark "on a diffuse apologia for ancient custom" (p. 85), and that D'Arcy himself should deplore, in a thoroughly English way, the idea of change: "Many

Public Schools have conceded to the vulgar clamour for change—change at any price. Carne, I am pleased to say, has not joined these Gadarene swine" (p. 56). Even Smiley's discussion about the murder with the chief constable, Brigadier Havelock, another spokesman for reactionary conservatism, becomes an extension of his encounters with school staff when Havelock declares: "Experiments never pay, do they. You can't experiment with tradition. . . . It takes centuries to make a gentleman" (pp. 129–30). The Sawley Arms, with its portraits of "a dozen generations of Lord Sawley's forbears, puffy men in crumbling pigment" (p. 86), also embodies reverence for the past, although by pinpointing the element of disintegration—"crumbling" paint—le Carré subtly undermines this attitude. Smiley finds the hotel "inefficient, antiquated and smug" (p. 91). Le Carré certainly presents the English devotion to tradition as the opposite of life-enhancing, perhaps even a form of the death wish, and his powerful description of the boys returning to school is shrouded in images of death:

> The trains would unload sad groups of black-coated boys on to the station platform. They came in great cars that shone with mournful purity. They came to bury poor King Edward, trundling handcarts over the cobbled streets or carrying tuck boxes like little coffins. Some wore gowns, and when they walked they looked like crows, or black angels come for the burying. Some followed singly like undertakers' mutes, and you could hear the clip of their boots as they went. They were always in mourning at Carne; the small boys because they must stay and the big boys because they must leave, the masters because mourning was respectable and the wives because respectability was underpaid. (pp. 1–2)

Considering this emphasis on the color of death, the title of the opening chapter, "Black Candles," is revealing. The candles are those the old homosexual Fielding burns at the dinner parties he is giving before his retirement after thirty years at the school; ostensibly they symbolize his sadness at leaving. There is something decidedly ostentatious about black candles, redolent of a black mass, and this fits in with the flamboyant, arty, fin de siècle diabolism Fielding cultivates: "Alcoholique et poète" (p. 45), he calls himself in a moment of self-dramatization as though he is a leftover from the Aesthetes and Decadents of the 1890s. Then there is the amazing, quasi-religious garment he wears in his capacity as senior housemaster when Smiley dines with him: not "customary academic dress" but "a wonderful confection of heavy black skirts and legal bib, like a monk in evening dress" (p. 42), which he bizarrely adorns with flowers to soften its austere solemnity. Fielding likes visual effects, and the various references to painters in the novel are made by him. Yet the blackness of the candles conveys a morbidity that Fielding does not intend; just as his pseudomedieval costume, which makes him resemble Dracula (he actually calls himself "the Vampire of Carne" [p. 45]), is not only a display of status, but confirmation that he and his school belong to a dead past—and, what is more, a make-believe past that never was. In the closing pages of the novel when Smiley and Fielding meet for the last time, Smiley diagnoses the condition of living death, hinting but never stating that he is talking about Fielding himself:

> And there are some of us—aren't there?—who are nothing, who are so labile that we astound ourselves; we're the chameleons. . . . They can't feel anything inside them, no pleasure or pain, no love or hate; they're ashamed and frightened that they can't feel. And their shame, this shame, Fielding, drives them to extravagance and colour. . . . The world sees them as showmen, fantasists, liars, as sensualists perhaps, not for what they are: the living dead. (pp. 148–49)

Le Carré is careful not to equate Fielding with the whole school, since other people embody different aspects of the institution, but the emotional and spiritual emptiness at the heart of Fielding accords with a lack in the school itself for all its outward religious paraphernalia.

The three main representatives of the school, Fielding himself, Shane Hecht, and Felix D'Arcy, belong to a tradition of larger-than-life characterization descending from Ben Jonson's Jacobean plays such as *Volpone*. The arrogant and supercilious Shane, "massive and enveloping, like a faded Valkyrie" (p. 4), is truly grotesque, an almost Dickensian figure whose smile is "the slow rotten smile of a whore" and who "within her great ugly body . . . was as cunning as a snake" (p. 6). In describing her le Carré uses the exaggeration of caricature, but whenever she speaks she possesses a horrifying credibility. She is the embodiment of social superiority and snobbery, and her potential for sly malice and loathing emerges in everything she says, especially her contemptuous irony at the expense of Stella Rode: "such a nice person, I always thought . . . and so *unusual*. She did such clever things with the same dress" (p. 82). The apparent compliment is, in fact, a vicious sneer; she praises in order to damn. For Shane other people seem to exist to be ridiculed.

If le Carré is highly successful in providing Shane with an appropriate style of speech, he is no less successful in the very different case of D'Arcy. This is most obvious at Fielding's dinner party for Smiley and D'Arcy, when the latter's eloquent defense of Carne's standards is couched in formal, precise, and prim speech far removed from the colloquial: "I am sensible that this determination has made me on more than one occasion unpopular. But such comment or advice as I offer is never—I beg you to notice this—is *never* directed against personalities, only against behaviour, against unseemly lapses in conduct" (p. 48). "Unseemly" is one of D'Arcy's favorite words, and he emerges as the principal standard bearer of etiquette and protocol in Carne, sensitive to every nuance of conduct. Even though Fielding pokes fun at D'Arcy's obsession with decorum when describing him to Smiley—"If you wear a gown on a bicycle, reply incorrectly to an invitation, make a fault in the *placement* of your dinner guests or speak of a colleague as 'Mister,' D'Arcy will find you out and admonish you" (p. 45)—Carne does take its customs, manners, and refinement of social propriety very seriously indeed. Le Carré's description of D'Arcy is less grotesque than that of Shane, but the element of caricature is obvious in this piece of Dickensian portraiture:

> The skin of his face was so unlined that he somehow suggested fatness without being fat. His voice was pitched on one insinuating note, and he smiled all the time, whether he was speaking or not. The smile never left his smooth face, it was worked into the malleable fabric of his flesh, stretching his lips across his perfect teeth and opening the corners of his red mouth, so that it seemed to be held in place by the invisible fingers of his dentist. (p. 49)

The permanent smile makes him seem like a corpse that has been beautified by cosmetic morticians.

Fielding is an altogether more complex character than Shane or D'Arcy. Even in an environment where most people are expert at role-playing and at living at the level of pretense, Fielding is undoubtedly the master, which is why he also proves to be such a consummate hypocrite. One of his favorite parts is that of devil's advocate, putting the case against Carne School in order to provoke his more straightforward colleagues to anger. In the opening chapter he does this at his dinner party for the Hechts, claiming that all he has done with his life is to have "entrenched a ruling class which is distinguished by neither talent, culture, nor wit; kept alive for one more generation the distinctions of a dead age" (p. 6). This attack culminates in what appears to be a savage debunking of the school—"we haven't had an original thought between us for the last fifty years of our lives" (p. 7)—but is Fielding simply teasing Hecht and enjoying his victim rise to the bait, or is he saying what he really thinks under the guise of an elaborate joke? Or by presenting what he feels to be the truth in the form of a charade, is he trying to disguise the unacceptable truth from himself? Fielding puts on a very similar performance for Smiley at his next dinner party, and for Smiley the problem is to identify the elusive reality concealed beneath Fielding's theatrical virtuosity and "big-screen style" (p. 46), which he finds both fascinating and repellent.

Considering the importance of façades at Carne School, much of Smiley's effort in detection is concerned with peeling away layers of appearances to locate the truth buried within, rather than following a line of deduction on the basis of the physical evidence. For Smiley, therefore, the case becomes an investigation of people rather than clues, and critical discussion needs to focus on the characters in their environment, the victim as much as the suspects. Smiley does not, of course, neglect the clues, but on their own they can mislead and some were indeed designed by the murderer to mislead. The obvious inference that Stella was killed by Mad Janie, who is in possession of jewelry worn by Stella at the time of her death, is rejected by Smiley even though the local chief constable initially accepts it. Much more than in *Call for the Dead* Smiley is in pursuit of a motive, and the various interviews he conducts are ways of digging deeply into the characters of both victim and suspects. Yet here too Smiley initially encounters a stumbling block. In listing possible murderers of Stella, he concludes that "in a sane world" none of them could be said to have anything resembling an adequate motive, but this in turn prompts the question of whether Carne School is a sane world: "Year in year out they must share the same life, say the same things to the same people, sing the same hymns." In an attempt to define the nature of this closed, self-devouring community where utter trivialities can be so important and where normality is in abeyance, Smiley resorts to the metaphors of illness and of a sanatorium earlier used by Fielding:

> You had to be ill, you had to be sick to understand, you had to be there in the sanatorium, not for weeks, but for years, had to be one in the line of white beds, to know the smell of their food and the greed in their eyes. You had to hear it and see it, to be part of it, to know their rules and recognise their transgressions. This world was compressed into a mould of anomalous conventions: blind, pharasaical but real. (p. 93)

In building up his portrait of the school, le Carré does not neglect the relationship—or lack of one—between it and the town of Carne, especially as he makes this symbolic of other divisions in English society. Rigby, who collaborates with Smiley in a way not unlike Mendel in *Call for the Dead*, explains the "big gap between the Town and Gown" to Smiley, drawing attention to the self-contained nature of the school itself: "They've got their own community, see, and no one outside it can get in" (p. 28). The fact that most of the masters were themselves educated at Carne makes it almost incestuous. The "big gap" is reinforced by differences in religious affiliation, the distance between lower-class Town and upper-class Gown being confirmed by that between Chapel (Nonconformism) and Church (Church of England). Carne School is Establishment through and through; the townspeople of Carne, tradesmen and shopkeepers, inhabit a different world. At the funeral of Stella, who is the only person attached to the school to have had much to do with the town, schoolmasters and their wives occupy one part of the church while representatives of the town gather in another part. Even death fails to bring the two sides together. Referring to the public school where he taught, Eton, and the Foreign Office for which he worked, le Carré has commented on the "big gap" separating the English ruling class from the ordinary populace: "I found them two institutions so fortified against the outside world that they had no hope of personal contact with the people they were meant to govern."[4]

There is a further social dimension to this dichotomy, embodied in Stella herself. Her family comes from the North of England so that the familiar distinction between North and South is brought within the precincts of this bastion of southern superiority, Carne School. One of the outstanding works of Victorian fiction, Mrs. Gaskell's *North and South*, invokes the distinction in its very title. Put very crudely, the opposition is between the more heavily industrialized, working-class, deprived, and poorer North of England and the more rural, middle and upper-class, privileged, and wealthier South. Politically, the South is predominantly Conservative while the North is predominantly Labour. When the super snob Shane Hecht declares, "Only about three good families between Ipswich and Newcastle" (p. 82), she is dismissing the entire area betwen a line about forty miles north of London (on which Ipswich lies) and the Scottish border (Newcastle upon Tyne is the most northerly city in England) as a socially irrelevant waste land of boors: anyone of interest or importance is bound to be in the South. This is a case of Shane expressing in extreme form what in real life tends to be thought rather than stated.

This North-South contrast is not a simple geographical one but is emblematic of divisions throughout English society, a point le Carré makes with particularly cutting force in the opening paragraph of a chapter set in London rather than Carne, "The Quality of Mercy" (chapter 14). Here the contrast is between the social face of the Public Schools Committee for Refugee Relief, complete with aristocratic patroness (the Countess of Sawley) and occupying a smart office in fashionable and wealthy Belgravia (north of the Thames), and the business part of the organization, "relegated to the south of the river, to one of those untended squares in Kennington which are part of London's architectural schizophrenia" (p. 105). The schizophrenia is social as well as architectural.

As a writer le Carré is fascinated by the gradations of class in English society and by the ways in which these are transmitted through the minutiae of behavior, dress, and accent. In such a class-conscious society, deviations from a particular code are easily noticed, and Carne is as sensitive to minor breaches of protocol as the princess in the fairy tale is to a pea concealed beneath a mattress. The Rodes stand out at Carne because their backgrounds are entirely alien to the school, both coming from very ordinary families and being Baptists. Before coming to Carne, Rode has taught in a grammar school in the maintained or state system of education, of which he is a product, something Fielding points out in his characteristically sardonic way: "He'd never seen a game of rugger before he came here, you know. They don't play rugger at grammar schools—it's all soccer" (p.5). In England (though not in neighboring Wales) rugby, or rugger as it tends to be called in public schools, is a more socially prestigious form of football than soccer, which attracts a lot of working-class support. Even sport is riddled with class distinctions. It is symptomatic that the Rodes' dog was a nondescript mongrel whereas D'Arcy's sister, Dorothy, breeds pedigree dogs, a pursuit of many upper-crust women in the country, and not only wins prizes at regional dog shows for her King Charles spaniels but "was commended at Cruft's" (p. 51), England's premier show.

In a conversation between two schoolboys at the opening of the novel, one says of Rode: "He's so *keen*, bouncing about all the time. You can tell he's not a gentleman" (p.3). Even these adolescents can read conduct in class terms so that Rode's display of enthusiasm brands him as different and socially inferior. In citing Fielding's comment that "emotionalism is only for the lower classes," the boys are not thinking specifically of Rode, but the remark does embody the Carnian view of him. Rode gives himself away by trying so hard to keep up with the Carnians that he is obviously behaving in a way unnatural for him. Unlike Stella, Rode has succumbed to the seductive force of the school and tried to conform, even changing his religious allegiance to the Church of England, something regarded by Stella's father, Mr. Glaston, as a betrayal verging on treachery: "Where I come from in the North, we don't do that. Chapel was something we'd stood up for and won. Almost like the vote" (p. 79). Yet Rode fails to disguise what he is, as Smiley, that ultrasensitive surveyor of human behavior and social nuance, recognizes the first time he sees Rode at his wife's funeral and again during their conversation on the following day:

> If it is vulgar to wear a pen in the breast pocket of your jacket, to favour Fair Isle pullovers and brown ties, to bob a little and turn your feet out as you walk, then Rode beyond a shadow of doubt was vulgar, for though he did not now commit these sins, his manner implied them all. . . . You could tell all the time, from every word and gesture, what he was; from the angle of his elbow as he drank his coffee, from the swift, expert pluck at the knee of his trouser leg as he sat down. (pp. 71, 75)

Neither Smiley nor le Carré are upholding the accusation of vulgarity that snobbish Carne would level at Rode, and "sins" is used ironically to subvert Carne's solemn devotion to manners. It is not Rode's social background that bothers Smiley, but his attempt to conceal it and pretend to be what he is not. Finally, however, Smiley's response to Rode is not one of intellectual judgment but of compassion for a vulnerable fellow being whose isolation Smiley is familiar with: "Rode had tried so hard—he had used Carne's language, bought the right clothes, and thought as best he could the right thoughts, yet remained hopelessly apart, hopelessly alone" (pp. 140-41).

Unlike her husband, Stella made no effort to ingratiate herself with Carne by adopting its mores. As Fielding puts it: "She was everything we're forced to ignore—she was red-brick, council estates, new towns, the very antithesis of Carne!" (p. 47). Stella's adherence to Chapel, her mixing with the townspeople, her befriending of Mad Janie, all put her beyond the pale, but her social solecisms took innumerable forms so that as far as Carne was concerned she could not put a foot right. In his typically prissy way D'Arcy notes how the masters' wives responded to her: "Her clothes, I believe, were a source of distress to some of them. She also frequented the public laundry. This, too, would not make a favourable impression" (pp. 48–49). And the bitchiest of the wives, Shane Hecht, has her own sour comment to make: "I went to tea with Stella once. Milk in first and Indian. So different" (p. 83). "So different" could be an expression of unexpected delight, but coming from this master of verbal venom it is loaded with contempt for Stella's failure to observe the social niceties. For Shane, Stella's use of Indian rather than China tea and her habit of putting milk into the cup before the tea rather than the other way round mark her as irredeemably lower class. In English society even the most trivial things speak of class distinctions and indicate "background," a very important word in the novel.

The effect on the reader of all this antagonism towards Stella even after her murder is to attract sympathy for a woman who has apparently had the integrity to remain true to her convictions and not attempt to emulate the foreign ways of her supposed social superiors. Even D'Arcy's Carnian sister, Dorothy, adds to this impression in her rejoinder to Mrs. Hecht: "Stella Rode may have been damn' bad form, Shane, but she did a lot for my refugees. . . . Collecting for them. Clothes, furniture, money. One of the few wives who *did* anything" (p. 83). Initially, Stella emerges as a victim of Carne School—an uncomplicated, honest, generous, sincere, and devout woman who has been destroyed because she is such an intolerable outsider.

Yet Stella was not what she seemed. Her image as the only genuine person in the theatrical environment of Carne School proves false. The full revelation of what she really was comes only near the end in chapter 19, "Disposal of a Legend," in which Rode, now being pursued by the police to face a murder charge, tells Smiley the truth about Stella, although le Carré is careful to prepare for this volte-face so that it does not seem a trick ending. As early as chapter 4 there is a hint that Stella could be devious, when Smiley discovers that Stella's letter to Brim contains a lie. In the next chapter, "Cat and Dog," the story of Stella having her dog destroyed is inconclusive but it does leave a question mark hanging over her, especially as D'Arcy accuses Stella of having invented "an absolute string of lies from beginning to end" (p. 52). The testimony of such committed Carnians as D'Arcy and Shane Hecht is inevitably suspect, and their bad opinion of Stella could be interpreted as a guarantee of her worth, but it is possible that D'Arcy's remark, "She was a thoroughly mischievous woman, Smiley, who made it her business to hold her husband up to ridicule" (p. 56), and Shane's comment, "She was one of those tiresome little snobs who think that only the humble are virtuous" (p. 83) contain a grain of truth. The same can be said of Major Harriman's comments to Smiley when he visits this local vet in an attempt to learn more about Stella's dog:

> "She was trouble," he said crisply. "I can spot 'em. I've had a few in the regiment, wives who are trouble. Little simpering types. Butter-wouldn't-melt, holier-than-thou. Arrange the flowers in the church and all that—pious as you please. I'd say she was the hysterical kind, self-dramatising, weeping all over the house for days on end. Anything for a bit of drama." (p. 98)

More disturbing altogether is what emerges in the immediately ensuing conversation Smiley has with the local Baptist minister from the North, Cardew, whose indirectness seems to be a way of concealing something detrimental to Stella's memory: "I've never met an angel, and Stella Rode was no exception" (p. 100). This could mean, "Stella, like the rest of us, was not perfect," but the use of two negatives suggests something decidedly different: "Stella was very far from perfect."

The distance separating her not only from perfection but from the do-gooding moral rectitude and piety she assumed becomes clear only with Rode's outpourings to Smiley. Before marrying Stella, Rode himself was completely taken in by her and dismissed her father's warnings that "she was bad—bad in her heart" and "full of malice" (p. 136) as nonsense. Once at Carne, Rode learned the hard way that Stella's father knew her much better than he did, and that she was a supreme hypocrite, a woman in whom the gap between appearance and reality was even wider than that between Town and Gown in Carne: "She could spin a good tale about anything. . . . She kind of stepped into a part and played it right through" (p. 139). What gave her pleasure was having power over people so that she could hurt them socially. Under the mask of meekness she went out of her way to humiliate her husband as much as possible in the eyes of his colleagues. She was a psychological sadist of immense cunning who loved making her victims squirm. As such she hoarded "every drop of gossip and dirt," not to enjoy with the usual salacious enthusiasm of the gossip, but to use spitefully and vindictively against people: "anything decent, anything good, she'd drag it down and spoil it" (p. 138). Rode's revelations about Stella include the authentic versions of events described earlier in the novel, where Stella usually emerges with considerable credit. In Ann Snow's accounts of how Stella came to her assistance in her dealings with Mulligan over furniture removal and of how Stella helped the Hungarian refugees staying with the D'Arcys, Stella emerges as the savior of the situation, the role she self-righteously created for herself. The truth as revealed by Rode is very different. Stella used a form of blackmail in the case of Mulligan, and deliberately misled the Hungarians for the sole purpose of causing Miss D'Arcy great embarrassment. Even Stella's concern for Mad Janie was fraudulent; it was not motivated by kindness, as appears to be the case, but by cruelty, her desire to dominate completely another being. The true story about her dog is also thoroughly unpleasant and shows that her cruelty could take a physical as well as a psychological form.

It is only after Rode's startling confession that the connection between the two arch-hypocrites, Stella and Fielding, becomes clear, as does the motive for her murder. Stella happened to know the skeleton in Fielding's closet, his legal prosecution for a homosexual offense with a boy nearly thirty years earlier, and her arrival at Carne gave her a marvelous opportunity to exploit this well-kept secret. She practiced a particularly insidious form of blackmail against him, pursuing "something more pleasing, more gratifying to her twisted little mind" than money; in Smiley's words, what she wanted was "to command and own" Fielding (p. 147), to toy mercilessly with him like a cat with a mouse. Stella, having initially appeared as she would like to have been seen, finally emerges as a villain with Fielding as her victim.

The reversal that le Carré produces here, making the murdered Stella so unsympathetic that the murderer seems justified, is by no means unique in crime literature. Yet this is not a simple reversal of right and wrong, good and evil, since Fielding too is a corrupt figure. His killing of the schoolboy Tim Perkins, who really is an innocent victim, in order to protect himself is in a different category from his murder of Stella, but even this is not an impulsive response to a particularly unpleasant stimulus: it is a crime planned to the last detail so as to incriminate others. Although there is a fatalistic quality reminiscent of Hardy in the way that one long-concealed action in Fielding's past precipitates his downfall, he is completely lacking in the tragic stature of Henchard in *The Mayor of Casterbridge*. Fielding's finest performance as a hypocrite is in his second extended meeting with Smiley in chapter 16. There is a striking structural resemblance to *Call for the Dead* here, since in both novels Smiley has an early discussion with the person who eventually proves to be his quarry (Elsa the spy, Fielding the murderer) and much later, armed with more information, he returns for a more rigorous interview. Both Elsa and Fielding, as experts in the art of deception, attempt to mislead Smiley by confessing a lesser misdemeanor in order to lodge the main guilt elsewhere. By claiming to have altered Perkins's examination paper because of his love for the boy, Fielding is able to accuse Rode of Stella's murder and provide apparently incontrovertible evidence, but whereas Smiley is initially taken in by Elsa he is not fooled by Fielding in spite of the latter's convincing performance. Leaving Fielding, Smiley is "reasonably confident that Terence Fielding was the most accomplished liar he had met for a long time" (p. 125).

The end of *A Murder of Quality* also recalls that of *Call for the Dead* in that it is altogether less reassuring than those of "positive thrillers" or even "negative thrillers," to use Jerry Palmer's terms. The imagery of the final chapter, "The Dross of the River," is grim and depressing: the filthy Thames, the thick mist, the "foul morning"

(p. 144), the premonition of the hanging of the condemned murderer, and that extraordinarily bleak final sentence, "Only the half-lit street, and the shadows moving along it" (p. 151). The solution of the mystery with the unmasking of Fielding brings Smiley no satisfaction either at the personal or the public level: "He had come to the end of the chase, and was already sickened by the kill" (p. 143). What began as a phone call to Fielding, made because Smiley had been a close colleague of Fielding's heroic brother Adrian whose memory he reveres, leads with tragic irony to Fielding's arrest and probable execution. For Smiley the apparent success of his investigation is overshadowed by his distress at being responsible for the almost certain conviction of Adrian Fielding's brother. This is what sickens Smiley, but even at the public level there is little cause for rejoicing. A crime has been solved, the murderer apprehended, but the final picture of Fielding being bundled into a police car, shouting "They'll hang me" (p. 151), is of a pathetic victim of evil rather than its perpetrator. There is no sense of justice being done and moral order restored, because in the world depicted in the novel hypocrisy and corruption emerge as far more powerful forces than justice and order.

In *A Murder of Quality* le Carré exploits the formula of the classical detective story to present his personal vision of a world desperately in need of redemption but most unlikely to achieve it. Carne School emerges as a version of hell, a place of do-it-yourself damnation, not unlike Chandler's Bay City. For this reason, it falsifies the novel to interpret it too literally as being about the public school system or the condition of England, although it includes these themes. One could argue that the book is now dated because the public schools have changed considerably during the twenty years since it was written (although English society has an amazing ability to stay much the same beneath the surface for all the superficial transformations). However, this would miss the point. It would be like saying that Chandler wrote only realistic novels about Los Angeles. *A Murder of Quality* is a metaphysical novel as well as a social and satirical one, a remarkable fusion of orthodox crime fiction with an unblinkered and unblinking gaze at the enormous human potential for falsity and evil and for disguising that evil as good.

4

Blind Man's Double Bluff: *The Spy Who Came in from the Cold* (1963)

Both *Call for the Dead* and *A Murder of Quality* were warmly received, but neither attracted anything like the attention given to le Carré's third novel. With *The Spy Who Came in from the Cold* (subsequently referred to as *The Spy*), he achieved an extraordinary popular success, became a best-selling author, and established himself as a truly original writer of spy fiction. *The Spy* won a Crime Writers' Association Gold Dagger Award, a Somerset Maugham Award, and the Mystery Writers of America's Edgar Allan Poe Award. For many readers this novel remains his finest achievement, and even after the recent, widely seen television adaptations of two novels from his *Quest for Karla* trilogy, it is probably the book still most immediately associated with his name. *The Spy* departs from its predecessors in a number of ways, but one major difference is the absence of a murder inquiry and of the concomitant police presence. Le Carré now discards the formulas of detective fiction, which provide his previous novels with structural backbones, in order to concentrate wholeheartedly on the world of espionage, as he also does in the successor to *The Spy*, *The Looking Glass War*.

The great international success of *The Spy* liberated le Carré from the Foreign Service in 1964 and led his publishers to reissue his first two novels together in that year as *The Le Carré Omnibus* in Britain and *The Incongruous Spy* in the USA. But the most unexpected consequence was an article by V. Voinov in Moscow's *Literary Gazette* (14 October 1965), maintaining that le Carré had been a member of British Intelligence and accusing him of being an apologist for the Cold War. The first of these allegations was correct, although le Carré did not admit it publicly until 1983, but the second provoked a fascinating and pungently ironic response from le Carré in the form of an open letter published in *Encounter* (May 1966), "To Russia, with Greetings," a play on the title of Fleming's *From Russia, with Love* (1957). After agreeing with Voinov that he had "little good to say of the British power structure, or of the morals of British intelligence,"[1] and pointing out that he had been accused in the USA of writing a "pro-Communist" novel, le Carré goes on to expose the hypocrisy and humbug of the Soviet attitude towards him. Referring to the recently published *The Looking Glass War* (mentioned by Voinov) as well as *The Spy*, le Carré argues with force that, whereas Fleming's Bond novels can easily be accommodated to fit the morally facile and nationalistically heroic conception of spying fostered by Soviet ideology, his own novels present a truth inimical to that ideology:

> I now realise that both these books make an assumption which is anathema to a Communist, and directly contrary to the trend now established by the public relations team of the Soviet Secret Services: that the enemy is not outside us but within, that we fight not looking forward but looking back, not for the future but for the past. The problem of the Cold War is that, as Auden once wrote, we haunt a ruined century. Behind the little flags we wave, there are old faces weeping, and children mutilated by the fatuous conflicts of preachers. Mr. Voinov, I suspect, smelt in my writing the greatest heresy of all: that there is no victory and no virtue in the Cold War, only a condition of human illness and a political misery. And so he called me its apologist (he might as well have called Freud a lecher).[2]

As this makes clear, *The Spy* and *The Looking Glass War* aspire to the condition of serious fiction, not popular entertainment, and in looking back to these two books while reviewing *Tinker, Tailor, Soldier, Spy* Julian Symons rightly insists that "it was as a novelist that le Carré wanted to be considered, and these two books are surely very good novels, books that should be taken into account in any fictional view of the sixties. They use the spy story as a means of conveying an attitude towards life and society."[3] It is worth noting that as recently as 1981, after le Carré wrote a letter to *The Times* (1 July) protesting about the proposed cuts in the BBC's World Service, an English-language broadcast from Moscow accused him of being involved in a political campaign, obviously directed against the Soviet Union.

The spy or secret agent has a compelling attraction for many ordinary people, and because of the enormous expansion of intelligence and counterintelligence work during and since World War II, general interest has been greater than ever before. This is particularly true in Britain, partly because of the fascinating disclosures that have gradually been made about British Intelligence during the war, but also because of numerous postwar spy scandals of the Cold War from 1945 to the present day, as well as a curiosity about the gadgetry of intelligence work. At the time of writing (Easter Week 1984) a middle-ranking MI5 officer, Michael Bettaney, received a prison sentence of twenty-three years for a number of espionage offenses involving the Soviet Union in 1982 and 1983. George Orwell has usually been credited with coining the term "Cold War" in 1945 to describe the nonmilitary and ideological hostility that came into being between the Soviet bloc and the Western alliance after the defeat of Hitler. Walter Lippmann's influential study, *The Cold War*, dates from 1947. What the Cold War has ensured is a vast investment in intelligence, leading to the high-technology espionage we are familiar with today in the form of spy satellites.

In the immediate postwar period the British betrayers of atomic secrets to the Soviet Union, Alan Nunn May, Klaus Fuchs, and Bruno Pontecorvo, attracted most attention before the sensational defection in 1951 of Donald Maclean and Guy Burgess, two British diplomats who spied for the Russians and who were in imminent danger of exposure. Burgess had worked for MI6 and was therefore a double agent like his more senior associate Kim Philby, the so-called "Third Man." Philby, one-time Head of the Soviet section of MI6, was a classic example of a mole, supposedly masterminding British activities against the Soviet Union while secretly working for the Kremlin. Following the defection of Maclean and Burgess, Philby was suspected of being a double agent and dismissed, but he did not defect until 1963. As recently as 1979 repercussions of these defections caused widespread interest when Sir Anthony Blunt, one of the most eminent art historians in the world, one of Britain's leading cultural ambassadors, and a former director of the Courtauld Institute and surveyor of the Queen's Pictures, was publicly unveiled as a former double agent and was stripped of his knighthood by the Queen, sixteen years after Michael Straight named him to the FBI as an ex-mole. Like many young English intellectuals of the 1930s, the "Auden generation," Blunt had been attracted to Marxism as an undergraduate and had been recruited for Soviet Intelligence by Burgess at Cambridge before the war, during which he worked for MI5. After Straight's disclosures Blunt made a full confession to MI5 in 1964 on condition that he was guaranteed immunity from prosecution. What made these defections and revelations so disturbing, especially in the 1950s, was that Soviet penetration of the British Establishment has been perpetrated by men who on the surface were quintessential members of that Establishment, pillars of the community.

During the early 1960s when le Carré was launching his career as a novelist, there was a succession of spy trials, Cold War political crises, and related events that kept the world of intelligence more in the news than at any other time since the war. Philby's defection was only one of a number of sensations. The shooting down of an American U-2 high-altitude reconnaissance or "spy" plane (piloted by Gary Powers for the CIA) over the Soviet Union in May 1960, only weeks before a Paris summit meeting between President Eisenhower and Soviet Premier Khrushchev, dashed high hopes of improved relations between the two superpowers. It also provided the Russians with one of their best-ever propaganda coups. American spy planes played a crucial role in identifying the Soviet attempt to establish missile bases in Cuba in 1962 after Fidel Castro's successful revolution. This led to President Kennedy's military blockade of Cuba and the eventual climb-down by the Soviets, although the Cuban Missile Crisis nearly triggered off a third world war. There is a reference to U-2s in *The Looking Glass War*. Particularly relevant to *The Spy* was another development that contributed to the deteriorating relations between East and West during the early 1960s: the building of the Berlin Wall by the East Germans in 1961, effectively sealing West Berlin off from surrounding East German territory.

In Britain MI5's breaking up of the Portland Spy Ring, including the Soviet "illegal" Konon Molody, known as Gordon Lonsdale, led to a famous spy trial in 1961. It was followed by others in 1962. George Blake, an MI6 agent, was exposed as a double agent in 1961 after working for the Russians since 1953, and received an unprecedentedly long sentence of forty-two years' imprisonment because of the enormous damage he had done to British Intelligence. Blake escaped from prison in 1966 and made his way to Moscow. Later in 1962 John Vassall, who worked at the Admiralty and betrayed naval secrets to the Russians (as did Harry Houghton of the Portland Spy Ring), received an eighteen-year sentence, and Barbara Fell, an Assistant Overseas Controller of the Central Office of Information, was jailed for passing secrets to her lover at the Yugoslav Embassy. Also in 1962 Greville

Wynne, an MI6 agent operating behind the Iron Curtain as a businessman, and Colonel Oleg Penkovsky, a member of Soviet Military Intelligence also working for MI6 as a double agent, were arrested by the KGB. A show trial followed in 1963, resulting in a death sentence for Penkovsky and a prison term for Wynne, who was exchanged in 1964 for Lonsdale of the Portland Spy Ring. 1963 was, above all, the year of the Profumo Crisis, a most convoluted political, diplomatic, and sexual scandal involving a cabinet minister in Harold Macmillan's Conservative Government, John Profumo, his mistress Christine Keeler, and a Russian intelligence officer working at the London Embassy as a Naval Attaché, Eugene Ivanov, whom MI5 were trying to "turn" into a double agent by compromising him sexually, possibly using Miss Keeler whom he knew. Stephen Ward, a society osteopath who committed suicide after being convicted of living off immoral earnings in 1963, was involved in the MI5 operation. Profumo resigned from Parliament after his attempt to mislead the House of Commons was exposed, and the Crisis named after him, which became the subject of an official investigation (Denning Report), contributed to the defeat of Macmillan's Government at the General Election in 1964.

Three of the four novels le Carré wrote in the early 1960s are either partly (*Call for the Dead*) or wholly (*The Spy* and *The Looking Glass War*) about Cold War espionage and the ethics of spying. To some extent le Carré was writing about what he knew, as he was when he wrote about a public school in *A Murder of Quality*, but he was also in tune with the times. The immediate success of *The Spy* suggests that at a period when the possibility of a third world war loomed larger than usual, there was a sizable audience for a more serious fiction about Cold War espionage than Ian Fleming's escapist romances. This does not mean that le Carré's novels are semi-documentary or realistic transcriptions of the actual world of intelligence, even though they are much more true to life than the James Bond adventures. Le Carré's spy novels carry conviction and lead us back into the real world in a way that Fleming's fantasies do not even begin to, but this is not to say that British Intelligence has ever carried out an operation like the one described in *The Spy* or that the Department in *The Looking Glass War* corresponds to a real-life branch of British Intelligence.

Kim Philby, who had more than a little expertise in these matters, admired *The Spy* for its sophistication after "all that James Bond idiocy,"[4] but was convinced that an operation like the very devious one described in the novel would never have been put into effect, a view shared by le Carré himself. He told Miriam Gross that he did not think the mission in *The Spy* "could happen, because I don't believe that it's ever possible to operate such a clean conspiracy, where all the pieces fit together."[5] As le Carré explained to Paul Vaughan, elaborating a point he made in an earlier interview with Melvyn Bragg about "the writer's trade" being "plausibility" rather than "authenticity,"[6] he is not interested in naturalistic accuracy but in preserving "the air of banality":

> It is , I think, a very important factor of storytelling that the nearer you can bring the fantasy to the reality, the more people are willing to swallow the fantasy. Authenticity is frightfully boring but credibility is what novel writing is about, and plausibility; if you put two spies on a bus they're much more attractive to the general reader than if you put them in a jet aeroplane. I do place great emphasis on keeping the humdrum alive.[7]

Le Carré is a writer of fiction, not of history or journalism, and while drawing on his personal experience he also invents in order to create his own imaginative world. In this way he interprets rather than records the real world of intelligence, projecting his own vision of the contemporary world, especially England, through his fiction.

Although in one sense a strikingly new departure for le Carré, *The Spy* is also a sequel of sorts—an oblique sequel, perhaps—to *Call for the Dead* because the situation it deals with arises directly out of the Fennan case, to which there are several references. One of the East German agents in the earlier novel, the killer Mundt, has in the meantime been rapidly promoted to one of the most senior positions in the East German intelligence organization (Abteilung) and now becomes the crucial figure in an elaborate and subtle plot conceived by the Circus. Initially the operation seems to be directed against Mundt because of his success in smashing the Circus's spy networks in Berlin run for ten years by Alec Leamas, the spy of the title; but the real aim, paradoxically, is not to eliminate Mundt but to secure his position as one of the key people in the Establishment of the German Democratic Republic (GDR). This ruthless enemy is also an invaluable "friend" because he has been "turned" into a double agent, a transformation not at all rare in real-life intelligence.

Towards the end of *Call for the Dead*, Mundt leaves England for Berlin under an assumed name, and there is no suggestion that his departure is other than a successful escape by a hunted agent. *The Spy* offers a totally different interpretation of the same event, with Mundt, having been apprehended in Britain, returning to Germany with the connivance of the Circus on condition that he acts as a double agent. This is a closely guarded secret to which even Leamas in Berlin is not a party. Double agents lead a particularly hazardous existence, and by reintroducing Mundt as a British mole at the center of East German intelligence, le Carré creates a situation in which this superspy is in danger of being unmasked and has to be protected from the strong suspicion of his colleague and rival, Fiedler, about his treachery. For readers of *The Spy* who know *Call for the Dead* there is a chilling irony in the fact that Smiley now attempts to safeguard British interests by contributing so much to what amounts to the rescue of the very man who nearly murdered him in the earlier novel. Political expediency takes precedence over personal emotion.

If there is continuity between *Call for the Dead* and *The Spy*, there is also discontinuity, nowhere more evident than in the displacement of Smiley from the central position he holds in the earlier novel by Leamas, another member of the Circus. At the end of *Call for the Dead* Smiley resigns from the Circus, and in *The Spy* he is said to have retired and to be "doing things on seventeenth-century Germany,"[8] but his retirement takes the paradoxical form of deep involvement in the operation concerning Mundt. In *The Spy* Smiley is a shadowy and sinister figure who is only occasionally present or even referred to, and his role in the Circus's operation emerges only gradually. Le Carré never clarifies how much the extraordinarily clever but morally offensive operation owes to Smiley's intellect, the prime instigator apparently being the head of the Circus, known only as Control—there is no mention of Smiley's bête noire in *Call for the Dead*, the Ministers' Adviser on Intelligence, Maston. The head of MI6 has traditionally been designated by the code initial "C," a Civil Service abbreviation of "Chief," although some commentators have suggested that it derives from the name of the first man to hold the position, Sir Mansfield Cumming; "Control" is le Carré's fictional equivalent. When Control and Leamas are together in Smiley's house at the end of chapter 6, Control says that Smiley, although he knows all about it and "sees the necessity . . . doesn't like the operation . . . finds it distasteful . . . wants no part in it" (p. 49). Nevertheless it is essential to the success of the plan that the agent who carries it out, Leamas himself, should be deliberately misled about it by Control. Smiley does play a part, and it is significant that he is the only named character present at the tragic denouement in Berlin when the two main figures, Leamas and Liz Gold, are killed. It is also interesting that in the early stages Smiley is described without being named on several occasions so that only a reader familiar with the previous novels would realize who is meant:

> Some way down the road . . . stood the figure of a man in a raincoat, short and rather plump. (p. 32)
>
> Standing at the newspaper kiosk, deep in a copy of the *Continental Daily Mail*, stood a small froglike figure wearing glasses, an earnest, worried little man. He looked like a civil servant. (p. 65)
>
> But this little bloke who come round, funny little shy chap with specs. (p. 96)
>
> One was short and rather plump. He had glasses and wore odd, expensive clothes. (p. 97)

Here le Carré is doing in a deft way what all writers with series characters do: writing for his initiates.

In several respects Leamas is so unlike Smiley that it is easy to overlook the resemblances between them. Leamas is not university educated, let alone an Oxford man, and is no intellectual. He is physically strong with a brusque, no-nonsense manner and very much a man of action, as his violent attacks on a grocer and a fellow inmate of a London prison and his subsequent killing of an East German guard with his bare hands establish. During Leamas's interrogation in East Germany the head of counterintelligence, Fiedler, rightly classes him as an operator rather than an evaluator (a word that describes Smiley), and in le Carré's depiction of Leamas there is nothing comparable to those extended passages in *Call for the Dead* in which he articulates Smiley's thought processes. Nevertheless, in the context of the Circus, Leamas, being of the same generation as Smiley, also belongs to the old school of Fielding and Steed-Asprey (described in *Call for the Dead*) and is not one of the new men. Like Smiley, Leamas speaks German like a native and also spent some of the war years as an active agent in enemy territory without being caught. Again like Smiley, Leamas is too individual to be comfortable among the smooth sophisticates of the Civil Service who thrive in the corridors of power at Whitehall, a world of "tendentious theorizing and clandestine self-interest" as well as "sophistry" (pp. 9–10). Leamas's "utilitarian approach to clothes" (p. 11) may be quite unlike Smiley's taste for costly but ill-fitting suits, but both dress differently from their more standardized colleagues and consequently stand out as nonconformists. It is not surprising that Leamas is a spy who prefers being out in the cold of hazardous active service somewhere abroad to being in the cozy security of a London office. His straightforward loyalty to his agents in Berlin is in sharp contrast to the extreme callousness with which Control connives in their liquidation by Mundt, a brutal sacrifice designed to protect Mundt as a double agent by enhancing his position in the eyes of the East German Establishment as a ruthless enemy of the West.

The full title of the novel is rich in implications and ambiguities, and is a vast improvement on le Carré's first working title, *The Carcass of the Lion.* Early in the narrative Leamas comes in from the cold in the sense that he is withdrawn from operational work in Berlin and given a desk job in London. Yet, ironically, this is a preparation for one final mission, a return to the cold before he can finally come in, something he fails to do. In another sense Leamas comes in from the cold of his professional life, with its cynicism and amorality, to the human warmth of his relationship with the Communist librarian Liz Gold, which may be doomed but is the most positive value in the novel. The inclusion of the word "cold" in the title is appropriate for other reasons, not only because many readers have found *The Spy* as terrifyingly icy as those early reviewers who used phrases such as "chilling authenticity," "chilly hell," and "freezes me," but also because it is very much a novel of the Cold War.

The Spy was published not long after the Cuban Missile Crisis when the Cold War was in more danger of turning into a hot one than at any other time since Stalin's death, and although the novel is not directly about a political crisis between East and West, it is a response to a deeply divided Europe where power blocs play inhuman games of realpolitik in the name of some supposedly high-minded cause, whether Communism or liberal democracy. Le Carré does, however, include another contemporary manifestation of the Cold War—the Berlin Wall, that most potent symbol of the division between East and West and a physical embodiment of Winston Churchill's famous metaphor of an Iron Curtain splitting Europe into two opposed camps. *The Spy* opens at the Wall at night with the killing of Leamas's best agent, Karl Riemeck, shot by East German guards as he crosses into West Berlin in the presence of Leamas himself. Having come full circle, the novel ends there again at night with two more killings by East German guards, those of Leamas and Liz as they cross into West Berlin. All three are victims of the Cold War. Spy fiction almost inevitably contains a political dimension, and even the James Bond novels draw heavily on the Cold War, but *The Spy* offers an altogether more mature and thoughtful political evaluation than the facile distinctions of Ian Fleming. Le Carré subverts the nationalistic, even jingoistic, assumptions underlying normal spy fiction to cast a questioning eye on the ethics of the Cold War and on the West's overconfident beliefs that right must always be on its side and that its democractic hands are clean.

The chilliness that reviewers ascribed to *The Spy* may be inherent in its subject and in le Carré's interpretation of current political realities, but it also manifests itself in the form and style of the novel. When Martin Ritt made a somewhat stagey film of *The Spy* in 1965 with a star-studded cast headed by Richard Burton, he shot it in black and white rather than color, made effective use of bleak, wintry landscapes, and imposed a stark, formalized mode of visual presentation. In doing so, Ritt managed to recreate cinematically some of the qualities of the original, because *The Spy* is an austere piece of writing, almost classical in its formal patterning and its omission of anything not strictly relevant to the main narrative line. The prose is spare and sinewy, and lacks those bravura stylistic flourishes that occur in the earlier novels. Except for the minor character of Miss Crail at the Bayswater Library for Psychic Research, it also lacks the elements of caricature and the grotesque so evident in *A Murder of Quality*.

Le Carré's approach to characterization in *The Spy* is more functional than in its predecessors in that the characters are conceived strictly in terms of their role in the plot. Whereas in *Call for the Dead* he devotes a chapter to a short life history of Smiley, including an account of his wayward wife, le Carré does nothing comparable for the central character of *The Spy*, Leamas, about whose background, family, and personal life we are told very little. Mention of his ex-wife and children, for example, is limited to one sentence in chapter 2 and a brief remark by Smiley to Liz in chapter 11. An excellent example of le Carré's great verbal economy is the way he treats the time span from Leamas's assault on the grocer (the final sentences of chapter 5) to his release from prison some months later (after only four paragraphs of chapter 6). As far as the plot is concerned all that is significant is that Leamas goes to prison, and le Carré does not linger over the arrest, court proceedings, and period of imprisonment, as he might have done, except to describe one incident that defines Leamas as a man of action capable of violence and a loner full of inner resources—elsewhere he is described as having "the courage of a solitary" (p. 9).

If le Carré refrains from filling in Leamas's past, he tells us even less about Liz Gold, the young Jewess who becomes Leamas's mistress and whose fate becomes interwoven with his, although her Communist convictions and activities are stressed since these are crucial to the plot. Fiedler, another Jew and therefore having something in common with Liz, is one of the most important characters, yet again le Carré does not build up his family, social, or even political background. This refusal of every possibility that his narrative offers to elaborate or digress has the effect of isolating the main characters as moral and political agents, and indeed they are presented as outsiders, not social beings. Leamas is a British spy and supposed defector; Liz, a British Communist, a rarity after the exodus from the Party at the time of the Soviet suppression of the Hungarian Rising in 1956; Fiedler, a German Jew, another rarity after the Holocaust; Mundt, a high-ranking East German offiicial with a Nazi background and also a traitor.

An important consequence of le Carré's taut control of the narrative is that the groupings of characters and the patterns of opposition stand out clearly from the texture of the novel. On one side is the Circus, embodied in Control and Smiley; on the other side is the Abteilung, embodied in Fiedler and Mundt. These constitute one set of mighty opposites between which Leamas and Liz find themselves trapped. But because espionage is inseparable from deceit and double dealing, there is another set of mighty opposites within the East German camp: Fiedler, the true servant of Communism and the GDR, and Mundt, their false servant although successfully masking his treachery behind a façade of devoted loyalty. These two are involved in a power struggle to the death, exemplified in the rapid reversals of fortune described in chapters 16–18 and in the climactic Tribunal (chapters 20–23). It is because of this schematic arrangement that Andrew Rutherford feels *The Spy* to have been written "in the manner of a moral fable."[9]

Whereas the British agent Leamas pretends to disown his country's interests for money, Mundt pretends to uphold his government's cause while secretly working for the West for money. Leamas believes that his mission is to manipulate Fiedler into destroying Mundt, but in achieving something totally different he accomplishes what he was really sent to do—to manipulate Fiedler into saving Mundt and destroying himself because he poses a dangerous threat to Mundt. In the duel that is being fought at the level of international intelligence, Leamas and Liz resemble Romeo and Juliet, star-crossed lovers from rival families who are finally destroyed by the feud. At the more mundane level of imagery le Carré employs, they can be metaphorically linked with the small car containing four "waving and laughing" children that Leamas, after nearly colliding with it at high speed, imagines being caught in a "hurtling stream of giant lorries" and being "pounded and smashed, until there was nothing left, nothing but the frenetic whine of klaxons and the blue lights flashing; and the bodies of the children, torn, like the murdered refugees on the road across the dunes" (pp. 101–2). When Leamas dies in the final sentence of the novel, it is this image of inhuman destructive power and of helpless innocence that recurs to him: "As he fell, Leamas saw a small car smashed between great lorries, and the children waving cheerfully through the window" (p. 219). The related image of "murdered refugees" also emerges from Leamas's memory, this time of the bombing of defenseless refugees in wartime Holland.

On the surface Leamas and Liz are an ill-matched, even opposed pair, he a middle-aged British spy and she a young Communist dedicated to the overthrow of the existing order, but like Romeo and Juliet they find that their love for each other transcends their political roles. During his interrogation by Peters in Holland, Leamas suddenly comes to a conscious understanding of what "Liz had given him" through the transforming power of her love:

> It was the caring about little things—the faith in ordinary life; that simplicity that made you break up a bit of bread into a paper bag, walk down to the beach and throw it to the gulls. It was this respect for triviality which he had never been allowed to possess; whether it was bread for the sea gulls or love, whatever it was he would go back and find it; he would make Liz find it for him. (p. 89)

He is able to shed the dehumanizing blinkers of the hardened professional agent and experience the world with new eyes. He perceives a reality very different from that of his working life in which falsity becomes indistinguishable from truth, as le Carré argues in an important passage at the end of chapter 13 where he analyzes the spy as someone "permanently isolated in his deceit" and living a "great lie" (pp. 125–26).

Similarly, the politically naive Liz discovers that her devotion to an individual is deeper than her commitment to the Party or her Marxist belief in History. There are times when she feels that the cause she supports idealistically is tarnished with lies and is "a fraud" (p. 156), and her experiences in East Germany do nothing to reassure her, especially her encounter with that embodiment of totalitarianism, the inhuman, slogan-quoting commissar in chapter 24 who seems to be a close relation of Orwell's Big Brother in *1984*. While still in England she experiences a crisis of faith over the secrecy and dishonesty with which the Party conducts its affairs, and wonders whether Leamas was right when he commented cynically: "Some people keep canaries, some people join the Party" (p. 140). In East Germany she remembers similar remarks by Leamas about the psychology of political commitment: "A dog scratches where it itches. Different dogs scratch in different places" (p. 160); and although she rejects his notion that "you believed in things because you needed to; what you believed in had no value of its own, no function," she finds her former certainties about the Party as "the vanguard of history, the spearpoint in the fight for Peace" increasingly uncertain. Leamas and Liz's love, again like Romeo and Juliet's, shines out against the surrounding moral darkness of conflict and hate, but whereas Romeo and Juliet's suicides have a redemptive function in reconciling warring families, Leamas and Liz's deaths are no more than squalid killings and accomplish nothing. The one genuinely positive force in the novel is nihilistically snuffed out.

True to the elliptical mode of the novel, le Carré does not make it explicit in the final paragraphs that Mundt, in collaboration with the Circus, has Liz gunned down on the brink of her escape with Leamas over the Berlin Wall in order to eliminate someone who knows what he is and might well incriminate him, but this is obviously what happens. There is a symmetry with Mundt's liquidation of his fellow double agent, Karl Riemeck, in the opening chapter. Liz is a necessary sacrifice to expediency, an innocent slaughtered so that the devious and treacherous can survive. Smiley, who has helped to engineer her fate and must carry some of the responsibility for what happens to her, is present at her death. Leamas, unlike Liz, is supposed to escape. With Leamas perched on top of the Wall, Smiley on one side pleads with him to jump to safety, while the East Germans on the other side hold their fire after shooting Liz. In climbing back down into the East to join his dead mistress, Leamas is in effect committing suicide by forcing the East Germans to kill him. Le Carré's writing is so restrained and understated here that the reader is forced to interpret Leamas's psychological processes for himself, but it is clear that Leamas, fully aware of the sordid cynicism of the situation and the moral vacuum at the center of power politics and the world of intelligence, heroically chooses death with the one person he loves rather than live with the knowledge he has acquired. His last action is one of moral integrity in an amoral world, a gesture of defiance against the law that prevails on both sides of the Wall: the end justifies the means. It is an assertion of love in the face of everything that tries to deny its existence. In an important essay in which he argues that "le Carré's examinations of the health and psyche of his nation (and indeed of the West itself) are not so much spy thrillers as thoughtful, compassionate meditations on deception, illusion and defeat" that establish him as "one of the best living English writers," George Grella makes the interesting suggestion that there are echoes of the Orpheus and Eurydice legend at the end of *The Spy*: Leamas, "sickened by the betrayal and mourning the end of innocence, . . . turns back, like another Orpheus, to his lost love," and in doing so finds "the only way out of his underworld."[10]

That Leamas might be associated in any way with innocence seems at first sight to be absurd, but the way in which he is ruthlessly manipulated by his own intelligence service, being deliberately misled as to the real nature of his dangerous mission, establishes him as a victim of forces much more callous than himself. It is Leamas's hatred of Mundt, whom he regards as his arch-enemy in Berlin, and his consequent desire for revenge that make him such an eager participant in what he conceives the Circus's plan to be. Leamas is actually in the dark for most of the novel, as is the reader, who usually shares Leamas's understanding of events. Mystification in *The Spy* consequently derives mainly from the point of view offered to the reader, although early in the novel le Carré withholds from the reader all the information about the operation that Leamas does possess.

When Control interviews Leamas in chapter 2, there are indications of a Circus operation in East Germany involving Leamas, apparently directed against Mundt, but there is no hint as to what Leamas's role will be. Various details of the instructions given to Leamas emerge only later in brief flashbacks during the operation when Leamas recalls these discussions. As a result the first-time reader may be excused for regarding Leamas's decline leading to his imprisonment (described in chapters 3–5) as the real collapse of a disillusioned ex-agent following his withdrawal from active service, not the carefully planned first stage of an intelligence operation designed to hoodwink the enemy by producing a likely defector. Le Carré certainly hints at this: Leamas is said to acquire the features of an habitual drunk "with unnatural speed" (p. 20); Liz senses that he has "got something special to do", that he is "like a man who's . . . sworn vengeance or something" (p. 31); and his insistent good-byes to her on the night before he commits the assault leading to his prison sentence anticipate a premeditated action of some sort. Yet it is not until the end of chapter 6, when Leamas surreptitiously meets Control after his release from prison, that the full significance of Leamas's faked degeneration so as to attract the attention of the Abteilung, becomes clear.

From this point, with Leamas being picked up by the Abteilung, the reader shares his defective interpretation of what happens and his sense of mystification and confusion when things appear to go wrong. Whereas Smiley in le Carré's first two novels is in the usual position of fictional detectives, whether classical or hardboiled, of being presented with a puzzle that he has to solve, Leamas is in almost the converse position. At the outset Leamas believes that he knows exactly what he is doing and is in control of the situation. He sees himself as the manipulator, not the manipulated, and that in providing clues for the Abteilung to interpret by disclosing the Circus's Rolling Stone operation, he will lead them to solve the puzzle in the way that he wants them to. He conceives his mission to be the discrediting and consequent liquidation of Mundt, whom he views as a devastatingly effective East German intelligence officer and nothing else. He also comes to the erroneous conclusion that the British "special interest" in East Germany is Fiedler, whom the Circus is determined to safeguard.

In fact the situation is not in the least as Leamas understands it. The Rolling Stone operation is not a daring bluff to incriminate Mundt, but part of an even more daring double bluff to vindicate Mundt as unswervingly loyal to the GDR so that he can continue to serve the British interest. Far from being in control of the scheme, Leamas is a pawn in a strategy that he does not apprehend until he has served his purpose by playing his designated part as a metaphorically blind man without realizing it. He assumes that when things do not go as he expected, the plan itself is going wrong, whereas it is working perfectly. Liz, too, is a pawn, and although Control apparently agrees to Leamas's demand that she not be involved in any way, she is crucial to the Circus's operation and is destined to be involved unto death. It is because of Liz's unwitting participation, achieved in the most devious of ways so that she remains ignorant of how she is being used, that Leamas successfully accomplishes his mission, even though this is the opposite of what he had been led to believe it was. Indeed, when he makes his confession to the Tribunal, he assumes that the operation has failed disastrously. It is only when the mission is over that Leamas suddenly sees "the whole ghastly trick" (p. 198) and recognizes that he is at "the lousy end to a filthy, lousy operation to save Mundt's skin" (p. 206).

The reader, seeing events mainly from Leamas's position, apprehends the truly diabolical ingenuity of the operation only when he does. Mundt is such a valuable double agent that the Circus is prepared to go to any lengths to secure his position when Fiedler begins to suspect the truth. As Leamas finally explains to Liz, it was not sufficient for the Circus to dispose of Fiedler, because what had to be eliminated was suspicion itself: "Public rehabilitation, that's what they organized for Mundt" (p. 207). In order to deceive the East German authorities into believing that any suspicions concerning Mundt's loyalty are groundless, the Circus has to establish beyond doubt that such suspicions arise from a systematic British attempt to discredit Mundt because of his effectiveness as a Cold War warrior. To achieve this, the Circus has to fabricate a chain of circumstantial evidence implicating Mundt as a double agent and trick Leamas into his "defection" so that he can clinch the case againt Mundt. To complete the Circus's triple-crossing deception of the East Germans, all that is then required is to expose Leamas for what he actually is, an agent posing as a defector in order to complete a British plot to frame Mundt. By creating a situation in which Liz, a trusted Communist, will tell all she knows to the East German Tribunal, especially Smiley's activities on Leamas's behalf after his imprisonment, the Circus undermines Leamas's evidence and so convinces the Tribunal that Mundt is a victim of British Intelligence. Control, like a superb ringmaster, has flawlessly put his performing animals through an elaborate series of hoops and maneuvers.

The network of deception is so involved that the distinction between what is true and what is false dissolves. Truth is an essential weapon in establishing falsehood. This emerges most forcefully in the Tribunal, when Fiedler, aided by Leamas, puts his case against Mundt, only to be defeated by Mundt's counsel when he produces Liz as a surprise witness. What is particularly disturbing about these legal proceedings is that the cases for both the prosecution and the defense are, paradoxically, true. Fiedler's accusations that Mundt is a British agent are perfectly justified, but Mundt's defense that Leamas is not a defector but an agent provocateur in a British plot of "almost superhuman subtlety" (p. 178) to discredit him is also true, although not the whole truth since the Circus's plot is even more subtle than this. Truth, indeed, is the real victim in this bizarre court of enquiry. The false traitor, Mundt, a brutal and inhuman figure, is released, cleared of any stigma. The true patriot and committed Marxist, Fiedler, who emerges as sincere, sympathetic, and likable in his extended interrogation of Leamas, is himself discredited and destined for summary liquidation.

Two relevant points about espionage are repeatedly made in the novel. One is that "intelligence work has one moral law—it is justified by results" (p. 9). The other, a consequence of the first, is that in the methodology and morality of spying there is no difference between East and West. Control himself stresses both of these during his interview with Leamas in chapter 2. Admitting that "we do disagreeable things," even "very wicked things," and that "our methods—ours and those of the opposition—have become much the same," Control's only justification is that the end, being "defensive" and "benevolent," cannot be achieved without these means if "ordinary people here and elsewhere" are to "sleep safely in their beds at night" (p. 15). At the end of *The Spy*, Leamas, despite having been unscrupulously exploited by Control, uses exactly the same argument to Liz when trying to justify the Circus's operation on behalf of Mundt: "They need him so that the great moronic mass you admire can sleep soundly in their beds at night. They need him for the safety of ordinary, crummy people like you and me" (p. 211). Ironically, Fiedler, who approximates to an East German equivalent of Control, articulates an identical philosophy when interrogating Leamas:

> All our work—yours and mine—is rooted in the theory that the whole is more important than the individual. That is why a Communist sees his secret service as the natural extension of his arm, and that is why in your own country intelligence is shrouded in a kind of *pudeur anglaise*. The exploitation of individuals can only be justified by the collective need, can't it? (p. 110)

The main difference between Fiedler and his Western opposites is that as a Marxist he has no difficulty in constructing a cogent intellectual rationale for even the most violent aspects of intelligence work, including political terror and murder, something he does at the opening of chapter 13. Faced with such an articulate defense of the socialist end justifying any means, Leamas is immediately tangled in a web of contradictions when he attempts a reply from a Western and nominally Christian viewpoint. Later, when Fiedler forces Leamas to admit that the modus operandi of the Circus "depends on the need," he takes delight in pointing out that this is an exemplary Stalinist argument. Yet for all his ironic teasing of Leamas, Fiedler acknowledges their essential similarity: "We're all the same, you know, that's the joke" (p. 156). If it is a joke, it proves to be a peculiarly grim and black one in practice.

There is a horrifying contradiction in the fact that intelligence is devoid of morality yet is supposed to serve and uphold moral principles enshrined in different political creeds. It is morally repugnant that someone with a totalitarian, even SS mentality such as Mundt should be working for the preservation of British democracy, especially as he has to eliminate lesser British agents in East Germany with the connivance of Control in order to secure his position in the GDR. Yet as a spy he is invaluable. It is equally objectionable that the Circus should persuade one of its senior operatives to risk his life on a mission about which he is totally misled, while its manipulation of Liz is even more morally contemptible, since she is an innocent. Yet by the criteria of intelligence, both ploys are fully justified because they produce the desired result. As Leamas tells Liz in one of the most important passages of the novel, their discussion about the ethics of spying and politics in chapter 25 as they try to escape from the GDR with Mundt's assistance only to travel to their deaths: "It was a foul, foul operation. But it's paid off, and that's the only rule" (p. 209).

Liz cannot accept the double standard that something can be both foul and worth achieving: the end is bound to be contaminated by the means. If the Circus's operation virtually necessitates the death of Fiedler, whom she recognizes to be "kind and decent" (p. 210), in order to protect a two-faced, anti-Semitic Nazi in Communist clothing, then the entire British cause, relying as it does on such people as Mundt, must be highly suspect, to say the least. For the more experienced and cynical Leamas, on the other hand, it may be necessary in a hopelessly fallen world to employ what is foul to prevent something even worse: the Cold War is preferable to a third world war. In this debate Liz argues from the heart, Leamas from the head. Ironically, the Communist Liz adopts the position of a liberal idealist, taking a quasi-Christian stance on moral absolutes rooted in the sanctity of the individual and deploring any compromise with expediency. She sees with great clarity that what is good and true is being cynically perverted for destructive purposes. This is what makes her indictment so telling: "It's far more terrible, what they are doing; to find the humanity in people, in me and whoever else they use, to turn it like a weapon in their hands, and use it to hurt and kill" (p. 211). In "To Russia, with Greetings," le Carré says of Liz and Fiedler, "I used Jewish people because I felt that after Stalin and Hitler they should particularly engage our protective instincts,"[11] not be disposable pawns to advance Western interests, and it is indeed "terrible" that, however unwittingly, Leamas destroys the only two people in the novel he cares for.

Leamas, the official defender of Western values, has to contend in a relativistic way, resembling the dedicated Marxist Fiedler, that preferred ends may entail immoral means, however regrettable. His defense of intelligence is, of necessity, entirely pragmatic. He has no illusions about spies—"a squalid procession of vain fools, traitors too, yes; pansies, sadists and drunkards, people who play cowboys and

Indians to brighten their rotten lives"—but acknowledges that "they're the poor sods who try to keep the preachers from blowing each other sky high" (pp. 210–11). In Liz's eyes, however, the "poor sods" are irredeemably damned because of their "contempt for what is real and good; contempt for love." There can be no compromise with evil, and the dirty world of intelligence belongs, morally, to Satan. If Leamas wins the political argument, Liz certainly wins the moral one, but the debate is left unresolved because events rapidly overtake them.

Soon afterwards Liz, the opponent of expediency, is killed as a matter of expediency, and Leamas, the advocate of expediency, chooses to die with her in what is a morally and humanly courageous protest against the code of expediency and in support of Liz's rival code of love. At the end of *The Spy* le Carré upholds Liz's positive values while stressing their extreme vulnerability and helplessness in a world of power blocs, bureaucratic institutions, and political ideologies, whether Communist or democratic, poised on the brink of madness and universal destruction. She lives up to her surname in being a nugget of gold in a world of dross. The ironically entitled final chapter, "In from the Cold," leaves the two lovers very much out in the cold, lying dead at the foot of the Berlin Wall, victims of British democracy as much as East German Communism. There is consequently nothing reassuring in the pessimistic conclusion, only a grim foreboding about a Europe seemingly intent, after two catastrophic wars in living memory, on unleashing yet again its potential for mass violence. Le Carré has said that he wrote *The Spy*, unlike its predecessors, with passion, and this urgent intensity explains why the book has acquired the status of being *the* British novel of the Cold War, incisively anti-British as it is in certain respects. What fed that passion is le Carré's commitment to "the Christian and humanist ethic that the individual is worth more than the collective," as he explains in "To Russia, with Greetings":

> I sought to remove espionage from the sterile arguments of the cold war and concentrate the reader's eye on the cost to the West, in moral terms, of fighting the legitimised weapons of Communism. . . . I have posed this question: for how long can we defend ourselves . . . by methods of this kind, and still remain the kind of society that is worth defending? . . . In espionage as I have depicted it Western man sacrifices the individual to defend the individual's right against the collective. That is Western hypocrisy, and I condemned it because I felt it took us too far into the Communist evaluation of the individual's place in society.[12]

5

Peter Pan's Last Victim: *The Looking Glass War* (1965)

Explaining to Michael Dean in a television interview why he has not followed many commercially successful English writers into tax exile, le Carré said that he relied on "English life for my books," and explained that when he wrote his first novel as a full-time writer, *The Looking Glass War*, on Crete, "I had the greatest difficulty to remember even how the English talk to one another. It was awfully hard, for my material is here."[1] In his article for Moscow's *Literary Gazette* Voinov linked this novel with its predecessor, and le Carré acknowledged the connection in his reply:

> I tried to deal with a different aspect of the same Western predicament. The ideological deadlock which provided the background to *The Spy Who Came in from the Cold* is replaced by the psychological deadlock of men whose emotional experiences are drawn from an old war. . . . I tried to touch new ground when I discussed the phenomenon of committed men who are committed to nothing but one another and the dreams they collectively evoke. At heart, I said, professional combatants of the Cold War have no ideological involvement. Half the time they are fighting the enemy, a good deal of the time they are fighting rival departments. The source of their energy lies not in the war of ideas but in their own desolate mentalities; they are the tragic ghosts, the unfallen dead of the last war.[2]

This suggests that le Carré was attempting to blend tragedy and caricature or satire, a difficult combination to achieve, and one associated with Evelyn Waugh, especially his *Sword of Honour* trilogy; Waugh is very rarely linked with le Carré although he seems to be a significant influence on him.

Smiley's career continues to unfold in *The Looking Glass War*, but le Carré relegates the Circus to a subsidiary role and places at the center of his novel a previously unmentioned British intelligence organization. This "sister service" to the Circus is known as "the Department" or, more familiarly, "the outfit" and is headed by Leclerc. The distinction between the two organizations is that the Department, with responsibility to an unnamed Ministry (presumably Defence), is concerned with military intelligence, while the Circus concentrates on political intelligence; in *Call for the Dead* Fennan addresses a letter to Smiley at the Ministry of Defence, but in *The Looking Glass War* the Circus is much more closely linked with the Foreign Office. On the surface the relationship between the two organizations is one of polite cooperation in the national interest, but under the surface there is a deep-seated rivalry, even mutual hostility. This corresponds to the real-life rivalry between MI5 and MI6, but Leclerc's Department is no more a naturalistic portrait of a part of British Intelligence than Carne School is of a major English public school in *A Murder of Quality*. Like Carne, the Department is a grim caricature that must be interpreted metaphorically rather than literally. The reviewers who expressed disappointment at the novel after *The Spy* seem to have been expecting a rerun of the earlier book and were failing to accept *The Looking Glass War* on its own, rather different terms. About ten years later, however, George Grella described it as "le Carré's most eloquent novel"[3] in his thoughtful short essay on the novelist.

The heyday of the Department was World War II, its time of glory. During the uneasy peace since 1945 the Department has been on a downhill path, whereas the Circus has come into its own and is very much in the ascendant. The Department, largely staffed by old wartime hands, has become a research outfit with almost no operational capacity, the Circus having taken over this function. Whereas the Circus has a fleet of cars at its disposal, the Department initially lacks its own transport, a point made forcefully early in the novel when Avery, having lied to his wife about the Department's "masses of cars,"[4] has to trudge the streets of London at night looking for a taxi at a time of emergency following Taylor's death. The decline of the Department is symbolized by its change of address from Sherlock Holmes's

Baker Street in London's fashionable West End (part of the British Secret Service, the Special Operations Executive, actually had its offices in Baker Street after it was formed in 1940) to its present premises in Blackfriars Road in the distinctly unfashionable district of Southwark (south of the Thames in East Central London) and its current status is embodied in the depressing house itself. Le Carré's vivid descriptions of both the exterior and the interior of this "crabbed, sooty villa" with its "air of controlled dilapidation" and its garden in which "nothing grew . . . but grass which had worn away in patches like the coat of an old mongrel" (p. 24) recall the wasteland imagery of urban dereliction, living death, and spiritual sterility in T. S. Eliot's early poetry.

Like *The Spy, The Looking Glass War* is about a Cold War intelligence operation in the early 1960s, but the latter novel focuses on the group planning Operation Mayfly rather than the culminating mission itself or the spy who carries it out, Leiser (also code-named Mayfly), a British-naturalized Pole from Danzig. Whereas Leamas (whose death is mentioned in *The Looking Glass War*) is usually at the center of attention in *The Spy*, Leiser is not an active participant until nearly halfway through the novel and does not hold the foreground until the closing chapters. This shift away from the individual agent to the organization behind him is a more radical departure from literary convention than anything in *The Spy*, and is formally embodied in the tripartite structure and in the much greater intercutting between characters and situations than in the previous novels. Each of the three sections is named after the consecutive missions of three British agents, "Taylor's Run," "Avery's Run," and "Leiser's Run," titles indicating that no individual is central and that different individuals come into prominence at different stages. In an interesting comparison (complete with diagrams) between *The Looking Glass War* and Frederick Forsyth's *The Day of the Jackal* (1971), Bruce Merry establishes that the structure of le Carré's novel is virtually the reverse of Forsyth's superbly organized thriller, slowing down and opening out the narrative whereas *The Day of the Jackal* progressively accelerates and narrows in focus as it moves to its climactic showdown. Sadly, Merry's formalist preoccupations and adoption of Forsyth's novel as the apogee of the well-made thriller seem to blind him to the other enormous differences between the two books, so that his strictures on the form of *The Looking Glass War* ignore the point that le Carré's aims have nothing in common with Forsyth's and, indeed, that le Carré is deliberately thwarting conventional thriller expectations.[5]

Because the Department is a microcosm of the English ruling class, the effect of this change of emphasis from a central protagonist to a group is to make *The Looking Glass War* as much a "condition of England" novel as an example of spy fiction. In *A Murder of Quality* le Carré employs the formula of classical detective fiction to diagnose a microcosm of the English upper classes. He does something similar in *The Looking Glass War* through the vehicle of the spy story. In an introductory essay to Bruce Page, David Leitch, and Phillip Knightley's *Philby: The Spy Who Betrayed a Generation*, first published in 1968, three years after the novel, le Carré commends the authors for treating "the British secret services for what they surely are: microcosms of the British condition, of our social attitudes and vanities."[6] Speaking of the Circus in an interview with Michael Barber ten years later, le Carré said: "I thought that it would in time work itself into a very beautiful microcosm of English behaviour and English society altogether."[7] Earlier in his essay on Philby, le Carré makes some caustic comments about the world of British Intelligence that are particularly relevant to the Department in the novel, such as: "Once entered, it provides no further opportunity for spiritual development. The door that clanged behind the new entrant protected him as much from himself as from reality. . . . The posturing chauvinism of his superiors would long have passed for idiotic in the outside world; in the secret world it passed for real."[8] The 1968 Hollywood film of *The Looking Glass War*, starring Sir Ralph Richardson and directed by Frank Pierson, involved considerable changes (including the elimination of Smiley), mainly to give it more conspicuous international appeal by playing down the "condition of England" issue.

Stylistically *The Looking Glass War* is similar to *The Spy* in its clipped austerity, but the pervasive tone is even bleaker, more bitter. The title, with its allusion to Lewis Carroll's second Alice story, *Through the Looking Glass*, carries sour connotations since it suggests that the Cold War and its protagonists belong to the realm of surreal fantasy. The reality le Carré depicts does indeed have an air of nightmare lunacy, of Carroll's looking glass world, despite its drab, everyday exterior. *The Looking Glass War* is also very much a winter's tale, the dominant imagery being of cold, discomfort, and desolation. The opening description of a snow-covered airfield in Finland at night establishes the mood, which is sustained to the closing description of a deserted farmhouse buffetted by icy winds in a landscape of snow and freezing mud in Northern Germany. There is nothing comparable to the love of Leamas and Liz, or even the passionate commitment of the humane Fiedler, to offset the overwhelming force of negation. Calculatedly cynical as the Circus's operation is in *The Spy*, it is successful. The operation in *The Looking Glass War*, on the other hand, is a disastrous failure from beginning to end.

Leclerc's Department is largely an anachronism, a relic of World War II; and like so many things in a deeply conservative country like England, strongly resistant to any kind of change, it is allowed to survive long after it has served its purpose. The Department not only looks back to the past but seems to live in it. In breaking the news of Taylor's death to his widow, Leclerc talks of him dying "very gallantly," only to have his wartime vocabulary thrown back in his face: "What do you mean, gallantly? . . . We're not fighting a war. That's finished, all that fancy talk" (p. 73). References to the war and to how things were done in the war abound, and the word "old" recurs frequently. Hanging in Leclerc's room are signed wartime photographs of the young men who served under him, the signatures "brown and faded" (p. 28), and next to them is another reminder of the war, a model of a Wellington bomber covered in dust. The Alias Club, brilliantly evoked in chapter 7 and redolent of Leclerc's room with its photographs and mementos from the war, is an extraordinary manifestation of this nostalgic obsession with the past and the war by those who served in it, who form the Club's membership.

When Leclerc wants to find a suitable agent to send to East Germany, he consults "the old cards" (p. 25) that date back to the war, and chooses Leiser on the basis of information twenty years out of date. It is symptomatic of the Department that the house it rents at Oxford should possess an "air of old age" (p. 139) and that the tapes used in Leiser's training "were made from old phonograph records" (p. 153), obviously well-worn ones dating from the war. A more amusing example of the Department's old-fashioned ineptitude is Leclerc's inability either to think in meters when presented with a metric measurement by the Circus or to make the necessary conversion. The Department yearns to recapture its past prestige, but tragically it is unable to adjust to greatly changed circumstances and can think of doing so only in wartime terms. By sleeping in his office as he did in the war, by reviving the wartime Special Section, by mounting a clandestine mission on strictly wartime lines ("putting a man in" [p. 65]) with wartime equipment, and adhering to "the war rules" (p. 121), Leclerc is attempting to resuscitate the Department and score against the Circus, but he is really ringing the Department's death knell and playing into the hands of Control and Smiley. Leclerc injects the appearance of new vitality into the senile body, but this is not a rebirth, only a final flicker of life.

Nowhere is the absurdity and sadness of the Department more apparent than in the training of Leiser, described in the third section, "Leiser's Run," a veritable exercise in nostalgia although the Department does not recognize this. The epigraph to this section, two lines from one of Rupert Brooke's *1914* sonnets about the attractive purity and freshness of war ("swimmers into cleanness leaping"), conveys something of the dangerously ingenuous mentality prevalent among Leclerc and his colleagues. The Department obtains a house in Oxford "as they had done in the war" (p. 134), as well as the same gymnasium "they had used in the war" (p. 156), and even recalls its wartime instructors, who resort to the wartime slang of "Jerries" (p. 168) for Germans as though they are preparing Leiser for a mission against Nazi Germany. The target at the firing range where Leiser practices is a mock-up of a German soldier, apparently another relic of Hitler's war. Most bizarre of all, Leiser is equipped with exactly the same type of radio transmitter he used in the war, heavy, cumbersome, slow, and easily detected. The relevance of the epigraph from Tait's *Complete Morse Instructor* at the beginning of the novel, warning that good Morse cannot be produced by someone who is carrying heavy loads, now becomes clear. Even to obtain one of these old-fashioned machines, Leclerc has to approach Smiley, whose words, "no doubt we can dig one up" (p. 144), suggest an artefact of archaeological interest. At the end of the novel when the East Germans detect Leiser's transmissions, they first suspect a child since "no agent in his right mind would put out a signal like that" (p. 247), before recognizing with astonishment that Leiser is functioning in exactly the same way as wartime British agents. Considering the ease with which Leiser is traced, the reassuring and complacent words of one of his instructors before he sets out ring very hollow: "They're not supermen, Fred; they're like us. A dozy lot" (p. 194). The East Germans prove to be far from "dozy" and are not a bit "like us."

The total mismanagement of the operation does not necessarily mean that it is unjustified, but the evidence on which Leclerc decides to launch the final mission is far too flimsy to warrant Leiser's run. In treating some information obtained by the Department's agent in Hamburg, John Gorton, as high-grade intelligence when it has been rejected by other Western agencies, Leclerc is clutching at straws in a desperate attempt to find a way of reestablishing the credibility of his Department in the eyes of Whitehall, where he and his colleagues are disparagingly called "the Grace and Favor boys" (p. 68). Despite the more sceptical common sense of Haldane, Leclerc induces a mood of communal self-deception in the Department, which rejects reason in favor of a form of blind faith. The sensational suggestion is that a rocket site for medium-range nuclear missiles of the type the Soviets tried to install in Cuba in 1962 is being built just inside East Germany under German, not Soviet, control, thus producing a dangerous situation analogous to the Cuban Missile Crisis. For Leclerc, who calls the Russian rocket "the linear descendant of the wartime German V-2" (p. 55), there is, however, a more potent parallel, as Haldane guesses: one with the Allies' discovery of the top-secret Nazi rocket research project at Peenemünde in World War II. If the Department can substantiate Gorton's claim, it will have proved its usefulness and ensured its future, but Gorton's report, based on evidence supplied by a supposed East German refugee, Fritsche, is suspect on various counts, not least because of Gorton's own position, as Haldane recognizes at once. Gorton, another old wartime hand, is so inactive that Woodford is surprised to learn that he still belongs to the Department, but because his contract is coming up for renewal and he is financially dependent on his Department sinecure, he is under pressure to make himself seem indispensable. There is virtually nothing to support Fritsche's claims and the photographs he provides leave as much to the imagination as a Rorschach test. Immediately before Leiser begins his run, Haldane discovers among his "Deception" files, containing the attempts by a "depressing miscellany of rogues, double agents and lunatics . . . to delude the Western intelligence agencies" (p. 191), a report and a set of photographs bearing the hallmarks of Fritsche's. The photographs are labeled "Fishy" and the report marked "Fabrication" (p. 192). Before Leiser sets out, it is a foregone conclusion, except to the self-deceivers of the Department, that he will find nothing to support Fritsche's bogus intelligence.

Le Carré establishes the incompetence of the Department in the short first section, "Taylor's Run," even before he reveals the reasons for the operation, which become clear in the second section, "Avery's Run." Taylor's task is to collect a film in Finland from a Scandinavian pilot, Lansen, who has flown his charter flight from West Germany off course over East Germany in order to photograph a specific area for the Department. "Taylor's Run" does create suspense and even mystery (is Taylor's death murder or accident?), but the overriding impression is of Taylor's inadequacy for this fairly simple task. Taylor, who cultivates his image as "a military man . . . decent regiment, decent club, knocked around in the war" (pp. 3-4), is representative of a certain kind of English establishment mind, myopically insular, complacent, patronizing, insensitive, priding itself on its basic decency at the expense of intellect or even intelligence. Taylor bears a strong resemblance to Kim Philby's description, in his autobiography *My Silent War*, of what he expected a British Secret Service man to be like: "lean, and bronzed, of course, with a clipped moustache, clipped accents and, most probably, a clipped mind."[9]

While waiting for Lansen, Taylor foolishly proceeds to get drunk on a German drink that he mistakenly assumes to be Finnish ("some of these foreign hooches, drunk in their own country, weren't at all bad" [p. 4]) and that he describes to the Finnish bartender as "your local poison" (p. 6), a slang phrase not intended to be insulting but seeming so in context. Taylor's actual contact with Lansen is conducted without any concern for secrecy, and even Taylor, who has already breached security by revealing his destination to his wife, recognizes that his mission is a parody of what it should be. The comic moment of panic when Taylor cannot find the money he is supposed to give Lansen, who tells him to try another pocket, confirms Taylor's bungling amateurishness. Taylor's death shortly afterwards is not without a touch of black comedy. Just as he is congratulating himself on not being fuddled in spite of his drinking, he is struck from behind by a car while walking on the wrong side of the road to his hotel at night and killed instantly. The precious film, for which Lansen has taken great risks, rolls away into the snow and is irrevocably lost.

Yet if Taylor is the wrong man for the job, it is not his fault. He has always been involved in routine courier work, never with an operational mission such as this, and the blame for its failure must rest with those who sanctioned his involvement. Haldane subsequently tells Leclerc that "we broke a first principle of intelligence" (p. 47) in using a courier on a secret mission. Taylor himself acknowledges that the Circus, not the Department, is the organization with the appropriate expertise for this kind of activity, a point reinforced later in the novel when it is revealed by the Finnish police investigating his death that everything he is carrying except his false passport establishes him as Taylor, not Malherbe, the alias he has adopted for the mission. No attempt has been made to protect the alias from misadventure. Even the Department's choice of one of those esoteric, upper-class English names pronounced very differently from the way they are spelled (Malherbe is pronounced Mallaby) is supremely foolish since it not only attracts attention, the opposite of what it should do, but causes the agent unnecessary difficulty. It subsequently emerges that Leclerc has hit on this name for reasons of personal nostalgia, Malherbe being the name of a close friend who was killed on active service for the Department during World War II.

As for the "mystery" of Taylor's death, which gives rise to speculation throughout the novel, le Carré never resolves the ambiguity by saying whether it is an unfortunate accident or a deliberate killing. Leclerc wants to interpret it as murder by enemy agents in order to justify his faith in the entire operation, but the reader may well decode the hints in another way. Since Taylor was probably killed by a Citroen, the sudden appearance of a Citroen when Avery is retracing Taylor's steps in Finland is momentarily menacing, but does not amount to anything. The final sentence of the penultimate paragraph of "Taylor's Run" in the British paperback, which is omitted from the American paperback, seems to rule out murder: "It is quite possible that the driver was unaware of what he had done; that the impact of the body on the car was not to be distinguished from a thud of loose snow against the axle."[10]

Avery's embarrassingly unsuccessful attempt to recover Lansen's film in Finland is described in "Avery's Run." Like Taylor, Avery has no operational experience and is untrained for such a task, but Leclerc, despite his view of Taylor's death, rashly decides to send him without even ensuring that his cover story holds water. In order to make his run, Avery has to secure the active cooperation of Smiley, who is to organize the safe return of Lansen's film if recovered, although he is supposed to regard this as nothing more than an exercise. Smiley, whose exact relationship with the Circus in *The Spy* is uncertain, is now firmly back and in charge of the North European work. Whereas in *The Spy* Smiley is often only hinted at and his role is enigmatic, in *The Looking Glass War* he is given the social and intellectual identity established in *Call for the Dead*. His academic devotion to German baroque literature emerges in discussions with both Avery and Leclerc, and his eccentric "unrespectable club," as it is called in *Call for the Dead*, is where he entertains Leclerc to dinner. There is even a fleeting reminder of Smiley's wife Ann, who is not mentioned in *The Spy*.

It is profoundly ironic that the Department's attempt to reassert itself as an intelligence organization comparable to the Circus should depend so heavily on the assistance of the Circus, if assistance is the right word. After the loss of Lansen's film and the impossibility of a second photographic overflight because of the political risks involved, the most down-to-earth member of the Department, Haldane, realizes that the scheme Leclerc has in mind is beyond their capabilities and should be undertaken by the much more professional Circus, if undertaken at all. In preparing Leiser for his run, Leclerc relies heavily on the expertise of the Circus while withholding the nature of his operation from Control and Smiley. This attempt to pull the wool over the Circus's eyes by maintaining that the operation is an elaborate training scheme backfires, and the Circus repays the dissimulation of the Department with its own brand, pretending to be deceived though not being taken in at all. The two wartime rivals are involved in a game of power, which the Department, fighting from a position of weakness, is bound to lose. "There used to be a time," Smiley tells Avery, "when our departments *competed*," but he suggests that the bad old days are over and that today "we want to give you all the help we can—*all* the help" (p. 60). Control's help finally proves to be like the proverbial rope given to someone to enable him to hang himself.

Believing that he receives the Circus's assistance on his own terms, Leclerc is grateful though puzzled, while Haldane, who discovers the Circus's deviousness over the cancellation of Taylor's passport, is much more suspicious. Control twice tells Smiley that his motive in helping the Department is "charity," but Haldane is right when he warns Leclerc early in the novel not to trust the Circus because "you'll get no charity from those people" (p. 67). The Circus's "charity" has to be interpreted as a form of euthanasia. Control's last words in the novel are: "It's not *my* fault they've taken so long to die" (p. 251). As in *The Spy* le Carré implies rather than states much of what is going on in the minds of his characters, but Control clearly allows what he contemptuously calls the Department's "war game" (p. 250) to proceed even though he could prevent it, knowing full well that it is virtually bound to end in humiliating failure. To complete the Circus's triumph over the Department, while washing his hands of any responsibility, all Control has to do is provide the assistance necessary for the Department to carry out its do-it-yourself political disgrace. Even Smiley is not exactly sure how cunning and calculating Control has been, as their final conversation at the opening of chapter 21 makes plain. If Smiley's conscience causes him to question Control, it does not hinder him in the task of wrapping up what is bound to be the Department's last operation. Leclerc, eager to pinpoint a nonexistent Cuban-style situation in East Germany, has precipitated a political crisis between East and West by sending Leiser through the Iron Curtain to certain capture, a misfortune compounded by his killing of a young East

German border guard. It takes the ingenuity of those masters of expediency at the Circus to rescue the situation by creating a cover story completely disowning Leiser.

The first epigraph to the novel (omitted from the American paperback), "I wouldn't mind being a Pawn, if only I might join,"[11] comes from Alice's excited response to the chessboard landscape in *Through the Looking Glass*, which makes her want to participate in the extraordinary game of chess as soon as she sees it, even if she has to be the humblest playing piece. This is particularly relevant to Leiser, who is lured into joining the Department for its extraordinary game, and then treated like a disposable pawn. During the war when he worked for the Department, Leiser was betrayed to the Nazis but escaped. Twenty years later he is recruited again, but so grossly misled that he is, in a sense, betrayed, and this time there is no escape. The title of the last subsection of "Leiser's Run," "Homecoming," is as loaded with tragic irony as that of the last chapter of *The Spy*, "In from the Cold." Having selected Leiser because he is the only former agent on the Department's old books who fits the bill, the Department has to make him want to commit himself, even though Leclerc argues that they are doing Leiser a favor by approaching him: "He'll be grateful, or should be" (p. 35). This commitment is achieved by a systematic policy of deception, involving flattery, concealing the truth, telling lies, and exploiting his strong pro-British sentiments. Leclerc's remarks about the Circus early in the novel—"Lying's second nature to them. Half of them don't know any longer when they're telling the truth" (p. 32)—are, ironically, equally applicable to the Department, which sustains the pretense, for the benefit of Leiser, that it is at least as large, active, and influential as it was during the war. There is a conspiracy to make Leiser believe that he is returning to the Department he knew, as though time has stood still, but what he is actually entering is the looking glass world.

The deviousness, falsehoods, and hypocrisy expended on Leiser make him appear almost as much of an innocent victim of the Department as Liz is of the Circus in *The Spy*. Although Leiser feels badly cheated just before he sets out when he is deprived of the gun he has been promised, he subsequently reverts to his more characteristic hero-worshiping of the Department: "what a team to work for, he thought; a man could go through life and never meet a set of blokes like that" (p. 241). This can (and should) be read ironically, but Leiser himself is sincere, and his innocence emerges poignantly because of the gap separating his interpretation of events from the reader's wider awareness of what is involved.

What makes the Department's exploitation of Leiser even more morally odious is the way in which it takes advantage of his naive, romantic assumptions about England and the English. Like many naturalized British subjects, Leiser resents being taken for a foreigner and wants to be regarded as an Englishman, yet his foreignness is immediately obvious in his unidiomatic speech (the exclamatory "God Christ" [p. 121]; "hanging cell" [p. 195] for "condemned cell") and in his appearance (on sight, a London pimp offers him a girl who "likes foreigners" and "gives it foreign," only to be told to "make it something English" [p. 170]). His arcadian reverie about the bygone days of the house at Oxford—"handsome women at croquet, handsome men at war, disdainful boys in boaters, girls at Cheltenham" (there is a famous girls' public school there; p. 174)—reveals how thoroughly sentimental he is about England. After being told by Haldane that Leiser is "British to the core" (p. 148), Avery informs Leiser that the Department's only worry about him is whether he's "too English" (p. 162), words that must be music to his ears. Leiser regards Haldane as the embodiment of the English gentleman, the epitome of "the old school" (p. 149), and has an unquestioning confidence in the "English gentlemen" (p. 135) of the Department whom he feels privileged to serve. Leiser's relationship with the Department is full of implications about social class. Yet Haldane, who regards Leiser as "a man to be handled, not known" (p. 137), is a sick wreck of a man, and his physical condition is symbolic of what the English gentleman has become. Leiser's credulous trust in his "betters" is without any foundation.

The essential irrationality of the Department in committing itself to the operation can be explained only as an example of justification by faith rather than works, and faith of a singularly mindless sort. Le Carré establishes the quasi-religious nature of the Department by ironically using religious terminology to describe it throughout the novel. During the war the Department developed a mystique that with the passage of time has hardened into a form of pseudomysticism and a private mythology, individual members taking on "legendary qualities" (p. 72). When Leclerc defends his determination to mount an operation without having much evidence to go on, he does so with a rhetorical question to Haldane: "Does every priest have to *prove* that Christ was born on Christmas Day?" (p. 68); these words recur to Haldane much later when he needs to justify himself. Leclerc, whose name itself suggests "cleric" or "clerk in holy orders," carries out his briefing in Germany, shortly before Leiser sets off, as though he is conducting a service or celebrating Mass: "as in the stillness of a church he read the liturgy of their devotion, moving his little hand across the map like a priest with the taper" (p. 209).

The analogy between the Department and the Church and between its staff and the priesthood or a religious order is developed elsewhere, as when Leiser looks to Haldane like "a sinner to his priest" (p. 163). The relationship between recruited agents such as Leiser and the Department is said to involve "vows," as though agents sacramentally enter into a marriage based on love, a word often used in connection with Leclerc and his colleagues, and memorably defined by Haldane as "whatever you can still betray" (p. 224). The Department is something to be believed in, a transcendent entity in which the individual can lose himself in order to find himself. What the important opening section of chapter 6 establishes is that Avery, the only recent recruit to the Department and indeed the only new recruit since the war, has undergone a form of conversion, discovered a vocation, and found not God but the Department, which offers its true devotees a sense of wholeness and inner peace. As his wife Sarah recognizes, Avery has fallen in love, but her rival is not another woman but the all-male world of the "black friars" as they are jokily called because of the Department's address. The witticism is more than mere wordplay, since at one point le Carré explicitly likens the members of the Department to monks, and the house comes to resemble a monastery when Leclerc decides that he and Avery must live there during the crisis, virtually renouncing the outside world, including Avery's wife and child.

"Above All, My Country" was the motto of MI6, according to Nigel West in the first of his three books to date about the British secret services, *MI5: British Security Service Operations, 1909–1945.*[12] The religion that sustains the Department is that secular mutation of religion known as patriotism, a belief in what le Carré calls "the mystery of England" in a passage describing how even the gloomy house on Blackfriars Road has taken on pseudomystical as well as maternal significance for its occupants: "its mystery was like the mystery of motherhood, its survival like the mystery of England. It shrouded and contained them, cradled them and, with sweet anachronism, gave them the illusion of nourishment" (p. 24). This passage not only hints at the all-embracing cocoon of self-deception with which the Department surrounds itself, but carries the wider implication that the Department is in some ways emblematic of postwar and postimperialist England, a country living not in the present but in its collective memory of greatness, protected from reality by its illusion of itself. For people like Leclerc, English tradition, however irrelevant and ludicrous it may appear from the outside, guarantees everything, as in the almost surreal remark he makes to Avery when he gives him a special Ministry pass at the end of "Avery's Run": "You're safe with that. . . . The Minister signed it. He uses red ink, you know. It's tradition" (p. 115); the head of MI6 traditionally used green ink, a practice established by its first Chief, Sir Mansfield Cumming. Several of le Carré's descriptions of London, like those of the Department's house, serve to undermine the illusion of "the mystery of England," as though the buildings and streets themselves define the social and spiritual malaise of a nation experiencing its decline and fall. Images of hopelessness and death pervade the passage in chapter 8 about Western Avenue (a long road leading from the center of London through the western suburbs) and there is no possibility of change from a condition of stagnation. Lambeth Road (in Lambeth, a district adjacent to Southwark), described in chapter 9, is even more conspicuously in a terminal state of decay. The new block of high-rise flats where Leclerc and Avery go in search of Taylor's widow in chapter 3 (le Carré places Roxburgh Gardens in Kennington, the district immediately south of Lambeth) is so irrevocably contaminated by its dingy, squalid surroundings that it too exudes despair, and for Leclerc there is no possible connection between contemporary reality, represented by "these slums with their Babel's Tower" (pp. 38–39), and his conception of the England he believes he is protecting, an England of wartime fantasy.

The call of patriotism, whether "my country—right or wrong" or "the mystery of England," usually has a much stronger appeal for men than for women. Here it is worth recalling the famous last words of Edith Cavell, the English nurse shot by the Germans in 1915 for harboring refugees in occupied Belgium during World War I: "I realize that patriotism is not enough. I must have no hatred or bitterness towards any one." In *The Looking Glass War* "the mystery of England" is clearly linked with the notion of male comradeship, which is strongly fostered in the English public school system. In describing Leclerc's wartime photographs of himself and his young protégés in the Department, le Carré says that "he might have been their schoolmaster" (p. 28) and subsequently refers to him as a "master of the public school catchword" (p. 213). Although no one woman is as prominent in *The Looking Glass War* as Liz is in *The Spy*, Sarah Avery, Mrs. Taylor, and even the Department's secretary, Carol, play an important collective part in undercutting the illusions and pretensions of the "black friars." All three women are much more in touch with reality than the men of the Department, who are only too eager to embrace fantasy and make-believe by rushing into the looking glass world.

Mrs. Taylor's demolition of Leclerc's pompous Churchillian phraseology has already been mentioned. Carol's common sense is evident in the way she questions the rationale behind both Taylor's and Avery's runs, since she knows that the Circus, with agents in Finland, could easily have collected Lansen's film in the first place. Avery's curt response, "You don't understand," is patronizing and chauvinist, an attempt to silence this threat to male knowingness and dominance posed by female rationality. Carol's diagnosis of Leclerc's obsession with the operation, "he's building one of his card houses" (p. 59), is only too accurate. Although also treated with condescension by Avery ("More important than you can possibly understand" [p. 110]), Sarah probes and exposes the immature, schoolboyish enthusiasm with which he flings himself into the Department's war game, like a swimmer "into cleanness leaping," at the expense of their marriage. Her reasonableness contrasts with his absurdly inflated interpretation of what he is doing as a member of a "secret elite" (p. 72), but, as she herself recognizes, what she is up against is not even "double-think" but "unthink" (p. 189), masquerading as masculine superthink.

This does not mean that the Department is without divisions and tensions. If Leclerc is its High Priest, Haldane is its Doubting Thomas. Yet although he persistently challenges Leclerc's opinions and decisions, Haldane's whole existence is too bound up with the Department for him to put up a stiff resistance. He prefers to acquiesce. It is in the relative newcomer, Avery, torn between his conflicting loyalties to the Department and to Sarah, that the tensions show most clearly and sometimes reach breaking point. At the end of "Avery's Run," when his laughable mission is capped by the grotesque incident in which the police wake Sarah in the middle of the night to inform her about the return of Taylor's body, Avery's consciousness of the Department's almost farcical incompetence and insensitivity causes him to explode angrily against Leclerc and Haldane. His tirade, ridiculing Gorton's report and the idea that Taylor was murdered, ends: "It's easy here, in the dream factory . . . but they're people out there, real people!" (p. 113). It is a dream factory, but dreams are potent and often irresistible: "this was how, in some clean and magic place, it really ought to be" (p. 210). Even Avery, who knows "the fatal disproportion between the dream and reality, between motive and action" better than anyone in the Department and who recognizes how reality is falsely "remade into the images of Leclerc's world," prefers the dream to reality.

Nevertheless Avery, unlike the others, is incapable of completely reconciling himself to the looking glass world, however appealing. Just before Leiser sets out, Avery acknowledges to himself that "while his own mission had unfolded as comedy, Leiser was to play the same part as tragedy; that he was witnessing an insane relay race in which each contestant ran faster and longer than the last, arriving nowhere but at his own destruction" (p. 212). Implicit in this comment is an ironic inversion of Marx's famous reinterpretation of Hegel's view that history repeats itself, major events occurring twice: Marx adds that the first appearance is tragic, the second farcical. This prefigures le Carré's explicit inversion of Marx's dictum in *A Small Town in Germany*. Avery's apostasy, which provokes Haldane's wrath ("you wanted an eleventh Commandment that would match your rare soul!" [p. 264]), finally occurs when Smiley dismantles the operation, leaving Leiser to his fate. The casualness with which Leiser is discarded, especially by Leclerc whose behavior in this crisis is so irrational as to verge on insanity, is too much for Avery, whose cri de coeur on behalf of Leiser and reality in the face of squalid expediency and looking glass rhetoric recalls Liz's similar outburst to Leamas near the end of *The Spy*:

> You made me do it for you, made me love him! It wasn't in you anymore! I brought him to you, I kept him in your house, made him dance to the music of your bloody war! I piped for him, but there's no breath in me now. He's Peter Pan's last victim, Haldane, the last one, the last love; the last music gone. (p. 265)

Avery's human commitment to Leiser is in sharp contrast to the Department's retreat into their collective dream, and amounts to a repudiation of the amoral criteria governing intelligence work, with individuals being sacrified to such abstractions as national interest. Avery's insight into how he has been manipulated by the aging warriors of World War II into manipulating Leiser, so that the Department can cling to its fantasy of glory, is simultaneously an epitaph for Leiser and the Department. The final image of Avery is of him weeping, ignored by the others, while Leclerc, "a man intent upon appearances, conscious of tradition" (p. 266), optimistically contemplates the future of the Department, which has no future. Ironically, the final words about Leiser, who also has no future, are exactly the same as those about Leclerc: "intent upon appearances, conscious of tradition" (p. 274).

It is sometimes said that Britain won the war but lost the peace. Victory in both World Wars has meant that Britain has not undergone such massive social and political convulsions as most of the European continent has experienced in the twentieth century. In one way this has been a blessing, but it has meant that Britain, despite the postwar transformation of its colonial Empire into a Commonwealth of independent nations, has not been forced into a comprehensively radical reconsideration of itself in the way that many European countries have been. Beneath the numerous superficial changes of recent decades, an essentially conservative consensus has been maintained, largely concerned with keeping things as they are. In conceiving a novel about Cold War espionage, le Carré hit on a way of diagnosing an important aspect of English life: its love of looking back, not in anger, but with rose-tinted nostalgia, perhaps in the hope that national greatness will once again reassert itself. One of the things that Mrs. Thatcher's Conservative Government was advocating prior to the General Election of 1983 was a return to Victorian values, while the Labour Opposition was invoking the spirit of 1945 when the Party won a landslide victory. The Department's attempt to relive World War II twenty years later is a microcosmic example of this phenomenon. In a television interview with Melvyn Bragg less than a year after the British-Argentine war over the Falkland Islands in 1982, le Carré responded as follows to a question about Britain in the 1950s:

> What was terrible was the extent to which the upper classes were feeding the imperial political tradition. But then I don't think England has changed very much. That is the most awful thing. We still respond in our postimperialist sleepwalk to battle cries like the Falklands. At the time of Suez, which was very little different from the Falklands in terms of national mood, I suspect, although the reasons for being there were different, I remember going to some pub and trying to find out what the lower classes were thinking—an arrogant step by a young master at Eton. There was an old servant of the College roosted in the corner of the bar. "Hello, sir, hello," he said, "Wonderful to see the old country on the march again." I think you could hear that today.[13]

With the substitution of "Department" for "country," the servant's words are spoken by his fictional equivalent in *The Looking Glass War*, the Department's porter, Pine. In addition to being as highly original a spy novel as *The Spy* itself and one that again debunks the glamorous conception of espionage purveyed by much popular fiction, this powerful and disturbing novel is a sour indictment of that "march" and of the sleepwalking mentality behind it. What *The Looking Glass War* communicates is le Carré's vision of national exhaustion and hopelessness. Eighteen years after the novel appeared, Anthony Verrier entitled his study of British foreign policy, including the role of MI6 in its formulation, between the end of World War II and the early 1970s (with a postscript on the Falklands War), *Through the Looking Glass: British Foreign Policy in an Age of Illusions* (1983).

6

Pursuing the Pursuer: *A Small Town in Germany* (1968)

In le Carré's first four novels George Smiley is either the central protagonist or an important minor figure, but he plays no part in the next two novels, *A Small Town in Germany* and *The Naive and Sentimental Lover*. Except for a single passing mention of Steed-Asprey, one of the people responsible for recruiting Smiley for the Secret Service in *Call for the Dead*, there are no direct links between *A Small Town in Germany* and its predecessors, although le Carré continues his indictment of the English Establishment (as embodied in the upper echelons of the Foreign Service), and his strong interest in Germany manifests itself again. Three of his earlier novels are concerned to a greater or lesser extent with Germany—the odd one out being *A Murder of Quality*—and both *The Spy* and *The Looking Glass War* are partly set there. The action of *A Small Town in Germany*, apart from one short chapter, takes place in and around Bonn, the capital of the Federal Republic since 1949, though not previously of much prominence in German history. Unlike such great German cities as Berlin, Hamburg, Frankfurt, and Munich, Bonn had never been a major center of population, industry, and culture, and its transformation into the political and diplomatic focal point of West Germany was an unexpected accident of history: le Carré observes that "the very choice of Bonn as the waiting house for Berlin has long been an anomaly; it is now an abuse."[1] Nevertheless Bonn is not exactly a small town, so the title, taken from a drinking song popular with the British Army of occupation after World War II, has strong ironic implications.

Le Carré's depiction of Bonn is even more relentlessly unflattering and sardonic than that of London in *The Looking Glass War*, a portrait of a stagnant sham of a place living a lie: "in Bonn movement has replaced progress, and whatever will not grow must die" (p. 17). In the first paragraph of the disturbing and haunting prologue, which reveals the influence of German Expressionism, le Carré's description of Bonn is sinister and grotesque, images of death being conspicuous: "Bonn was a Balkan city, stained and secret, drawn over with tramwire. Bonn was a dark house where someone had died, a house draped in Catholic black and guarded by policemen" (p. 3). Le Carré's Bonn is Kafkaesque, a disorienting place that seems unreal and approximates to nightmare, as de Lisle suggests to Turner when he collects him from the airport: "Sometimes the fog is a little colder . . . then we call it winter. Sometimes it's warmer, and that's summer. . . . An island cut off by fog, that's us. It's a very *metaphysical* spot; the dreams have quite replaced reality. We live somewhere between the recent future and the not so recent past" (p. 50). The almost monochrome world of officialdom and bureaucracy, as embodied in the Ministry of the Interior, can seem equally unreal: "the pale, functional interiors, the pale, functional reproductions on the wall, the pale, unpolished teak; the white shirts, the gray ties and faces pale as the moon" (p. 31). Yet in another way Bonn, with its "naked, comfortless and uncomforted" legislative assembly, the Bundestag, "a vast motel mourned by its own flags and painted in yellowing milk" (p. 274), is all too hideously real, as the extended description in chapter 1 of "this unnatural capital village . . . this island state, which lacks both political identity and social hinterland, and is permanently committed to the condition of impermanence" (pp. 16–17) makes clear. The notion of Bonn (and indeed Germany) as a place where reality and nightmare can become indistinguishable is important in a narrative that looks back to the Nazi past and forward to a possible neo-Nazi future.

The main events of *A Small Town in Germany* are limited to one week in what le Carré calls "the recent future" in the short preface he wrote for the American edition, probably meaning as little as a year or two in the future from the time of publication; the American edition makes the time scale more explicit than the British edition by prefacing each chapter with a temporal heading such as "Monday Morning" or

"Tuesday Night." During the week two different though not unrelated political developments are reaching their climaxes, producing "the hottest crisis" (p. 13) that the British Embassy staff in Bonn can remember. On the broad European front, difficult negotiations are taking place in Brussels about Britain's application to join the European Economic Community (EEC), more familiarly known as the Common Market, which in the late 1960s and early 1970s still consisted of the six founder nations and signatories of the 1958 Treaty of Rome. For a number of years before Britain finally joined the EEC in 1973, after earlier unsuccessful attempts to resolve such problems as Britain's trade with New Zealand, a topic mentioned in the novel, the issue of membership was a most controversial one in British politics, and it has become so again with the Labour Party advocating British withdrawal from the EEC.

The other development is the growing success within West Germany of an imaginary extraparliamentary political organization with neo-Nazi characteristics known as the Movement, which is mounting an anti-British and anti-EEC campaign of meetings and demonstrations intended to destabilize the political balance inside the country and to wreck the Brussels negotiations. During the week of the novel this campaign builds up to a climactic rally in Bonn itself. The charismatic leader of the Movement is Karfeld, described by the British diplomat Peter de Lisle as "isolationist, chauvinist, pacifist, revanchist" (p. 121), who in less than a year has been able to coordinate and discipline disparate groups of dissidents and protesters into a well-organized mass movement. De Lisle likens him to both Oswald Mosley, the hypnotic leader of the British Union of Fascists during the 1930s, and Pierre Poujade, the leader of petit bourgeois neofascist reaction in postwar France for a few years whose name has entered the French language as a way of referring to this political "philosophy." Karfeld's success is due partly to his ability to be all things to all men, progressive and reactionary at the same time, and partly to his reputation as a war hero uncontaminated by Nazism. This enables Karfeld to present himself not as a throwback to the Hitler era but as the prophet of a new, independent Germany of the future.

In creating the Movement, le Carré draws on those manifestations of neo-Nazism that periodically afflict West Germany, but his fictional organization is much more successful in attracting widespread support, especially from the student body, than actual neo-Nazi groups have been. Le Carré envisages a merging of political interests between Karfeld and the students' leader, Halbach, as the Movement crusades on behalf of a regenerated Germany no longer tied to the West and its postwar allegiances but instead looking to the East, including a Bonn-Moscow trade axis. This may seem an odd idea to attribute to a neo-Nazi movement, but history, as usual, is more bizarre than fiction. For many people in the 1930s the notion of a treaty between the apparent polar opposites of Hitler and Stalin was unthinkable, yet the impossible occurred in 1939 when Nazi Germany and the Communist Soviet Union signed a nonaggression pact, producing widespread disillusionment with Communism among the intelligentsia of Europe.

The year in which the novel was published, 1968, has, like 1789, already acquired mythic status because of what happened in France, even though a full-scale revolution was averted. The reference to Grosvenor Square at the opening of the novel, for example, is to the kind of large-scale anti-Vietnam demonstrations that took place outside the US Embassy in London at this time. The political background that le Carré establishes for the main action of *A Small Town in Germany* reflects many developments in the 1960s: the growing tensions in the Western alliance following the escalation of American involvement in the Vietnam War, the radical questioning of the political status quo, the politicizing of the student body, and the proliferation of sometimes violent protests and demonstrations. In West Germany the political unrest of the late 1960s and early 1970s, as disillusionment with the institutions of Bonn became more vocal, was spearheaded by the generation of radical students who have since been labeled "Hitler's Children," the most famous being members of the Red Army Faction such as Ulrike Meinhof, Andreas Baader, and Gudrun Ensslin. Most were born in the 1940s, felt alienated from their parents and their cultural inheritance because of the Nazi past, and were deeply suspicious of the capitalist panaceas of conspicuous consumption offered by the postwar German "economic miracle" to what their principal philosophical guru, Herbert Marcuse, called "one-dimensional man." As le Carré points out in the preface to the American edition, the formation in 1966 of a Grand Coalition between the two major political parties in West Germany, the Social Democrats and the Christian Democrats, had the effect of encouraging extraparliamentary opposition since there seemed to be no adequate outlet for dissent within the democratic structures, and the West Germany le Carré envisages in the novel is governed by just such a Grand Coalition.

For much of its length—and it is appreciably longer than any of its predecessors—*A Small Town in Germany* gives the impression that it is another novel about espionage, despite the absence of Smiley and the Circus, but it turns out to be something different, an explicitly political novel couched in the form of a mystery or thriller investigation. Reviewers, presumably expecting another spy novel, were unsure whether to treat it as a sophisticated thriller or as a serious novel, whereas it is both, something that even as perceptive a critic as the well-known crime novelist H. R. F. Keating failed to acknowledge. Approaching it as a thriller he found it pretentious, complaining that "the writing is overpoweringly literary," surely not a fault in a novel though it may be in a thriller, and that the puzzling prologue was "acceptable for god-literature, outrageous for entertainment literature."[2] Such a polarized distinction is completely irrelevant to le Carré, who is aiming at neither of these extremes but at being both serious and entertaining, as important novelists from Fielding to Graham Greene have been.

A Small Town in Germany is a novel of pursuit, indeed of multiple pursuit, as the title ("The Hunter and the Hunted") of the short prologue suggests, although the full significance of the pursuit described in this eerie, atmospheric piece of writing becomes clear only towards the end of the novel. The unnamed "hunter" of the prologue proves to be Leo Harting, a child refugee to Britain from Nazi Germany in the 1930s who has worked in Germany for the British authorities in various capacities since the war without reverting to German nationality. His present post is a sinecure in the British Embassy at Bonn as a temporary Second Secretary, which gives him diplomatic status but no prestige in the hierarchy of the British Foreign Service. The unnamed "hunted" of the prologue turns out to be Karfeld himself. Yet during the week the novel encompasses, Leo the hunter is himself being hunted, and in the closing stages it is he who is hunted to death while his quarry escapes with his life. After Leo's surprising disappearance, he is pursued by the British authorities in the form of Alan Turner, a counterintelligence officer from the Security Department with a reputation for accomplishing his missions successfully if ruthlessly, and also by Karfeld's Movement in secret collaboration with the West German police.

An unusual feature of the novel is that two of the central characters, the protagonist Leo and his antagonist Karfeld, are discussed a great deal during Turner's investigation but are dramatically foregrounded as participants only in the prologue, where neither is identified, and in the epilogue, where Leo is killed as soon as he enters the narrative in the last few paragraphs. As a result, the viewpoints and motivations of both Leo and Karfeld are presented indirectly, except for the speech

Karfeld makes in the epilogue. The reader sees Leo through the eyes of Turner, who provides the main point of view in much the same way as Smiley does in le Carré's first two novels. Le Carré's decision not to describe Leo's actions or thoughts during the week ensures that the mystery surrounding him is sustained for most of the novel, but it has several disadvantages. The dramatic action centers on Leo, but by keeping him offstage le Carré also deprives his own narrative of that dramatic action. Much of the novel is set in the Bonn Embassy and in premises occupied by Embassy staff, resulting in much less variety than in *The Spy* and *The Looking Glass War*, and le Carré's reliance on a series of extended and somewhat monotonous interviews conducted by Turner after he reaches Germany produces a related lack of narrative variety. Had le Carré written the novel in another way, for example by alternating the narrative between Leo's pursuit and Turner's investigation, he would have lost the element of mystery but he would probably have achieved a novel with far more momentum and dramatic interplay than the one he has written, which is less compellingly powerful than its two predecessors.

The prologue immediately creates a sense of mystery, which is sustained in the less heightened opening chapters as a number of unexplained disappearances from the British Embassy are revealed, beginning with such humble ones as cups from the canteen and a two-bar electric fire but culminating with a top-secret file and Leo Harting himself. The immediate assumption is that Leo is a Soviet spy who has hurriedly defected, taking information likely to have serious and embarrassing repercussions for the British government, especially at a time of delicate European negotiations. The British response is to send Turner to Bonn in order to track down Leo. The journalist Sam Allerton uses the nickname "Security Turner" (p. 130) and calls him "a bloodhound" (p. 129), and on a previous mission to Warsaw Turner's methods led to the mental breakdown of Myra Meadowes, the daughter of a diplomat now at the Bonn Embassy. What emerges as early as chapter 3, in which Turner is briefed in London by his superior, Lumley, before flying to Germany is the status of both Leo and his pursuer Turner as social outsiders in the snobbish eyes of the British Establishment, although both are useful to it, just as Leiser, another outsider, is in *The Looking Glass War*. One of the first things that Lumley says of Leo, a one-time refugee brought up in England by his Communist uncle, is: "There's a smell, that's all. A foreign smell" (p. 45). Lumley's xenophobic and patronizing description of Leo establishes him as deeply suspect, a man insufficiently British to be trusted.

It later emerges that in terms of the strict social hierarchy in the Embassy at Bonn, with its sharp division between "dips" and "non-dips" (those with diplomatic status and those without), Leo was not acceptable at the higher levels even though technically a "dip"—not "quite dinner party material" (p. 58) according to Rawley Bradfield, who heads Chancery (political section). Bradfield's attitude towards Leo is extremely condescending, even contemptuous: "His English was never perfect. He was socially energetic at a certain level; mainly in the less discriminating embassies. They say he got on well with the South Americans" (p. 64). The final remark, in which Bradfield carefully distances himself by the use of "They say" from the allegedly disreputable rabble of Latin American diplomats, is supposed to be damning but reveals Bradfield's exalted assumption of his own British superiority.

If Leo is not "dinner party material" in Bradfield's eyes, then neither is the "clever, predatory and vulgar" Turner (p. 56), who is no gentleman and is labeled a "Bevin boy" (p. 130) by Allerton, a phrase alluding to a senior Labour Party Minister in the wartime and postwar governments, Ernest Bevin, and therefore indicative of Turner's ungenteel, working-class origins. Turner is a tougher, more abrasive, more aggressive, lower-class version of Smiley, intellectual and academic as well as intelligent ("a former Fellow of Saint Anthony's College, Oxford" [p. 38]) and not at one with the Foreign Office for which he works even though he serves it most efficiently. Like Smiley, he has abandoned "the *contemplative* life of the academic in favor of the *functional* life of the civil servant" (p. 153). Also like Smiley, Turner is separated from his wife who has another man. As he despatches Turner to the Embassy in Bonn, Lumley tells him, "Try and look as though you belong" (p. 48), while realizing that Turner's cloth cap or working-class identity cannot be masked by a suit of clothes. Turner is clearly a product of the postwar meritocracy, which advanced the educational and career prospects of clever children who lacked the advantages of their social "superiors" in birth, wealth, and privilege. Even so, when le Carré notes that Saint Anthony's College "takes all kinds of people," he is implying that Turner would not have been socially acceptable to some Oxford colleges, and the snobbery inseparable from class bias in the Establishment is also evident in his ironic comment about official Foreign Office publications: "While they shed a merciless light on the origin of all their other Turners, in the matter of Alan they remained tight-lipped, as if, having considered all the facts, they felt that silence was the kindest policy" (p. 38). By creating

Turner, le Carré makes the issue of social class more central than anywhere else in his fiction, except perhaps for *A Murder of Quality*.

There is a telling comparison in chapter 3 between Turner and his colleague in the Security Department, Shawn, who has been posted there from the Brigade of Guards, one of the most socially prestigious units in the British Army. Unlike Turner, Shawn comes from the right background and possesses all the desirable social attributes. Nevertheless Shawn is an upper-class "twit" who fails to grasp the significance of the telegrams received by the Security Department from Bonn about Leo's disappearance. When Turner asks Lumley why he does not send Shawn on such a politically delicate mission—"He's tactful. Charm them all, he would"—Lumley replies: "Because you'll find him and Shawn won't" (p. 48). There is a suggestion in what Lumley says about Turner's intense motivation to succeed that this is a form of compensation, that Turner has to make himself invaluable and prove his worth in a way that would not occur to Shawn.

Turner does find Leo, although too late to save his life, but his visit to the Embassy in Bonn is characterized by neither tact nor charm. After arriving there Turner conducts a series of interviews with the staff, including Bradfield, de Lisle, Arthur Meadowes (Chancery Registrar), Jenny Pargiter (Information Officer) and John Gaunt (Chancery Guard), in an attempt to build up a full picture of Leo and his activities so that he can explain the circumstances of his disappearance and discover his present whereabouts. Turner is brusque, outspoken, even accusatory and insulting, and refuses to indulge in the polite display of deference that senior diplomats such as Bradfield regard as their due. The last thing that Turner observes is the hypocritical ritual of diplomatic niceties institutionalized in the British Foreign Service, with the result that Bradfield eventually calls him "a political primitive" (p. 199), complains "that manners mean nothing to you whatever", and expostulates that "it will take a long time to sweep up the mess you have left behind you in this Embassy" (p. 200). Turner is an intruder into the refined world of the diplomats—for Bradfield's wife, Hazel, he is the equivalent of an impertinent tradesman—and when passing two office girls in the Embassy, Turner experiences a sense of fellow feeling at having found his social level: "This was his world. Second class and foreign. One carried a thermos; the other labored under a stack of files" (p. 77). The more Turner learns about Leo, including his black-market business deals, the more he becomes aware that they belong together as "second class and foreign." Meadowes actually tells Turner that Leo "wasn't like us. He tried to be, but he wasn't. More like you, I suppose, in some ways" (p. 108). In a short interior monologue after interviewing Meadowes, Turner acknowledges to himself this sense of identity with Leo: "Come on, Leo, we're of one blood, you and I: underground men, that's us. I'll chase you through the sewers, Leo; that's why I smell so lovely. We've got the earth's dirt on us, you and I" (p. 115).

From the early description of the Embassy building, le Carré, who at one time worked there although he insists in his preface that his novel is not a roman à clef, presents the official British presence in West Germany with acidic humor and irony:

> Imagine a sprawling factory block of no merit, the kind of building you see in dozens on the Western bypass, usually with a symbol of its product set out on the roof . . . and you have portrayed with fair accuracy the mind and force of England in the Federal Republic. With one sprawling limb it holds down the past, with another it smooths the present; while a third searches anxiously in the wet Rhenish earth to find what is buried for the future. (p. 17)

His account in chapter 2 of Sunday morning churchgoing at the Embassy Chapel, as the staff members emerge from their homes in the "modest piece of suburban Surrey" the British have created in Germany where "dogs of unmistakably English breed ramble in the long gardens," is caustically witty. Le Carré has a sharp and unmerciful eye for the elaborate codes of social behavior typical of the English upper classes, an excellent example being the entry of the wives into the Church in strict pecking order while pretending that it is all very casual and spontaneous:

> Reaching the church steps they all pause, smiling invitingly at the senior wife present. She, with a little gesture of surprise, climbs the steps ahead of them and disappears through the green curtain, leaving her inferiors to follow, quite by accident, the order of succession which protocol, had they cared about such things, would exactly have demanded. (p. 34)

Le Carré's irony is at its most incisive in such phrases as "a little gesture of surprise" (a standard weekly routine completely devoid of surprise to acknowledge the preferment the others always accord her), "quite by accident" (self-conscious and deliberate), and "had they cared about such things" (they are obsessed with protocol). Turner's eruption into this world of communal artifice and role-playing is bound to be disruptive because he refuses to abide by the rules and sees the charade for what it is. De Lisle's attempt to conceal information about Bradfield because he is "my colleague, my superior," information that might help to apprehend a supposed spy at a time of national emergency, provokes Turner into a bitter attack on what he regards as the self-perpetuating oligarchy of the British Establishment, primarily concerned with protecting itself and looking after its own interests:

> Who do you represent out here? Yourselves or the poor bloody taxpayer? I'll tell you who: the club. *Your* club. The bloody Foreign Office; and if you saw Rawley Bradfield standing on Westminster Bridge hawking his files for an extra pension, you'd bloody well look the other way. . . . You make me puke. All of you. The whole sodding circus. You didn't give a twopenny damn for Leo, any of you, while he was here. Common as dirt, wasn't he? No background, no childhood, no nothing. Shove him the other side of the river where he won't be noticed! Tuck him away in the catacombs with the German staff! Worth a drink but not worth dinner. What happens now? He bolts, and he takes half your secrets with him for good measure, and suddenly you've got the guilts and you're blushing like a lot of virgins holding your hands over your fannies and not talking to strange men. (p. 133)

Despite the problems he faces, Turner rapidly accumulates evidence concerning Leo that he then has to interpret, and his procedures, especially his extended struggle "to make order out of chaos" (p. 152) in chapter 9, recall those of Smiley, another Oxford-trained intellectual, in le Carré's first two novels. As he speculatively juggles the facts into theories, Turner concludes that although, superficially, everything points to Leo being a defector, this obvious solution is an untenable hypothesis. Turner's subsequent unauthorized visit to Leo's house in Königswinter on the opposite side of the Rhine serves to confirm his conclusion. Bradfield, Gaunt, and Meadowes all acknowledge a new urgency in Leo in the recent past, and Meadowes explains that Leo "went on a track" (p. 104) in the Embassy archives, meaning that he was pursuing a complex line of inquiry in the hope of being able to establish something. Meadowes's further remarks about Leo seeming "happy" and "serene" (p. 109) shortly before his disappearance indicates a satisfactory end of the track. When evaluating the evidence, Turner again feels a sense of identity with Leo in that Leo's behavior accords with his being "a hunter, a pursuer" (p. 161), not the opposite, as he would be if he were a vulnerable spy. What Turner cannot fathom at this halfway stage is the identity of Leo's target. The mystery remains and the suspense continues.

Turner's further inquiries lead him into trouble with the German police and with Bradfield as Head of Chancery, and he is violently attacked in his hotel in an attempt to terminate his investigation; but he discovers from Mickie Crabbe, a junior member of Chancery, the reason for Leo's notorious brawl at a Cologne nightclub some years previously; from Hazel Bradfield that she is Leo's mistress; and from his search of Leo's house the missing Embassy key, which literally and metaphorically unlocks Leo's secret and leads Turner to the solution of the mystery. The extraordinary discovery that Turner makes in the disused basement of the Embassy is that Leo has established a secret office in what is known as "the Glory Hole" (p. 249) and that everything missing from the Embassy, except for the top-secret Green File, is there. Turner is then able to retrace Leo's path through archive material to find "a missing truth" (p. 251) by correlating widely dispersed evidence, making his sense of involvement and even identification with his official quarry more complete. The "missing truth," revealed to the reader when Turner reveals it to Bradfield in a dramatic showdown after Bradfield has forbidden him to enter the Embassy and has ordered him to return to London, is that Karfeld is not the patriotic but non-Nazi war hero he purports to be, but a Nazi war criminal guilty of experiments in human extermination who has successfully concealed his past and created a new identity for himself. Le Carré achieves a superb fusion of narration and symbolism in Turner's descent to the underworld of the Embassy, the basement which has been sealed off from the visible superstructure of diplomatic life yet which contains a disturbing truth that the Embassy staff, with their penchant for conspiratorial secrecy, would prefer to repress, like an undesirable manifestation of the subconscious. Much of the evidence Turner has previously collected now falls into place: Leo's first-hand knowledge of Nazi atrocities at the end of the war in 1945; his frequent talk about Fascism; his fear that "it could happen again," as Gaunt notes, "and the West would just stand by" (p. 88), as the West did during the 1930s with its policy of appeasing Hitler; his provocative use of the wooden buttons used as money in Nazi concentration camps, when encountering reminders of Nazi behavior in postwar Germany as in the Cologne nightclub incident.

Yet the ghastly irony of the situation is that under the Statute of Limitations concerning war crimes by former Nazis, Karfeld is now immune from prosecution. It emerges in Turner's interview with Praschko in the last chapter before the epilogue that Leo sought legal advice on this point from Praschko, an old friend and a fellow refugee from the Nazis whose postwar career in Germany has nevertheless been totally different from Leo's. Praschko, now a member of the Bundestag, has moved away from his early left-wing views to become very much part of the new Germany, a pragmatist keen to put the past behind him rather than a moralist determined not to forget the past and its obscenities. The empty gun holster that Turner and de Lisle are given by the boiler man during their search of Leo's house suggests that Leo has decided to take justice into his own hands now that the state cannot uphold it, and that his disappearance is that of a one-man jury, judge, and executioner. Leo, a fairly insignificant man whom few people take seriously, has found himself with the weight of history and morality on his shoulders and has risen to the challenge by deciding to kill Karfeld, whom he sees as a second Hitler, in order to prevent the evil of the recent past from "all happening again" (p. 285).

The culmination of the Movement's rally in Bonn displays many features typical of similar Nazi displays, from the flags and the torchlight to Karfeld's nationalistic rhetoric and the militaristic music, "a raucous, crude, deafening roar, a call to battle and a call to anger, a call to kill ugliness, to destroy the sick and the unwieldy, the maimed, the loathsome and the incompetent" (p. 310). The soothing element of rationality and moderation in Karfeld's speech is undermined by everything else in his Nuremberg-style rally. Another thing that lends credibilty to Leo's fears is the revelation that the Bonn Establishment is willing to cooperate with Karfeld. For example, Ludwig Siebkron, a senior official at the Ministry of the Interior, has been aiding Karfeld by setting up a police manhunt for Leo even before he learns that Leo was attempting to assassinate Karfeld in Bonn just after midnight on the day of his disappearance and actually shot at Karfeld during a rally of the Movement in Hanover on the following day. Several unexplained incidents early in the novel become clear in retrospect: the prologue describes the attempted assassination in Bonn; the plainclothesman seizes Mickie Crabbe at the Commonwealth Sports because he suspects him of being Leo; the mob attack on the British Library at Hanover and the killing of the librarian, Fräulein Eich, formerly Leo's fiancée, are a response by Karfeld's stormtrooping bodyguard to Leo's attempt on his life from the Library.

One of William Faulkner's most memorable statements comes from *Requiem for a Nun*: "The past is never dead. It's not even past."[3] One of the main characteristics of civilized man is his communal memory, his sense of history, and his ability to relate the present to the past rather than live in a perpetual, virtually mindless present, which is what the Western popular media encourage. It is possible to take the present seriously only if the past is also taken seriously. Leo is known as "the memory man" and sees the Movement in relation to the past, giving him an essentially moral perspective of contemporary events.

Leo's decision to act against a possible new Führer is a moral decision, which can be justified in much the same way that the conspiracy and attempted assassination of Hitler in 1944 were justified by the great German theologian and Protestant martyr, Dietrich Bonhoeffer. The alternative position to Leo's is the respectable, law-abiding but immoral one of turning a blind eye to the past in the name of prudent self-interest and political expediency that is adopted by Praschko, a representative of the Bonn Establishment, and by Bradfield, the spokesman for the British Establishment. Modern German history presents the problem in an extreme form because a nominally Christian nation priding itself on its centrality to Western civilization proved to be capable of barbarism on such a massive scale that many people refused to believe it during World War II even though strong evidence was emerging from Nazi-held territory.

In *The Spy, The Looking Glass War*, and *A Small Town in Germany* the conflicts between morality and expediency and between individual values and political necessity emerge as important themes, and in the closing stages of all three novels there is a major confrontation between proponents of different opinions. In the first of these novels this takes place in a context of espionage although it has wider implications, whereas in *A Small Town in Germany* it directly confronts the broad political questions. Leamas and Liz argue passionately as they drive to the Berlin Wall; *The Spy* then concludes with their violent deaths. Avery, revolted by the casual way in which his colleagues abandon Leiser, attacks them; this is followed by the final pursuit of Leiser with which *The Looking Glass War* ends. In *A Small Town in Germany* Turner and Bradfield engage in an extended debate of great dramatic power, one of the high points of the narrative, after which the novel ends with the final pursuit and violent death of Leo at the hands of Karfeld's supporters during the Bonn rally. Unlike Leamas, Liz, and Leisier, Leo is a relatively free agent, not a Cold War pawn who is ruthlessly manipulated from beginning to end, but his ultimate powerlessness makes him just as much a tragic victim of political forces devoted to their own survival irrespective of their concern for the greater good of the world or of mankind. In some ways the denouement of *A Small Town in Germany*, with its final image of Leo's broken body, is as bleak as those of its two predecessors, the individual agent of morality and justice being destroyed by the mass forces of hatred and violence, but in another way the ending is more open because, in theory, Turner still has the power to expose Karfeld, although whether he would be able to do so is uncertain. Nothing can restore Leamas and Liz to life, and nothing can save Leiser, but even though Leo is lost, his cause remains alive in Turner.

If Leo's fate is terrible, so is the relevation that comes to Turner in his final discussion with Bradfield when he has an inspired intuition about the contents of the missing Green File. It is a revelation of Perfidious Albion at her most perfidious, because the Green File contains information about a secret meeting between Karfeld and Bradfield intended to appease Karfeld and to ensure British interests should Karfeld come to power in West Germany. This brings to mind the British Prime Minister Neville Chamberlain's policy of appeasement towards Hitler at the time of the Munich Agreement of 1938, and for Leo it must have been the final confirmation that history was repeating itself and that it was "all happening again." Turner speculates to Bradfield that Leo's purpose in taking the Green File was to reveal how history is actually being reenacted as tragedy, in flat contradiction to Marx's view that when history repeats itself it does so as comedy or farce, not as the initial tragedy—de Lisle quotes Marx during his conversation with Turner in chapter 7. For Bradfield, on the other hand, Leo's moral conscience poses an anarchic threat to this British exercise in realpolitik, and he is able to disown Leo without a qualm, just as Leclerc disowns Leiser in *The Looking Glass War*. The moral individual has to be sacrified to the amoral state. Turner can score a moral victory over Bradfield in their vehement argument, but there is a kind of honesty in Bradfield's confession of his deeply pessimistic conservatism, which gives his case intellectual coherence, however callous it seems in other ways:

> I am a hypocrite . . . I'm a great believer in hypocrisy. It's the nearest we ever get to virtue. . . . I serve the appearance of things. It is the worst of systems; it is better than the others. That is my profession, and that is my philosophy. And unlike yourself . . . I did not contract to serve a powerful nation, least of all a virtuous one. All power corrupts. The loss of power corrupts even more. We thank an American for that advice. It's quite true. We are a corrupt nation, and we need all the help we can get. That is lamentable and, I confess, occasionally humiliating. However, I would rather fail as a power than survive by impotence. I would rather be vanquished than neutral. I would rather be English than Swiss. And unlike you, I expect nothing. I expect no more from institutions than I expect from people. (p. 291)

What Bradfield articulates so well in his encounter with the morally outraged Turner is his conviction that in the modern world of complex international relationships and diplomacy, a world in which a declining

Britain has lost both its Empire and its role as a world power, moral absolutes are not only irrelevant but positively dangerous because they work "against the order that results from chaos; against the built-in moderation of an aimless society." Bradfield defends the art of the possible in the here and now, not a conception of an ideal, utopian society in some undefined future:

> You speak as if there were those who contribute and those who do not. As if we were all working for the day when we are no longer needed; when the world could pack up and cultivate its allotment. There *is* no product. There *is* no final day. This *is* the life we work for. Now. At this moment. . . . That's the limit of our action. Beyond it is anarchy, and all the romantic claptrap of protest and conscience. We are all looking for the wider freedom, every one of us. It doesn't exist. (p. 292)

It is significant that in their verbal battle Bradfield, not Turner, has the last word: "Either you're in or you're out. Either you're involved or you're not. . . . Or would you rather be Swiss?" (p. 296). The debate ends with a question, and the novel itself ends shortly afterwards with the questions it raises in a state of unresolved tension. Le Carré is not, of course, endorsing Bradfield here at the expense of the much more sympathetic Turner, but through him he puts the case of the political "realist" without illusions, for whom some truths are better not known or suppressed, and he therefore does justice to the complexity of the important contemporary issues he confronts.

7

To Catch a Mole: *Tinker, Tailor, Soldier, Spy* (1974)

Interlude: The Naive and the Sentimental

Le Carré is not thought of as a short story writer, but he published two stories in the *Saturday Evening Post* in 1967 and 1968. The first, "Dare I Weep, Dare I Mourn?" (28 January 1967), is an ironic and distinctly black comedy about an impulsive and unpremeditated perfect murder of someone officially dead. After receiving news from East Germany that his father has died and that permission has been obtained for him to be buried in West Germany, Dietrich Koorp drives across the border to collect the coffin, only to find that his father is alive and that his "death" is an ingenious scheme for illegally escaping to the West. Dietrich finds the prospect of being burdened with his objectionable father so unappealing that, when he makes the return journey, he ensures that his father suffocates in the coffin. Recrossing the border, he is indeed transporting a corpse. Although this slight though clever story is not about espionage, the German setting and the border crossing between East and West inevitably recall several of le Carré's novels.

The second story, "What Ritual Is Being Observed Tonight?" (2 November 1968), is totally different and reveals a sentimental side of le Carré virtually invisible in the five novels published at the time. This is a highly romantic story about the chance and almost miraculous recovery of a love seemingly lost forever. Not until fourteen years later with the end of *The Little Drummer Girl*, and then only in heavily muted form, does le Carré convey anything remotely like the sense of securely achieved love presented at the close of "What Ritual Is Being Observed Tonight?" Love, in le Carré, is whatever can and usually is betrayed, if not by the lovers themselves (as in the case of Ann Smiley), then by the world surrounding them (Liz and Leamas). The first-person narrator recalls his infatuation with a French girl, Marie-Louise, while working in Provence in 1954 prior to going to Oxford, and his mistaken assumption that she did not reciprocate his feelings. Believing himself to be an unrequited lover, he concentrates on his intellectual pursuits and enters on an academic career as a Germanist. Invited to speak at a French university, he discovers that Marie-Louise is the wife of his insufferably arid host, Du Chêne, whom she married on the rebound. The course of true love has not run smooth, but the true lovers are finally reunited. This is lightweight stuff and le Carré may not wish to be reminded of it, but in one way it prefigures his next novel, *The Naive and Sentimental Lover*. The narrator of the story is an expert on Schiller and has written on the famous "Schillerian distinction between the naive and the sentimental."[1] Furthermore one character talks of making "a bridge between the naive and the sentimental. Between the intellect and the body" (p. 65). This, as the title indicates, is the theme of the next novel, but the typically Romantic distinction underlies the continuing debate running through his fiction, whether internalized (as in Smiley's case) or externalized (the argument between Liz and Leamas at the end of *The Spy*), between trusting the impulses of the heart and complying with the dictates of the intellect.

Altogether more characteristic of le Carré in subject is his television play with the punning title *The End of the Line*, broadcast on 29 June 1970 in the Armchair Theatre series on ITV (Thames). Set on a train, this is a claustrophobic duologue in which a young man attached to the British Security Service but disguised as a clergyman, Bagley, uses his own cowardice and sexual ambiguity to secure the breakdown and force a confession from a mathematician, Frayne, who has been passing secrets to the Russians after being compromised in a homosexual affair. Le Carré emphasizes the resemblances between the two men, the spy-catcher and the traitor being two sides of the same coin. It is all too easy to imagine the roles being reversed, and both men inhabit the same moral limbo. Seven years later le Carré partly dramatized *Call for the Dead* for a television program about himself in the BBC series *The Lively Arts* (25 September 1977), his only other example of television drama.

Three years after *A Small Town in Germany* le Carré published *The Naive and Sentimental Lover*, his one novel to date that is completely divorced from the conventions of mystery and spy fiction. *The Naive and Sentimental Lover* has its admirers, some of them fulsomely enthusiastic, but because le Carré subsequently reverted to spy fiction, this one "straight" novel has increasingly looked like an artistic aberration, and an undistinguished one at that. What *The Naive and Sentimental Lover* suggests is that when le Carré deprives himself of a particular set of literary conventions, he also deprives his distinctive talents of the stimulus they need to flourish fully. There can be no doubt that his decision to resurrect Smiley and the Circus after the experiment of *The Naive and Sentimental Lover* was absolutely right. Nevertheless the assumption today that its critical reception was unmitigatedly hostile, something encouraged by le Carré himself in such statements as "I was extremely hurt by the awful reception which *The Naive and Sentimental Lover* got at the time"[2] (radio interview with Paul Vaughan in 1979), is by no means the whole truth. Some reviewers welcomed this new departure with its unexpected elements of fantasy and magic, and there were even complimentary comparisons to Joyce and Hesse.

The Naive and Sentimental Lover was evidently a major undertaking for le Carré and he lavished a good deal of time and effort on it. It is considerably longer than the longest of his previous novels, and although shorter than *The Honourable Schoolboy* and *The Little Drummer Girl* it is, by contemporary British standards, a blockbuster of a novel. At the same time it lacks the wider moral and political dimensions of its three immediate predecessors, being essentially domestic in focus. As such it has been regarded as his most personal and autobiographical novel, with much less distance between his own experience and his imaginary world than in his other books. The real-life source of *The Naive and Sentimental Lover* was the friendship that developed between le Carré and the very gifted Scottish novelist James Kennaway and their triangular relationship involving Kennaway's wife Susan. Le Carré dedicated *The Looking Glass War* to Kennaway, whom he first met in 1963, only a few years before Kennaway's tragically early death in 1968 at the age of forty. Le Carré's involvement with the Kennaways received considerable, even sensational, publicity in 1981 with the publication of *The Kennaway Papers*, compiled by Susan from her husband's writings, especially his notebooks, with a running commentary by herself. In his biography of Kennaway, *James and Jim* (1983), Trevor Royle shows how both writers transmuted this experience into fiction, Kennaway in *Some Gor-*

geous Accident (1967) and le Carré in *The Naive and Sentimental Lover*.

In le Carré's novel Aldo Cassidy, a conventional and successful young businessman who, like le Carré, attended Sherborne School before going to one of the less well-known Oxford colleges, finds his life profoundly transformed by a chance encounter with a wild bohemian writer, Shamus, and his wife Helen. Shamus virtually lives a life of fantasy, and he reminded reviewers of such fictional creations as the artist Gulley Jimson in Joyce Cary's *The Horse's Mouth* (1944) and of such real yet quasi-legendary people as Dylan Thomas and Brendan Behan. Kennaway himself, like so many Scottish writers and artists, was a deeply divided man—Royle's title *James and Jim* recalls *Dr. Jekyll and Mr. Hyde* by another important Scottish writer, Robert Louis Stevenson—and at times seemed intent on being to Scotland what Thomas was to Wales and Behan was to Ireland. Shamus approximates to Cassidy's alter ego or submerged self, and under this anarchic and disruptive influence Cassidy begins to abandon his respectable, bourgeois life-style for something much less inhibited. In terms of the Schillerian dichotomy, Cassidy is a sentimental lover (the product of education who consciously cultivates feeling) aspiring to be a naive lover (spontaneous and instinctive) and failing. In a prepublication letter to booksellers le Carré eloquently explained his intentions in the new novel:

> In *The Naive and Sentimental Lover* there are no secret services, no gothic intrigues to subject the doubting individual to the needs of society. Aldo Cassidy, the central character, is not blessed with such convenient excuses for setting aside his longing for personal fulfilment. He is not enmeshed by spies; he is not visited, at untimely moments, by pledges from a former life. Cassidy is the victim not of society, but of himself; of his origin, his profession, his fantasies and his longings. True, Cassidy like his predecessors is a dreamer obliged to conform. But with this difference: he could, he really could, be free. What defeats him is not a latterday Machiavelli but the impossibility of middle-class love. In Cassidy perhaps this paradox comes to life: that in the process of seeking freedom the striver has lost the power to be free.
>
> In theme, therefore, this book is not as far from its predecessors as you might suppose. In treatment, it is vastly different. I found great relief in being able to remove at last that vast superstructure of plot and politics, and reveal beneath it the man I have always known: bewildered, aspiring, comic, loving, weak and oddly loyal.[3]

An interesting short novel about the contradictoriness of human nature could have been produced from this material, but le Carré's excessively expansive handling is too undisciplined and self-indulgent to justify its length. After the crisp and ironic laconicism of *The Spy* and *The Looking Glass War*, the prose of *The Naive and Sentimental Lover* is wordy and, what is worse, at times exhibits something new and unwelcome in le Carré's writing, a coy whimsicality and soft-centered affectation. Chapter 23 opens, "An unusual silence fills the house and no birds sing,"[4] the last four words being a quotation from Keats's ballad *La Belle Dame Sans Merci*, but it is difficult to see what purpose, ironical or otherwise, this serves except as a piece of gratuitous jokiness, and consequently it seems meretriciously showy. In comparison the phrase from *Macbeth* at the end of the following sentence from *The Little Drummer Girl* about the Israeli Ambassador in Bonn, "He was an ambassador, after all, as well as a Jew, and here in double trust,"[5] is neatly pointed and resonates with implications; Shakespeare's words occur in a soliloquy by Macbeth in which he contemplates murdering the virtuous Duncan who is both his king and his guest. Another brief quotation from *Macbeth*, about Macduff's unnatural birth, occurs at the end of Craw's imitation of Sherlock Holmes, "Remark first the empty cages over the window, whence air-conditioners have been untimely ripped,"[6] in *The Honourable Schoolboy*, a characteristic example of his flamboyant style of speech and therefore entirely justified.

There are compensations in *The Naive and Sentimental Lover*, but it did not point the way forward for le Carré; in his next novel, *Tinker, Tailor, Soldier, Spy*, he returned to where he started in *Call for the Dead*, the figure of George Smiley, who continued to preoccupy him throughout the 1970s. For le Carré the literary legacy of *The Naive and Sentimental Lover* is twofold. First is its leisurely, almost Victorian expansiveness, a quality that characterizes his four subsequent novels but not his five novels of the 1960s, although the last of these, *A Small Town in Germany*, moves in this direction. Whether this has been entirely for the good is a matter of debate, but if le Carré inevitably sacrifices the high-pressure intensity and tautness of *The Spy* and *The Looking Glass War*, he does provide many of the satisfactions associated with the traditional novel as opposed to the spy thriller. Second is an injection into his later fiction of some romance elements and conventions, a feature noted by H. R. F. Keating in his enthusiastic review of *Tinker, Tailor, Soldier, Spy*. Praising *The Naive and Sentimental Lover* as a "splendid romantic fantasy," Keating argued that in *Tinker, Tailor, Soldier, Spy* "the spinner of spy-stories and the poet of fantasy have met to produce a novel that shoulders its way into the front ranks of the art."[7]

Smiley Redivivus

Tinker, Tailor, Soldier, Spy is the first of a trilogy of novels about Smiley and the Circus that was eventually published in an omnibus edition with the overall title *The Quest for Karla* (1982). In an interview with Nicholas Wapshott after the completion of *The Little Drummer Girl* in 1982, le Carré said that initially he "tried writing *Tinker, Tailor* without Smiley,"[8] but found that "it didn't work" without his series character. As le Carré told Paul Vaughan in 1979, the "extremely labyrinthine plot" needed Smiley "as a central intellect in whom the reader has so much confidence. When Smiley is becoming analytical and intuitive about things you more or less leave the reasoning to him."[9] Like its two successors *Tinker, Tailor, Soldier, Spy* can stand on its own, but there is a connecting theme running through the trilogy that binds it together in a way significantly different from three novels about the same series character, such as Hercule Poirot or Philip Marlowe. The title of the trilogy clarifies this unifying thread, the quest being Smiley's pursuit of his Soviet counterpart known only as Karla, with whom he has been engaged in a long-distance intellectual duel for many years in the Cold War struggle between the Circus and its Soviet equivalent, Moscow Centre.

In *Tinker, Tailor, Soldier, Spy* Smiley claims that Karla is less "fireproof" than he seems and predicts that his fanaticism will, "if I have anything to do with it,"[10] lead to his undoing. At the end of *Smiley's People* Smiley finally achieves victory over his old foe, with whom he identifies in some respects, by locating the chink in Karla's almost perfect armor and manipulating him into a position where he has to defect to the West. It is this quest that justifies the numerous references to Karla in *Tinker, Tailor, Soldier, Spy*, including Connie Sachs's apparent digression about Moscow Centre in chapter 12 and especially Smiley's extended account to Guillam in chapter 23 of his only personal encounter with Karla in India in 1955 when he made a strenuous but unsuccessful attempt to persuade him to defect. It was on this occasion that Smiley lent Karla his cigarette lighter, a present from Ann, and allowed him to keep it as an unspoken expression of the bond between them. The symbolism of the cigarette lighter is vitally important in the denouement of *Smiley's People*, illustrating the care with which le Carré has developed the trilogy as a whole. First-time readers of *Tinker, Tailor, Soldier, Spy* may find the passages referring to Karla distracting since they are rarely relevant to Smiley's primary quest in this novel, the unearthing of a Soviet mole or deep-penetration agent in the senior ranks of the Circus itself, but the importance attached to Karla in this first novel is crucial to the trilogy.

What the publication of the omnibus *Quest for Karla* did was to emphasize that the trilogy is more than the sum of its parts. The Irish poet Tom Paulin acknowledged this in a review of *Smiley's People* that looks back to its predecessors. For Paulin, le Carré "is a devout and brilliant myth-maker who has raised the jargon of office politics into the terms of a national epic." This suggestion understandably leads Paulin to compare le Carré with Edmund Spenser, whose own national epic *The Faerie Queene*

> offers a myth of the English consciousness struggling to achieve its Anglican identity. Karla is the Leninist equivalent of Spenser's Papal Archimago, while Ann Smiley is the false Duessa, a neurotic metamorphosis of Una who is Truth and the soul of the nation. Smiley is the Red Cross Knight.[11]

One can challenge Paulin's specific suggestions without questioning his insights that le Carré is exploiting the literary convention of romance as well as realism and that the trilogy possesses mythic, perhaps even epic, dimensions. The elements of romance and myth, especially allusions to the Arthurian legends or "the matter of Britain," become increasingly obvious as the trilogy progresses, perhaps because le Carré gradually became more aware of the archetypes underpinning his work, and they help to transform what in other hands might have been ephemeral topicality (a fictionalizing of journalistic mole hunts) into art that transcends the limitations of the spy genre.

What remains unclear is the stage during his writing of the Smiley saga when le Carré settled on a trilogy. On the publication of *The Little Drummer Girl* in 1983, le Carré gave a television interview to Melvyn Bragg in which he talked about the television serializations of *Tinker, Tailor, Soldier, Spy* (1979 in the UK) and *Smiley's People* (1982 in the UK). Sir Alec Guinness took the part of Smiley in both productions, and le Carré was full of praise for this great actor's subtle performances. At the same time he argued that Sir Alec

> also took the character away from me. I found that writing Smiley after Smiley, through Guinness, had entered the public domain was very difficult, and I was beginning in my mind to caricature myself and him. The secrecy we spoke of earlier had been taken away from me. I had originally intended to write Smiley-Karla novels which might run to a dozen or more, and take me to different theaters of the world. I could do it in South America, I could do it in the Middle East, I could do it here and there. The bright lights that were shone on Smiley made him

> unattractive to me, and I defected from him. The success blew the operation in a way, for me, and so I closed the series down, made it a trilogy, and tucked Smiley up in bed. One day when he's a little forgotten again, I'll get him out, but for the time being we are not on terms.[12]

Television and film adaptations of novels inevitably impose particular visual schemata on the originals, whereas prose encourages readers' imaginations to create their own images. Le Carré clearly found that Sir Alec's interpretation of Smiley had imposed itself on the character in such a way that it was difficult to think of Smiley except as Guinness. In an article about the seven-part adaptation of *Tinker, Tailor, Soldier, Spy* that he published during its first run on television, le Carré said that although Guinness was the only actor he "seriously considered" for the part, he found that after "a day's shooting" he was "writing Guinness, not Smiley"[13] when he returned to *Smiley's People*, the book on which he was working.

Nevertheless le Carré's remarks to Bragg about closing the series down as a trilogy might be a case of *post hoc ergo propter hoc, hoc* being Guinness. Philip Oakes, who interviewed le Carré when *The Honourable Schoolboy* was published in September 1977, reported that it "is the second book in what Le Carré plans to be a quartet."[14] After completing *The Honourable Schoolboy* le Carré toured the Middle East with a view to writing a Smiley-Karla novel in that setting, but abandoned this in favor of *Smiley's People*, reserving the Israeli-Palestinian conflict for a non-Smiley novel, *The Little Drummer Girl*. Exactly two years after talking to Oakes, le Carré told Paul Vaughan shortly before *Tinker, Tailor, Soldier, Spy* was televised that after *The Naive and Sentimental Lover*

> I did decide, secretly, that I would write three books which formed a crude trilogy—*Tinker, Tailor*, then *The Honourable Schoolboy*, and the third one which I've just completed. For good trade reasons one doesn't like to announce one's going to write a trilogy. If the book's a flop you're landed with the other two, or you have to crawl out of the tunnel. Another reason is that there is a resistance from people, feeling they're coming in in the middle of a trilogy or even buying the last one in a trilogy. So one has to be jolly careful. But I thought I would write those three, which I've now done, and then I would hang Smiley's boots up, at least for a while.[15]

Whether le Carré did or did not begin this series of novels with the clear idea of writing a trilogy entitled *The Quest for Karla*, the three books do form a coherent and unified sequence for all their diversity.

In returning to Smiley's world with *Tinker, Tailor, Soldier, Spy,* le Carré reintroduces a number of familiar characters, notably Peter Guillam who now plays a key part as Smiley's right-hand man. The expansiveness mentioned above is obvious in le Carré's periodic accounts of Guillam's uneasy relationship with his flute-playing girlfriend Camilla, which shed light on his private life and thus make him a fuller character but have no connection whatever with the main narrative. Other figures from the early novels include the former policeman Mendel, who helps Smiley as he did in *Call for the Dead*, and Ailsa Brimley from *A Murder of Quality*, who provides Smiley with a safe house for an agent in trouble, Ricki Tarr, while there is even a brief mention of Smiley's much-despised superior, Maston, in *Call for the Dead*, here described as "a figure of no account" (p. 130). Nevertheless, because *Tinker, Tailor, Soldier, Spy* is not about an operation mounted by the Circus but about an internal investigation of the Circus, this closed and secret world, complete with its personal tensions, rivalries, and intrigues, is described much more fully than in any earlier novel. A host of new Circus characters are introduced for the first time, including such top men as Bill Haydon, Roy Bland, Toby Esterhase, and the present head, Percy Alleline, as well as a number of less senior agents and personnel such as the "babysitter" or bodyguard Fawn and the journalist-spy Jerry Westerby, who becomes a major character in the second novel of the trilogy, being "the honourable schoolboy" of the title.

It is partly because of this focus on the structure and workings of the Circus that le Carré's now famous spy slang receives its first airing in *Tinker, Tailor, Soldier, Spy*, including "branch lines," "burned," "handwriting," "honey trap," "inquisitors," "lamplighters," "mothers," "scalphunters," "stock," "tradecraft," and of course "mole" itself, for which the CIA word is "sleeper." The meanings of these words, some invented and some taken from genuine "spyspeak," are clear in context, but le Carré himself glossed a number of them in his 1976 interview with Melvyn Bragg,[16] and a fuller glossary is included in the cover story *Time* ran on le Carré when *The Honourable Schoolboy* was published.[17] Le Carré has so popularized "mole" that it has become standard English, but the term is not his. Marx used it metaphorically in a context of political subversion, and Soviet Intelligence subsequently applied it to a particularly dangerous kind of spy or double agent, one deeply embedded in the secret services or government apparatus of one's opponents and therefore capable of inflicting untold damage to his own country from within. Michael Straight, the American intellectual whose evidence led MI5 to identify Anthony Blunt as a former Soviet mole in 1964, points out in his political memoir *After Long Silence* that in student Communist circles in Cambridge during the 1930s those "preparing to earn their livings as barristers or as civil servants" were known as "moles."[18]

The extraordinary fascination that moles have had for the British during the Cold War since 1945 really dates from the defection of Guy Burgess and Donald Maclean in 1951, although the betrayal of Western military secrets to the Soviet Union for ideological reasons by the so-called atom spies of the late 1940s no doubt played a part. The double defection of 1951 was an immense shock to national pride because men ostensibly serving their country in positions of great trust turned out to be the opposite of what they seemed. The outcries of bewildered disbelief at the time are echoed in *Tinker, Tailor, Soldier, Spy* when the staunchly patriotic spy Jim Prideaux refuses to believe that anyone in the Circus, let alone a senior and much-respected member, could be anything as perfidiously un-British as a double agent. Smiley's response questions the naive nationalism at the heart of Prideaux's response: "We've turned enough members of other outfits: Russians, Poles, Czechs, French. Even the odd American. What's so special about the British, all of a sudden?" (p. 284). What bothered people in 1951 so much was the sense that the ground was slipping from under their feet, that something as supposedly stable and reliable as the Civil Service was not built on true British rock but on shifting sand. If men whose loyalty could be taken for granted proved disloyal, how far might the rot go? Did Burgess and Maclean represent the tip of an iceberg? These were among the issues raised by their flight to Moscow, and the subsequent detection and unmasking of other moles from the same background, notably Kim Philby, has continued to the present time.

Because of his eminence as the finest of all British-born art historians, the case of Blunt caused a sensation when Mrs. Thatcher made a statement to the House of Commons about it in November 1979, following Andrew Boyle's oblique exposure of Blunt in *The Climate of Treason* (1979). The timing of this seemed like a superb piece of "tradecraft" by le Carré and the BBC because it virtually coincided with the television serialization of *Tinker, Tailor, Soldier, Spy* in the fall of that year, and preceded the publication of *Smiley's People* by only a few months. Further revelations ensued, and in a book published not long afterwards, *Their Trade Was Treachery* (1981), Chapman Pincher speculates about whether Sir Roger Hollis, a member of MI5 for nearly thirty years after his recruitment in the 1930s and its

Director General for about a third of that time, was a KGB "super-mole." Pincher's somewhat sensational book and Nigel West's more scholarly *A Matter of Trust: MI5, 1945–72* (1982) have done much to stir up the muddy water yet again, as has *After Long Silence* in which Michael Straight describes how Blunt recruited him as a potential Soviet mole. Le Carré had a number of interesting things to say about Blunt in his 1980 interview with Miriam Gross— "One forgets nowadays the extent to which homosexuality, at that period, was of itself a commitment to a secret world"[19]—and he drew attention to the fortuitous resemblances between his fictional mole and Blunt, both being painters, art connoisseurs, and homosexuals.

Since the defection of Philby the British moles have provoked a great deal of discussion about what motivated their allegiance to Moscow. In his introductory essay to Philby's own selective autobiography *My Silent War*, Graham Greene presents Philby in patently Greenean terms as a committed individual serving what he thought to be the higher good. Le Carré himself takes a very different view in his 1968 Introduction to Page, Leitch, and Knightley's *Philby: The Spy Who Betrayed a Generation*, arguing that he did "not much believe in the political motive of Kim Philby"[20] and preferred to seem him as a symptom of national malaise. Although it was not realized at the time, le Carré had left intelligence work only four years before this and could therefore be said to be writing from the inside. In assessing the rival interpretations of Greene and le Carré, the former American intelligence officer Miles Copeland, who claims that he knew Philby "as well as anyone did — especially during the period just before he fled to Moscow,"[21] comes down heavily on le Carré's side. Le Carré was nevertheless attacked in *The Philby Affair* (1968) by the well-known historian and one-time MI6 colleague of Philby's, Hugh Trevor-Roper (now Lord Dacre), who accuses him of presenting the Secret Service as "a rotten microcosm of a rotten society";[22] but this crudely oversimplifies le Carré's argument, which is indubitably critical of England but also upholds the democratic principles enshrined in Britain's unwritten constitution:

> We shall never, I hope, create a society that is proof against his kind: the little man who found a big name for cheating. Philby is the price we pay for being moderately free; for being able to read this book; and there is a side to Philby's head which knows it, and will know it till he dies. Stupid, credulous, smug and torpid as the establishment may have been, it erred on the side of trust. [23]

Le Carré may be "a disgusted patriot,"[24] as David Caute perceptively labeled him in his review of *Smiley's People*, but however disgusted, he remains a true-born Englishman.

The ease with which the Soviet Union could recruit potential spies among upper-class university students, especially at Cambridge, during the 1930s—men and women likely to enter the Civil Service or even Parliament and reach top positions—is now all too familiar. In *Tinker, Tailor, Soldier, Spy* the remarks in the Soviet agent Irina's diary about such recruitment are true to the historical record:

> Most of the English moles were recruited by Karla before the war and came from the higher bourgeoisie, even aristocrats and nobles who were disgusted with their origins, and became secretly fanatic, much more fanatic than their working-class English comrades, who are slothful. Several were applying to join the Party when Karla stopped them in time and directed them to special work. Some fought in Spain against Franco Fascism, and Karla's talent-spotters found them there and turned them over to Karla for recruitment. Others were recruited in the war during the alliance of expediency between Soviet Russia and Britain. (p. 59)

When Smiley is invited to undertake the task of identifying the Circus mole, he is told: "It's your generation, after all. Your legacy" (p. 74). In chapter 29 the references to a student group at Oxford during the late 1930s known as The Optimates, founded by Bill Haydon and described as "an upper-class Christ Church Club, mainly old Etonian" (p. 261), are presumably intended to bring to mind the actual and equally exclusive group at Cambridge usually known as the Apostles, although officially the Cambridge Conversazione Society, of which Blunt, Burgess, and Straight were members. Among the founders of the Apostles a century earlier were the future Poet Laureate Alfred Tennyson and his brother Charles, and many outstanding Cambridge men had belonged to the Society in the intervening period and still did belong, including the historian G. M. Trevelyan, the economist John Maynard Keynes, the novelist E. M. Forster, and the philosopher G. E. Moore. Contrary to what is sometimes thought today, the Apostles was not a front for left-wing activists in the 1930s, but a number of young Apostles were either Communists or fellow travelers, including Virginia Woolf's nephew Julian Bell, who was killed in action during the Spanish Civil War. Although The Optimates is said to be a politically conservative club, readers familiar with the cases of Philby and Burgess, for example, will know that this need not be taken completely at face value. Both men, although openly socialist in the early 1930s, subsequently concealed their Communist beliefs not only by avoiding left-wing organizations but by associating to some extent with right-wing ones, thus nullifying any suspicions about their loyalty.

Nine years separate *Tinker, Tailor, Soldier, Spy* from le Carré's last novel involving Smiley and the Circus, so it is not surprising that there have been major changes in the Circus, now under new management. Control has died and his "high chamberlain" (p. 131) Smiley has left the Circus because of a major disagreement, as he did once before in *Call for the Dead.* Control, suffering from ill health, was forced to retire after a mission in Czechoslovakia known as Operation Testify, which he was masterminding, went disastrously wrong. The British government suffered serious embarrassment when a senior agent who had worked with the Czech resistance during World War II, Jim Prideaux (work name, Ellis), was shot and captured by the Russians, though he was subsequently repatriated. In chapter 10 it emerges that Smiley's departure from the Circus stemmed from the same crisis. Convinced that Operation Testify (or the Ellis scandal) must have been betrayed to the Russians by an informer within the Circus, Smiley took his suspicions to Oliver Lacon of the Cabinet Office, "a senior adviser to various mixed committees and a watchdog of intelligence affairs" or "less reverentially, Whitehall's head prefect" (p. 29), only to be rebuffed and told to drop his inquiries. Smiley's response was to retire and to put his professional life completely behind him, predictably devoting himself to his scholarly pursuits in German culture, "which had served him well enough as a distraction while he was at the Circus, but which now that he was unemployed were nothing, absolutely nothing" (p. 75).

Smiley's retirement proves to be no more lasting than his earlier one, during which he turned private detective in *A Murder of Quality* before resuming his work for the Circus in *The Spy.* Smiley's latest retirement comes to an abrupt end in chapter 3 when Guillam appears as if by magic in Smiley's house to whisk him off to a highly confidential meeting with an apologetic Lacon and Ricki Tarr, a Circus agent who vanished some months earlier while on a mission in Hong Kong and who now produces evidence supporting Smiley's hunch about a Soviet mole in the Circus. Lacon, who attributes his earlier failure to take Smiley seriously to the inherent duplicity of all secret service work ("It's a little difficult to know when to trust you people and when not. You do live by rather different standards, don't you? I mean you have to" [p. 70]), now invites Smiley to carry out a top-secret investigation of the Circus without its knowledge in order to identify the mole, if one exists. Smiley is recalled because he is the only person above suspicion with the expertise to carry out such a probe who is likely to do it with the tact and delicacy demanded by the Minister so as to minimize any scandal. As in *Call for the Dead* Smiley is in pursuit of a hostile agent, but this time the detective work has to be clandestine. Smiley cannot function as a member of the Circus and has no access to its records except through Lacon and Guillam, who has to maintain his position within the Circus while covertly aiding and abetting Smiley. By stressing Smiley's physical isolation and the essentially lonely nature of much of his enquiry, le Carré establishes his individualism and his reluctance to be associated with the herd.

If the Circus has undergone a transformation, Smiley himself has not. As Guillam explains to Smiley, since Control's departure the Circus has been restructured according to the prevailing doctrine of "lateralism" so that operations are no longer organized regionally but are grouped together under London Station, headed by Bill Haydon with Bland and Esterhase as his chief assistants. This arrangement gives Haydon a great deal of power and independence. Smiley, on the other hand, has undergone little change and is instantly recognizable from the first description of him hurrying in the rain: "Small, podgy, and at best middle-aged, he was by appearance one of London's meek who do not inherit the earth. His legs were short, his gait anything but agile, his dress costly, ill-fitting and extremely wet" (p. 18). Here as throughout *The Quest for Karla* le Carré is careful to blur the question of Smiley's age, giving him a kind of ageless late middle age. Smiley has not advanced appreciably in years since le Carré's early novels, in which he must be in his middle to late fifties (according to *Call for the Dead* he was recruited for the Circus as a graduate in 1928), even though *Tinker, Tailor, Soldier, Spy* is set about ten years later in the early 1970s. Had le Carré been completely faithful to his original conception, Smiley would have been entering old age in *Tinker, Tailor, Soldier, Spy* and been well over seventy in *Smiley's People*. As in *Call for the Dead* there are many references in *Tinker, Tailor, Soldier, Spy* to Ann, "the last illusion of the illusionless man" (p. 364), but since she is as usual engaged on one of her affairs, she is conspicuous by her absence except for Smiley's sighting of her at the very end of the novel when, devoted as ever, he travels to the East Coast port of Immingham where he knows her to be. This journey again recalls *Call for the Dead*, which ends with Smiley flying to Zurich in pursuit of Ann. The crucial difference between the Smiley of *Call for the Dead* and the Smiley of *Tinker, Tailor, Soldier, Spy* is that in 1961 he was partly an antitype of the conventional spy of fiction and an antidote to James Bond, whereas in 1974 he returned as an established figure, not a novel one; an eccentric hero rather than an antihero. By 1974 the vogue for Bondian spy fantasies, against which le Carré reacted so strongly in his early work, was well past its peak and very much in decline, despite the continuing popularity of Ian Fleming's original creation, especially in film versions.

In *Tinker, Tailor, Soldier, Spy* le Carré employs two parallel narrative threads, the main one dealing with Smiley's investigation and the other focusing on another quirky and unusual middle-aged man, Jim Prideaux, with whom the novel opens and ends. The description of Prideaux's extraordinary arrival at Thursgood's School in the first chapter, "driving an old red Alvis and towing a second-hand trailer that had once been blue" (p. 4) and establishing himself in what is called the Dip, a large hole in the school grounds dug years ago for a swimming pool that has not been installed, is most memorable. Prideaux is evidently a completely independent man who makes his own decisions and is beholden to no one. Initially, the treatment of Prideaux at Thursgood's in the rural West Country county of Somerset (there are references to the town of Taunton and to the Quantock Hills), where he obtains temporary employment as a master, has no obvious connection with the Circus, but the mystery of his former life and the cause of his injured back become evident when Smiley looks into Operation Testify. Prideaux is virtually in hiding from his Circus past, which he understandably wants to put behind him considering its ignominious end, and he organizes some of the schoolboys into a form of spy network to warn him of anyone in the area interested in him. Prideaux has endured a succession of traumatic experiences as a result of Testify, physical as well as psychological. After being shot by the Russians, he was lucky to escape with his life and has been left with a permanently damaged back; but he has also undergone a grueling interrogation by Moscow Centre, another interrogation by the Circus's "inquisitors" on his return, and has been humiliatingly pensioned off as "the Circus's Number One leper" (p. 302) and told to reveal nothing about Testify to anyone. Despite his efforts Prideaux, who knows nothing about Control's disgrace and death or about Smiley's exit from the Circus, cannot avoid the past, and the two narratives converge as Mendel tracks him down so that Smiley can interview him at length in the third and final part of the novel. This is a turning point for Prideaux who now feels compelled to right a terrible wrong done to him and to his much-loved Czech spy networks by the mole. Ultimate responsibility for the Russian ambush Prideaux walked into rests with the mole, who has also betrayed the Czech networks, thus ensuring the deaths of Prideaux's friends and agents, and moreover has completely discredited Prideaux by suggesting that he informed against them to save himself while in Russian hands.

From this point Prideaux becomes a pursuer rather than someone in fear of being pursued, although like Smiley in *The Spy* he is more of a shadow than a presence as he patiently waits for Smiley to close in on the mole before doing so himself: the apparently disappearing man that "Guillam saw, or thought he saw, a tall crooked figure in a dark coat" (p. 327), at the end of chapter 34 must be Prideaux. It is Prideaux who carries out a form of unofficial execution combined with a revenge killing of the mole at the very end of the novel when he is supposedly in safe custody after his arrest, but le Carré does not name Prideaux, and Smiley, who obviously intuits what has happened, declines to offer an opinion when asked—presumably because he recognizes that justice, albeit of the rougher sort, has been done. Ostensibly, the mole has been Prideaux's lifelong friend since their undergraduate days at Oxford during the 1930s, when they were also lovers, so that Prideaux's sense of personal and national outrage—he is a profoundly patriotic man—is easy to understand. What clinches the identity of the mole's killer is the manner of his death. When his body is discovered, "his eyes were open and his head was propped unnaturally to one side, like the head of a bird when its neck has been expertly broken" (p. 365), words that immediately recall the incident 350 pages earlier in chapter 1 when Prideaux disposes of an injured owl at the school: "It's neck, as the braver ones established, was snapped. Only a gamekeeper, declared Sudeley, who had one, would know how to kill an owl so well" (p. 14).

By developing the Prideaux narrative independently of the Smiley narrative for much of the novel, le Carré diversifies the interest by allowing himself scope to develop characters and situations not germane to the main story line. The schoolboy Bill Roach, who becomes Prideaux's main helper, is an example of how le Carré now gives some prominence to figures irrelevant to the primary theme of detection in a way that is substantially different from the more functional approach to narrative in his early novels, especially *The Spy*. One of the main bonuses of this expansiveness is the gently satirical treatment of that distinctly English educational institution, the Prep or Preparatory School. Thursgood's is a mild caricature of these private, single-sex establishments catering to wealthy children aged between six and thirteen who are destined for English public schools, about which le Carré had some caustic things to say in *A Murder of Quality*. Thursgood's is therefore a complement to Carne School (geographically they are not far apart), although le Carré's descriptions are characterized by wry amusement, not the bitter indignation with which he presented aspects of Carne. Prideaux, whose previous teaching experience is nil, not surprisingly arrives at Thursgood's "through one of the shiftier agencies specialising in supply teachers for prep schools" and is immediately recognized by the staff to be "a poor white of the teaching community" who "belonged to the same sad bunch as the late Mrs. Loveday, who had a Persian-lamb coat and stood in for junior divinity until her cheques bounced, or the late Mr. Maltby, the pianist who had been called from choir practice to help the police with their inquiries, and as far as anyone knew was helping them to this day" (p. 3). What puzzles Thursgood about Prideaux is that although his past is a complete mystery he is not one of the standard con men in the profession with whom Thursgood is all too familiar: "bogus Oxford men" and "classics masters who had no Greek and parsons who had no divinity," men who when exposed "broke down and wept and left, or stayed on half-pay" (p. 15). The last point is telling, because Thursgood is obviously prepared to employ rogues at reduced rates to avoid paying a full salary to a properly qualified teacher. Here as elsewhere in le Carré's fiction the influence of Evelyn Waugh's witty style can be felt.

Many readers have found the complex main narrative of *Tinker, Tailor, Soldier, Spy* intriguing but also baffling, and le Carré has undoubtedly constructed an intricate puzzle of considerable intellectual ingenuity that requires the brainpower of Smiley to solve and also requires of the reader the concentration demanded by serious literary fiction, not the sun-drugged doziness with which many thrillers are read on holiday beaches. One reason for this is that le Carré is trying to give Smiley's search for the mole as much verisimilitude as possible, so it is not a straightforward linear journey but more of a zigzag that advances slowly and indirectly, or even a trek through a maze complete with cul-de-sacs. Smiley is not in the advantageous position of Alan Turner who has carte blanche to interrogate whomever he likes in his quest for a supposed double agent in *A Small Town in Germany*. Within the confines of the Embassy Turner's investigation is open, whereas Smiley's is of necessity secret, and he cannot question anyone in the Circus without alerting the very person he is trying to identify. What Smiley has to do is to collect scraps of evidence from people who can help him without setting off alarm bells in the Circus, and piece them together with information derived from a painstaking comparative analysis of various files and records in the hope that the solution will emerge.

Because of the context in which he functions, Smiley's methods are different from those of the sleuth in classical detective fiction, but there are obvious parallels. Like *Call for the Dead* and *A Small Town in Germany, Tinker, Tailor, Soldier, Spy* is an unusual transformation of the classical detective formula into a security investigation of supposed treachery. Turner's inquiry takes an unorthodox turn when the supposed spy proves to be innocent, but Smiley's mole hunt conforms closely to the underlying formula in that there are only four suspects, all within the closed world of the Circus: Alleline, Haydon, Bland, Esterhase. This pattern is strikingly similar to Smiley's search for Stella Rode's murderer among a small number of suspects in the confines of Carne School. Where *Tinker, Tailor, Soldier, Spy* differs markedly from the formula is that the four suspects, who might be expected to figure prominently, only rarely occupy the foreground, and until chapter 34 in the closing stages of the novel, when Smiley speculates to Toby Esterhase, there is no communication or confrontation between Smiley and any of the suspects. Given the nature of Smiley's investigation and le Carré's decision to present much of the narrative from Smiley's viewpoint, this is inevitable, but it does mean that the suspects make less impact and are altogether less substantial and vivid than characters such as Connie Sachs and Jerry Westerby, who as far as the plot is concerned are much less important. Alleline, for example, is little more than a caricature, and Bland, true to his name, is almost invisible. The four suspects bear some resemblance to the major character of Leo in *A Small Town in Germany* in being absentees rather than presences, and there is consequently something of a vacuum in the novel, although le Carré disguises this to a great extent by involving the reader in the processes of Smiley's inquiry.

The intellectual nature of that inquiry means that there is little action in *Tinker, Tailor, Soldier, Spy*, but le Carré succeeds in injecting more variety into the novel than in *A Small Town in Germany*, with its succession of similar interviews. Smiley's inquiry in *Tinker, Tailor, Soldier, Spy* brings him into contact with a wider and more interesting spectrum of humanity than Turner encounters, and what they have to tell him is more diverse than is the case with Turner's informants, all of whom concentrate on one topic, Leo. Indeed the plenitude of detail in *Tinker, Tailor, Soldier, Spy* is one reason why readers have difficulty in seeing the wood for the trees. Le Carré does seem to be carried away by the complicating possiblities of some of his subnarratives, as in the case of Ricki Tarr's story about his involvement with a Soviet agent, Irina, in Hong Kong and about her subsequent forcible removal to Moscow. This contains a nugget of gold in the form of strong evidence that Karla has been running a mole known as Gerald within the Circus and that one of Karla's right-hand men, Colonel Viktorov, is using diplomatic cover as Cultural Attaché Polyakov at the Russian Embassy in London to control Gerald. It is on the basis of Tarr's information to Guillam that Lacon summons Smiley to "clean the stables" (p. 74) in Herculean style, yet le Carré lavishes over five chapters on Tarr in the early part of the novel (end of chapter 4 and chapters 5–9), including his reading to Smiley, Lacon, and Guillam of extended passages from Irina's diary. In the early 1960s, le Carré would probably have presented Tarr's story in condensed form so as to highlight its value as intelligence and consequently its relevance to the unmasking of the mole, but he now gives it value as a story in itself in a way that is typical of his more recent fiction.

Chapter 22, describing Smiley's second encounter with Tarr when he is in hiding from both the Circus and Moscow Centre in Ailsa Brimley's house, produces only minor additions to his earlier account and contributes very little to Smiley's investigation, but it does serve as a reminder of the numerous balls Smiley is juggling in the air at the same time. Most of chapters 12 and 13 is about Smiley's visit to Oxford to pick the brains of Connie Sachs, the retired one-woman memory bank of the Circus and former "queen of research" (p. 97), who plays an important part in *The Honourable Schoolboy* and makes an appearance in *Smiley's People*. Reg Gadney has suggested that in choosing the names Connie and Jim Ellis, le Carré was consciously or unconsciously drawing on the Philby affair, since " 'Connie' . . . was an alias given to Philby's mistress" and one of Guy Burgess's cover names "was Jim Andreyevitch Eliot."[25] As far as the investigation goes, Connie's remarks about Moscow Centre and Polyakov, especially her suspicion that he was running a mole, provide Smiley with independent confirmation of Irina's revelations rather than anything new, but Connie, whose style of speech is as individual as Tarr's or Westerby's or Max's or Esterhase's, emerges as an interesting character in her own right, unlike some of the rather faceless people questioned by Turner in *A Small Town in Germany*. In *Tinker, Tailor, Soldier, Spy* le Carré gives more individuality to his many minor characters than in his early fiction by dwelling on them for longer and by equipping them with verbal mannerisms of their own. In delineating characters, writers of detective and spy fiction usually rely much more on dialogue and speech idiom, just as dramatists have to do, than on passages of description, analysis, and stream of consciousness as in straight fiction, and while le Carré employs a variety of techniques he has always made extensive use of dialogue. In *Tinker, Tailor, Soldier, Spy* le Carré is also discursive in presenting incidents that might well have received summary treatment in his early fiction. In chapters 11 and 20 he describes in some detail how Guillam obtains information for Smiley from Circus records by underhand means, chapter 20 being largely devoted to the precise mechanics of Guillam's clever theft of the Testify file in the presence of the Circus archivists.

Smiley's investigation is really a journey into the past with new eyes, and in particular involves a complete revaluation of the two major Circus operations concerning Eastern Europe at the end of Control's career, Witchcraft and Testify. As Smiley pursues his quarry he beomes aware that he is virtually repeating a search that Control was secretly conducting before Testify brought his career to an abrupt halt and prematurely terminated his own hunt for the mole when he had narrowed the suspects down to five top men. Smiley therefore senses "that Control's ghost was his companion into all but the furthest reaches" (p. 140). The conventional Whitehall wisdom is that Operation Witchcraft, involving a mysterious, high-level Russian source of Kremlin secrets called Merlin, is one of the best intelligence coups in the Circus's history. The Cabinet Minister with whom Smiley and Lacon discuss the Operation, Miles Sercombe, a cousin of Ann's, as is Bill Haydon, exclaims: "That Witchcraft stuff is bloody marvellous!" (p. 222). Yet Smiley's patient reexamination of Witchcraft in his hideout or "operational headquarters" (p. 123) at the Hotel Islay, where he goes under the name of Barraclough, leads him to the conclusion that it is a most subtle Russian scheme to hoodwink the Circus by providing sufficiently good information for Merlin to seem a genuinely pro-Western or at least anti-Soviet agent within the Soviet ranks. In fact Witchcraft is a Moscow Centre, not a Circus, success, because by creating a direct link between the Circus and Merlin, including his London representative, Polyakov, it provides perfect cover for mole Gerald's contacts with his controller. The Circus, blinded by its apparent triumph and lavishing funds on the Operation, including the purchase of an expensive London house solely for Witchcraft, has fallen victim to a brilliant deception by Karla and has played into his hands. Significantly, Witchcraft is not associated with Control, who has remained sceptical of it, but with Alleline, who has taken the credit for it. Indeed part of Karla's purpose in Witchcraft was to secure the imperceptive and credulous Alleline as Control's heir apparent so that the Circus would not be in the hands of someone like Smiley. When Smiley puts his hypothesis about Witchcraft to Toby Esterhase in chapter 34, he gives hints about who he thinks the mole is although he avoids naming anyone by talking only of Gerald.

Operation Testify, over which "the Foreign Office and the Defence Ministry had jointly blown a gasket" (p. 78), also turns out to be totally different from the received Whitehall version, which Lacon expresses when he talks of Control's "gross incompetence" in launching "a private war against the Czechs" (p. 71) in an apparent attempt to kidnap a Czech general. Control has taken full responsibility for the catastrophe of Testify, but Smiley's researches, including interviews with Sam Collins, duty officer at the Circus on the night Prideaux was wounded and captured (chapter 26), with Max, Prideaux's "babysitter" in Czechoslovakia (chapter 27), with Jerry Westerby, who has picked up a Czech account of Testify in Prague (chapter 28), and with Jim Prideaux himself (chapters 31–32), reveal that it was not "launched by an old man for his dying glory" (p. 78), as Haydon tells Guillam. On the contrary, Control's aim was to obtain the identity of the mole from the Czech general, who has worked in Moscow Centre's England section and who is believed to be willing to betray its secrets, so totally disenchanted has he become with the Communist cause since the Warsaw Pact military suppression of the Prague Spring in 1968, when Dubček attempted to give socialism a human face in his country by a policy of liberalization. The title of the novel comes from the code that Control and Prideaux used on Testify, suspects in the Circus being labeled according to the children's fortune-telling rhyme, "Tinker, Tailor, Soldier, Sailor, Rich Man, Poor Man, Beggarman, Thief," which is too well-known in Britain to warrant the inclusion in the British edition of the explanatory note found at the beginning of the American edition. Smiley, it should be noted, was humbly coded Beggarman, a touch of affectionate irony on Control's part.

Once in Czechoslovakia, Prideaux realized that his mission had been compromised and that he was probably walking into a trap, but did not grasp the extraordinary truth deduced by Smiley that Control had already been lured into a trap by Karla, who is as much behind Testify as Witchcraft. Although Prideaux was not aware of it, part of his interrogation was by Karla himself, as Smiley immediately recognizes from Prideaux's description of the chain-smoking "cold little fellow" (p.

297) with Smiley's lighter. Karla, alerted to the danger his mole is in from Control, has skillfully used disinformation to trick Control into launching Testify, thus ensuring his own downfall as a result of the inevitable political scandal and eliminating the only threat to Gerald. Operation Testify is another handsome intelligence victory for Karla over the Circus. With Control and Smiley out of the way, the Circus can virtually be run to suit Moscow Centre, especially against its main target, the Americans. It is only through Tarr's stroke of luck that Smiley, a worthy combatant for Karla, can be brought back to redeem the situation, and it is fitting that Smiley should employ Tarr in chapter 35 to set up his own trap to ensnare the mole at the Circus's safe house reserved for contacts with Polyakov as part of Witchcraft. Writing about the world "of multiple betrayals—of treason, infidelity, disloyalty and broken faith" presented in the novel, Andrew Rutherford, who argues that "*Tinker Tailor Soldier Spy* achieves a perfect fusion of spy plot and universal theme, as it explores the antithetical phenomena of treason and fidelity," says: "Examples of treachery, of obligations broken and trust betrayed, proliferate like the metaphorical extensions of sin and disorder in Shakespearean tragedy. There is a sense of corruption at the very heart of things; and Smiley's search for the source of evil has affinities with Oedipus's quest for truth or Hamlet's for revenge."[26]

Le Carré does not reveal that the aristocractic Haydon is the mole until this point, although devotees of mystery stories, familiar with the convention of "the least likely suspect," will probably guess correctly long before this. For much of the novel the "ubiquitous and charming" Haydon with his "grand designs for restoring England to influence and greatness" (p. 155), appears as the quintessential, upper-class Englishman, much as Kim Philby did in real life, and he was a "least likely suspect" if there ever was one. For Guillam, "Haydon was of that unrepeatable, fading Circus generation, to which his parents and George Smiley also belonged" (p. 86), a view shared by Connie Sachs for whom Haydon exemplifies the old, original Circus of Fielding, Jebedee, and Steed-Asprey; and for Lauder Strickland, Haydon is a "fantastic fellow . . . London Station could not be in better hands. Incredible ability. Incredible record. Brilliant" (p. 87). Even Smiley, who has reason to hold a grudge against Haydon because of his affair with Ann, an affair cynically planned in order to confuse Smiley's emotions and distract him from any mole scent, acknowledges that "the comparison with Lawrence was inevitable" (p. 155)—that is, T. E. Lawrence (of Arabia), an almost mythical figure in twentieth-century

British history. It is not surprising that Guillam feels "not merely betrayed but orphaned" when the man who "was his inspiration, the torch-bearer of a certain kind of antiquated romanticism, a notion of English calling" (p. 347) emerges as the mole. Yet when early in the novel Guillam thinks of Haydon having "a slightly Dorian Gray look" (p. 89), he is much closer to the mark than he realizes, because Oscar Wilde's eponymous character in *The Picture of Dorian Gray* is the literary epitome of a man being the opposite of what he seems.

After the successful springing of Smiley's mole trap, there is a most revealing passage:

> He knew, of course. He had always known it was Bill. Just as Control had known, and Lacon in Mendel's house. Just as Connie and Jim had known, and Alleline and Esterhase; all of them had tacitly shared that unexpressed half-knowledge which like an illness they hoped would go away if it was never owned to, never diagnosed. (p. 346)

Bruce Merry identifies this phenomenon as "the old English malaise . . . the insistence on settling things behind doors, pulling strings for guilty friends, overlooking an admired colleague's fist in the petty cash."[27] What le Carré has to say in his essay on Philby about British intelligence officers identifying "class with loyalty" and being so preoccupied "with the modalities of national self-advancement" that "they are professionally incapable of comprehending ideology, however it was born, as a serious motivating force in people of their own kind,"[28] is pertinent in Haydon's case.

Le Carré's heavy concentration on the mechanics of Smiley's investigation does mean that some of its moral and political dimensions are not given much prominence until after the mole has been caught. There are two principal issues, one concerning the mole and the other the mole-catcher. First is the mind and political motivation of the ideological spy who has to maintain a double life with all its psychological tensions even though he may feel fully justified in what he is doing. In this connection, part of le Carré's diagnosis of Philby is particularly relevant to Haydon:

> It is, I am sure, part of the ambivalence of Philby's position that he never altogether took leave of the world he forswore. He enjoyed the establishment; he enjoyed its camaraderie, its inside track, its institutional warmth, its comforting distaste for intellectual pyrotechnics; to the very end he remained dependent on the very people he deceived.[29]

Second is the conflict between human and political values in Smiley as spy-hunter, knowing that the mole is bound to be a colleague of long standing who has shared much of his own Circus experience, a personal associate as well as a national enemy. There is a resemblance here to Smiley's crisis of conscience over his old friend and official enemy Dieter Frey in *Call for the Dead.*

Haydon's explanation of his decision to work for the Russians and his account of Operations Witchcraft and Testify emerge in his confession to Smiley in chapter 38, although le Carré gives this much less space than several inteviews earlier in the novel that, thematically at any rate, are much less important. Faced with a world in which the Britain he was reared to serve has shrunk from a great world power to a nation in postimperialist decline, increasingly subservient to a loathsome United States and exhibiting the unacceptable face of capitalism, Haydon has linked his destiny with the Eastern bloc rather than the West. Britain's serious political miscalculation over the Suez Crisis in 1956 was, for Haydon, the last straw, the dying wag of the imperial bulldog's mangy tail. Haydon's defense brings to mind Connie's sad words about a generation (Haydon's, Smiley's, and her own) "trained to Empire, trained to rule the waves," only to find it vanishing before their eyes: "All gone. All taken away. Bye-bye, world" (p. 113). These remarks recur to Smiley as a way of understanding Haydon before he interviews him at the end of the novel: "He saw with painful clarity an ambitious man born to the big canvas, brought up to rule, divide and conquer, whose visions and vanities all were fixed, like Percy's, upon the world's game; for whom the reality was a poor island with scarcely a voice that would carry across the water" (p. 345). If Haydon is a traitor, there is also a sense in which, as Smiley acknowledges, he has been betrayed by history. Haydon belongs to a generation that inherited the quasi-religious nationalistic faith of Victorian England and was expected to uphold it, but found it no longer tenable and sought another substitute religion—in his case, Communism. To use a theological analogy, Haydon came to the conclusion that his primary obedience was not to Caesar, the nation state where he was born, but to God, in the form of Marxism-Leninism.

As in the passage quoted above, it is partly through Smiley's speculations rather than directly that Haydon's mentality is mediated, and because Smiley sees Haydon as contradictory and paradoxical he refuses to pass conventional judgment on him by simply labeling him a traitor. "Distrustful as ever of the standard shapes of human motive," what Smiley sees is "a picture of one of those wooden Russian dolls that open up, revealing one person inside the other, and another inside him" (p. 367). This is why the supremely self-conscious Smiley himself feels so divided and experiences qualms of conscience about what he has done as his political duty, even while deploring the "appalling duplicity" of Haydon: "Nothing is worth the destruction of another human being. Somewhere the path of pain and betrayal must end . . . . It was the treason, not the man, that belonged to the public domain" (p. 345). The anarchic side of Smiley is aware that even "the public domain" can be called in question, as he does when he experiences "a surge of resentment against the institutions he was supposed to be protecting: 'The social contract cuts both ways, you know,' said Lacon. The Minister's lolling mendacity, Lacon's tight-lipped moral complacency, the bludgeoning greed of Percy Alleline: such men invalidated any contract—why should anyone be loyal to them?" (pp. 345–46). Here Smiley comes close to exonerating Haydon by undermining the basis of any form of loyalty to the public or the state, although another side of Smiley cannot condone the systematic duplicity that has made Haydon's life at the Circus one monumental lie. Smiley's conception of his secret service work as a regrettable necessity does not accord with Haydon's conviction "that secret services were the only real measure of a nation's political health, the only real expression of its subconscious" (p. 355), a belief that would be shared by Fiedler in *The Spy*. With Smiley's acute sense of moral ambiguity, it is no wonder that he refuses to be a judge, let alone a hanging judge. That role is left to Prideaux.

The obvious ease with which Prideaux gains access to Haydon without being detected is puzzling, considering Smiley's deep concern about Haydon's safety while in custody at the Circus's "Nursery" at Sarratt and his determination to ensure that no harm comes to him before he is sent to Russia as part of a deal with Karla. When he first visits Haydon at Sarratt, Smiley is "angry at Haydon's physical condition, but when he taxed the guards they professed mystification. He was angrier still to learn that the additional security precautions he had insisted on had been relaxed after the first day. When he demanded to see Craddox, head of Nursery, Craddox was unavailable and his assistant acted dumb" (p. 354). Is this deliberate carelessness on the part of the authorities, almost in the hope that something will happen to Haydon to ease the government's embarrassment? Or is the laxness merely symptomatic of the debilitated condition of the Circus? Le Carré's description of Sarratt certainly emphsizes decay and dereliction:

> Sarratt was a sorry place after the grandeur that Smiley remembered. Most of the elms had gone with the disease; pylons burgeoned over the

> old cricket field. The house itself, a sprawling brick mansion, had also come down a lot since the heyday of the cold war in Europe, and most of the better furniture seemed to have disappeared, he supposed into one of Alleline's houses. (p. 353)

Here as so often in le Carré's fiction the description of a place carries metaphorical significance, and if Sarratt is emblematic of the Circus, it also implies that something is rotten in the state of Britain. At the end of the novel Smiley is left with the gargantuan task of cleaning up what Lacon calls "the mess at Cambridge Circus" (p. 352), if he wants to accept the challenge, pending the appointment of a new, permanent head.

Like *The Looking Glass War*—and unlike *Call for the Dead, The Spy, The Honourable Schoolboy*, and *Smiley's People*—*Tinker, Tailor, Soldier, Spy* is a novel that unremittingly holds a mirror up to England by concentrating on the Circus itself rather than presenting an action about the Circus involved with an external threat. Admittedly Karla, like an evil genius, casts a dark shadow over the Circus, but Smiley's actual quest does not begin in earnest until after the mole has been brought to light and is therefore more central to the other two novels in the trilogy. Because of le Carré's focus, *Tinker, Tailor, Soldier, Spy* contains strong undertones of the Arthurian legends, especially of the final catastrophe that destroys Arthur's court and that emanates from within rather than from without. Le Carré's description of Haydon "as a member of that inestimable body that Ann loosely called the Set" (p. 345) clearly suggests the Knights of the Round Table, something reinforced by "Circus" itself, meaning a circular space. Just as the Arthurian knights were supposedly dedicated to chivalric ideals and the good of the kingdom, the Circus is, in theory, devoted to upholding the values of a liberal democracy and preserving the nation state. For Guillam the Circus at its best is the modern embodiment of a long tradition of nobility and heroism, and the exposure of Haydon, the "model on which he built his life" (p. 347) and a Lancelot figure on the surface, as a traitor makes him turn all his resentment against "the Circus and the failed magic that had formed his faith" (p. 348).

In the Arthurian legends it is an insider, Mordred, who brings about the final destruction of Camelot, and by the end of *Tinker, Tailor, Soldier, Spy* the Circus is in total disarray. Haydon's "blowing" to the Russians of most of the Circus's activities is subsequently described in the trilogy in mythical terms as "the fall." Even before Mordred's treachery, however, there are premonitions of disintegration at Camelot, as in Lancelot's adulterous relationship with Queen Guinevere, the nearest equivalent being Haydon's affair with Ann Smiley. The way in which le Carré handles the intertwining of personal and public betrayals and evasions is similar to what occurs in the Arthurian legends. As Tom Paulin notes, Haydon has wounded "the English psyche and at the end of le Carré's masterpiece, *Tinker, Tailor, Soldier, Spy*, the wounded patriot, Jim Prideaux, avenges the betrayed consciousness of Albion."[30] Prideaux's private revenge, like Hamlet's, is simultaneously a public and political act. George Grella sums up this connection better than anyone:

> In Smiley's tortured humanity we see the reason for le Carré's obsession with the relationship between love and betrayal—treason is not only an act against a nation and for an ideology, but also an act against a faith and against human emotion. E.M. Forster once wrote in a famous essay, "if I had to choose between betraying my country and betraying my friend I hope I should have the guts to betray my country." What he didn't realize is what John le Carré demonstrates: there is no ultimate difference between the two—to betray one's country *is* to betray one's friend. Love, after all, is whatever you can still betray.[31]

What le Carré achieves by triggering off mythic resonances is the transformation of the particular into the universal. However much he draws on recent British spy scandals, *Tinker, Tailor, Soldier, Spy* is much more than a fictionalized case history, and John Halperin is thoroughly misguided in discussing it as though it were a roman à clef, "the painstaking recreation of the Kim Philby story" in which "Haydon is Philby . . . and Smiley is Dick White, with a little of Sir Maurice Oldfield thrown in."[32] To relate the novel very specifically to real-life British Intelligence, of which both White and Oldfield were heads, is to claim the kind of authenticity for le Carré's novel that he himself has more than once disowned.

8

The Spy Who Went into the Heat: *The Honourable Schoolboy* (1977)

When listening to Sam Collins's story in chapter 4 of *The Honourable Schoolboy* about his investigation into a Moscow Centre "goldseam" in Laos, involving the movement of clandestine funds into normal banking channels, Smiley encourages Collins to tell it as fully as possible: "It's the *detail* I'm enjoying."[1] In the following chapter when the "honourable schoolboy" himself, Jerry Westerby, visits his literary agent Mencken in London, he receives the following advice about the novel he is writing:

> Nobody's brought off the Eastern novel recently, my view. Greene managed it, if you can take Greene, which I can't—too much popery. Malraux, if you like philosophy, which I don't. Maugham you can *have*, and before that it's back to Conrad. . . . Go easy on the Hemingway stuff. All that grace under pressure, love with your balls shot off. . . . Longer sentences. Moment you journalist chappies turn your hand to novels, you write too short. Short paragraphs, short sentences, short chapters. You see the stuff in column inches, 'stead of across the page. Hemingway was just the same. Always trying to write novels on the back of a matchbox. Spread yourself, my view. (p. 97)

Even though another of le Carré's major characters, Shamus in *The Naive and Sentimental Lover*, is a novelist, he normally refrains from making any comment within his fiction about the literary form he employs, so these remarks in a book that can itself be described as an "Eastern novel" are most conspicuous.

By describing Mencken as "one of those natural fools for whom English society, and the publishing world in particular, is ever ready to make a comfortable space" (p. 96), le Carré defensively distances himself from his character's words, but he would presumably endorse some of what Mencken is saying since it accords with his own practice in *The Quest for Karla*, especially in his longest novel, *The Honourable Schoolboy*. Like Smiley, le Carré clearly enjoys the detail, and he certainly spreads himself. The last thing that le Carré is doing is writing the trilogy on the back of a matchbox, and of all his novels *The Honourable Schoolboy* is one that might be said to contain everything. Indeed for some reviewers it contained too much, the most common complaint about this and other novels after *A Small Town in Germany* being that they are too long. Yet much of the pleasure of reading the novel stems from its expansiveness, from the accumulation of detail le Carré lavishes on the bare bones of his story and from the care with which he individualizes his very large and diverse cast of characters. *The Honourable Schoolboy*, which like *The Spy* won two British literary awards, another Crime Writers' Association Gold Dagger and a James Tait Black Memorial Prize, comprehensively encompasses a world in the manner of nineteenth-century fiction. Mencken's reference to Conrad, a novelist who also enjoyed detail and spread himself, is not the only hint in *The Honourable Schoolboy* that le Carré had that major writer in mind. During his travels in Southeast Asia, Jerry reads Conrad and regards Phnom Penh, the capital of Cambodia, as "the last of the true Conrad river ports" (p. 330). In an interview with Michael Barber after the novel appeared, le Carré said that he found himself "referring to Jerry and George as 'my secret sharers,' "[2] an obvious allusion to one of Conrad's most important shorter works, "The Secret Sharer."

A fascinating feature of *The Honourable Schoolboy* is the linguistic virtuosity reminiscent of such Victorian novelists as Dickens that le Carré displays in providing his cosmopolitan cast with such a diversified range of English speech idioms, something he attempts on a much larger scale than ever before. Many characters, including Jerry Westerby with his aging British slang, Ricardo with his Latin-American-tinged variety of American colloquial speech, and Murphy with his polite American pedantry and bureaucratic jargon, have a distinctive style of speech. There is Tiu's syntactically elliptical Chinese version of English: "Some horse-writer ask pretty damn questions" (p. 298); and Sol Eckland's aggressive American style, so different from Murphy's verbose formality: "And do we go for his jugular? . . . Do we, hell. We pussyfoot. We stand on the sidelines. . . . We float like a butterfly and sting like one. Jesus, if *we'd* been handling this thing we'd have had that bastard trussed over a barrel months ago" (p. 270). The most extraordinary examples are probably Charlie Marshall's idiosyncratic and exotic mélange of slang, hyperbole, and incongruity: "But Jesus, Voltaire, you screw it out of me, they will kill you very completely, because that Mr. Tiu, he's a business-like and very philosophical gentleman, hear me? They kill *me*, they kill *Ricardo*, they kill *you*, they kill the whole damn human race!" (p. 383); and Craw's equally idiosyncratic, sonorous rhetoric with its highly cultivated blend of pseudo-Elizabethan eloquence and jokiness: "Your Graces. . . . Pray silence for my son. I fear he would have parley with us. Brother Luke, you have committed several acts of war today and one more will meet with our severe disfavour. Speak clearly and concisely omitting no detail, however slight, and thereafter hold your water, sir" (p. 9).

Until *The Honourable Schoolboy* le Carré had never placed his characters outside Northern Europe, mainly England and Germany, except for Smiley's reminiscences about his encounter with Karla in India in *Tinker, Tailor, Soldier, Spy*. When this novel was published, there was some criticism that le Carré was still nagging away at the European arena of the Cold War, which he knew very well, instead of accepting the challenge of its worldwide and Third World dimensions. A related though more interesting complaint was voiced by Reg Gadney in a review article, in which he argues that the historical subject matter le Carré draws on, the hunting of 1930s moles, already belonged to the past, not the early 1970s when the novel is set, so that there is a discrepancy between historical actuality and fictional reality, something not apparent in, for example, *The Spy*.[3] Whether or not one regards these as flaws, le Carré more than answered such criticisms in *The Honourable Schoolboy*, which geographically encompasses much of Southeast Asia (concentrating in particular on Hong Kong) as well as the familiar territory of Smiley's London, and which is not open to Gadney's charge of slight anachronism. The original hardback came equipped with two maps, one of Southeast Asia and the other of the Hong Kong region, to help the Western reader follow the action through unfamiliar territory; neither is included in the American paperback although one is retained in the British paperback. It is most unusual for a novel to contain an authorial preface acknowledging indebtedness to various people, but le Carré's foreward to *The Honourable Schoolboy* does just that in connection with his travels throughout Southeast Asia to carry out the necessary research for the book.

The action of *The Honourable Schoolboy* in 1974–5 coincides with the closing stages of the war in Indo-China in which South Vietnam fell to the Viet Cong and North Vietnamese, and Cambodia to the Khmer Rouge. Jerry Westerby, who travels widely in Southeast Asia, is a foreign correspondent, at least on the surface, and the part of the novel devoted to his pursuit of Ricardo in Thailand, Laos, Cambodia, and Vietnam possesses the qualities of vivid reporting, especially war reporting, as well as advancing the narrative. Just as Graham Greene's study a of a double agent, *The Human Factor* (1978), brings le Carré to mind, *The Honourable Schoolboy* recalls Greene's *The Quiet American* (1955), narrated by an English journalist in Saigon during an earlier war in Vietnam, between the French colonial power and the Communist Vietminh. There is a further reminder of Greene in that le Carré's title closely resembles Greene's *The Honorary Consul* (1973). The panoramic sweep of *The Honourable Schoolboy* goes far beyond any of le Carré's earlier novels, and includes many aspects of life in Hong Kong (from the millionaire Drake Ko to the "free-lance gossip writer" Phoebe Wayfarer [p. 195] to the international press corps), opium smuggling as well as the war in Southeast Asia, rivalry between the Circus and its American counterpart known as "the Cousins," interdepartmental wrangling in Whitehall, and even life in a gossipy Italian village. The organization known as "the Cousins" is closely based on the CIA; like the CIA, it is sometimes called "the Company" and has its headquarters in Langley, Virginia. By expanding his scope to include previously untouched geographical and political areas, le Carré is able to introduce new themes into his fiction, especially Britain's colonial history and the often uneasy relationship, indeed friction, between Western and Oriental cultures.

After le Carré's concentration on closed worlds in *Tinker, Tailor, Soldier, Spy*, *A Small Town in Germany*, and *The Looking Glass War*, the unexpected release into globe-trotting and multifarious settings in *The Honourable Schoolboy* produces a sense of artistic liberation and exuberance. There are hints of this possibility in *Tinker, Tailor, Soldier, Spy*, especially in Ricki Tarr's retrospective account of the Soviet agents in Hong Kong, but this lacks the dramatic immediacy of

Jerry's much more extended adventures in the Far East. What permits this new spaciousness and openness is le Carré's use of a genuine double narrative, one centering on the Circus and Smiley, the mastermind behind Operation Dolphin, and the other on Jerry, the agent in the field, to whom the title of the novel gives prominence. Again there are hints of this possibility in *Tinker, Tailor, Soldier, Spy* with its two narratives, one concentrating on Prideaux and the other on Smiley, but the latter so overshadows the former that the relationship is that of a main plot to a subplot. Prideaux is an ex-agent, not an active one like Jerry, and there can be no sustained counterpoint between the two intercut narratives as there is in *The Honourable Schoolboy*, because Prideaux's life at Thursgood's School has no direct connection with Smiley's search for the mole. It is significant that in referring to both Prideaux and Westerby, le Carré departs from his usual practice of using surnames for his male characters (Smiley is never "George" except in direct speech), preferring "Jim" and "Jerry" respectively, thus bringing them closer to the reader from their first appearances.

If *Tinker, Tailor, Soldier, Spy* has two openings, *The Honourable Schoolboy* has no fewer than three, chapter 1 establishing Hong Kong itself, the principal stage for the ensuing drama, chapter 2 introducing Jerry in Italy, and chapter 3 describing Smiley temporarily at the helm of the Circus. This arrangement has the advantage of stressing important elements and characters in the novel before Smiley and other Circus faces, both familiar and unfamiliar, make their presence felt. Chapter 1, for example, depicts the Foreign Correspondents' Club in Hong Kong, especially its extraordinary doyen and "Ancient Mariner" (p. 9), an aging Australian called Craw, whom le Carré based on a famous international journalist, Dick Hughes, also the model for Dikko Henderson in one of Fleming's James Bond novels, *You Only Live Twice* (1964). In his foreword le Carré says that he "shamelessly exaggerated" Hughes's "outward character and mannerisms" but "could not obey his urgent exhortion to libel him to the hilt" (pp. ix–x); when Hughes died in Hong Kong on 4 January 1984, le Carré wrote a short tribute for *The Sunday Times* (8 January).

Le Carré's use of a double narrative allows the plot to unfold on two fronts simultaneously. Smiley's "group of five" (p. 54) at the Circus rakes over the past, as Smiley does single-handedly in *Tinker, Tailor, Soldier, Spy*, delving into the archives and interviewing people in the hope of locating more pieces of the jigsaw they are trying to put together. Even in this narrative Smiley is less dominant than in *Tinker, Tailor, Soldier, Spy* since he is much more dependent on the expertise of others. In the other narrative Jerry does work almost entirely alone and in the opposite way to Smiley, although he receives some help from Craw, an old Circus hand as well as a newspaperman. If Smiley's methods are those of a dedicated researcher combing the past to understand the present, Jerry's are those of an empiricist operating in the present and gradually piecing together what has led up to it. As the novel moves towards its tragic denouement, the two narratives converge, especially with the arrival in Hong Kong of Smiley and other Circus personnel, yet at the same time the aims of Jerry and Smiley diverge as Jerry decides to break loose and undermine the operation.

A good example of the counterpointing of the two narratives occurs in the first of the novel's two parts, "Winding the Clock." Jerry, with time on his hands in Hong Kong after carrying out his first task for Smiley, institutes in chapter 7 his own unofficial investigation into the intriguing and paradoxical Chinese businessman Drake Ko, who is central to Operation Dolphin. Jerry contrives to meet him at the racecourse in Hong Kong, where Ko is a Jockey Club Steward, and subsequently observes him with a beautiful European blonde, with whom Ko is obviously on intimate terms. As Jerry later learns, she is Ricardo's ex-mistress Lizzie Worthington, known in Hong Kong as Liese Worth. Jerry also discovers the importance for Ko of the name Nelson (like Drake, the name of a great English sailor): he visits the grave of Ko's only son, Nelson; he bets on one of Ko's racehorses, Lucky Nelson; he sees Ko's oceangoing cruiser, *Admiral Nelson*.

Back in London, Smiley is following a parallel line of inquiry. From what he has heard about Lizzie from Collins and Craw, Smiley feels that she could be "a potential lever" (p. 209), and in chapter 10 he interviews Peter Worthington, the husband she walked out on (whose words, "nobody could have a girl like Elizabeth as a wife and expect to have her all to himself" [p. 215], apply equally well to Ann Smiley), and subsequently Lizzie's parents, the Pellings. For the first of these interviews Smiley uses the name Standfast, an ironic allusion to John Buchan's nationalistic spy adventure, *Mr. Standfast* (1919), from which le Carré took the epigraph to the second part of *The Looking Glass War*; for the second Smiley announces himself equally ironically as Oates, the name of the heroic member of Captain Scott's expedition to the South Pole who sacrificed himself in a vain attempt to save the lives of his companions in 1912.

The significance of "Nelson" becomes clear in chapter 11 during the far more revealing interview with a retired Baptist missionary from China, Mr. Hibbert, who is located because he once acted as a referee for Drake Ko. What Hibbert discloses to Smiley's representatives, Connie Sachs and Doc di Salis,[4], the Circus's chief experts on Moscow and Peking respectively, is the unrecorded fact that Drake Ko has a younger brother, Nelson, who was "Drake's whole life. . . . Do anything for him" (p. 240). Hibbert and his late wife—Liese, significantly—had acted almost like parents to the orphaned Ko brothers, and he is the source of a great deal of information about the rebellious and brilliant Nelson Ko, including his four years as a student in Russia. On the basis of what they learn from Hibbert, the Circus researchers are able to find a link between Nelson and Karla and to trace Nelson's career in China after Drake fled to Hong Kong from the Communist Peoples' Republic in 1951.

In addition to interweaving his two main narratives, le Carré sets these within a much more unusual framework that is unprecedented in his work. At both the beginning and the end of the novel as well as intermittently throughout, le Carré employs a narrative voice substantially different from that used in the bulk of the novel, an orthodox third-person narrator. The viewpoint of the opening narrative is both retrospective ("Afterwards" is the first word) and fluid, looking back on the events to be described, but with shifts from past to present tense, and rapid transitions between consciousnesses. This allows le Carré to provide very brief résumés of both *Tinker, Tailor, Soldier, Spy* and *The Honourable Schoolboy* itself, and mention Smiley, Karla, Haydon, Guillam, Jerry Westerby, the Cousins, and Hong Kong in the first couple of pages. More importantly, the narrative stance establishes at the outset the mythic status Operation Dolphin has assumed in intelligence circles since it was completed, with Smiley as "the last of the *true* greats" (p. 5). Yet if this voice tends to produce a choric effect, its chief characteristic is not omniscience but a floating uncertainty. The speculative aspect of this narrative voice is illustrated in the following passage in which questions remain unanswered:

> So how did Ricardo get through to Tiu so fast without the telephone? The most likely theory is the colonel's police link to Bangkok. And from Bangkok? Heaven knows. Trade telex, the exchange-rate network—anything is possible. The Chinese have their own ways of doing these things. (p. 432)

At other times, however, when the retrospective voice cuts in to pose questions that could be asked about Smiley's conduct of the operation, it is usually decisive, even dogmatic, in vindicating his decisions, emphasizing the difficulty of coping with a situation when so many factors were unknown:

> It has been laid at Smiley's door more than once since the curtain was rung down on the Dolphin case that now was the moment when George should have gone back to Sam Collins and hit him hard and straight just where it hurt. George could have cut a lot of corners that way, say the knowing; he could have saved vital time.
>
> They are talking simplistic nonsense. (p. 209)

Le Carré is more protective of Smiley in *The Honourable Schoolboy* than in any previous novel involving his series character.

The Honourable Schoolboy is by no means the first of le Carré's novels to feature a British agent in the field, but his handling of Jerry is very different from that of agents in earlier novels. *Tinker, Tailor, Soldier, Spy* contains reports from Tarr and Prideaux about their operations overseas, and *The Looking Glass War* describes no fewer than three runs, yet neither novel focuses for long on any one agent in the field and, with the exception of Tarr's, all these missions are miserable or disastrous failures. *The Spy* is manifestly different since it concentrates largely on Leamas, but because he is completely misled about the nature of his mission and because le Carré compounds the mystification by not enlightening the reader until the end of the novel, Leamas's situation as a supposed defector bears little resemblance to what we would normally think of as an agent in the field. In one sense Leamas is highly successful, but he is tricked into accomplishing the exact opposite of what he wants to achieve.

There is no such deception in the case of Jerry, who willingly acts as Smiley's long-distance operational arm and whose role conforms more closely to fictional stereotypes of the spy—the playboy-spy, rather than the gentleman-spy of pre-Fleming spy fiction (Smiley is an unorthodox example of this type). Until Jerry disobeys orders and takes things into his own hands towards the end of the novel, he is remarkably effective from the time he arrives in Hong Kong to commence his mission, and leads a charmed life in the turmoil of Southeast Asia. Jerry, a rather romantic and glamorous figure for all his journalistic dishevelment and passé upper-class slang (such as "super" and "sport"), is a born adventurer with a girl in every town, not to mention a bevy of cast-off wives. As a womanizing freebooter with a considerable amount of savoir faire and a high degree of professionalism as a spy, he bears more resemblance to James Bond than one would expect from a writer as averse to Ian Fleming as le Carré. Jerry is a much more complicated and contradictory figure than the supersuave, supersophisticated Bond, but le Carré's ability to create an agent like this at all indicates that he no longer felt constrained by his opposition to Fleming to restrict his palette to certain colors.

Leamas is also an adventurer at heart, an operational man who would probably share Jerry's anti-intellectual credo, "In the beginning was the deed" (a phrase from Goethe once quoted to him by Smiley, p. 121), but Leamas, unlike Jerry, is disillusioned and world-weary, and is a deliberately anti-romantic and unglamorous creation. In his previous novels le Carré suppresses any tendency towards adventure in the conventional sense, neither Leamas's nor Leiser's missions being presented in this way, but in *The Honourable Schoolboy* he relaxes his firm control to marry the intellectual processes familiar from his other Smiley novels with Jerry's freewheeling activities as a man of action rather than of thought. Some reviewers, especially in England, were not impressed by this development, probably because they felt that le Carré was betraying his own principles, but this is a negative way of interpreting a welcome opening-out of his fiction to include a much wider range of experience than usual.

Le Carré's presentation of Jerry is by no means lacking in irony, but he is careful not to undermine his character in a way that would make Jerry a parody figure or caricature, as he comes close to being in *Tinker, Tailor, Soldier, Spy* with his Red Indian routine, fortunately abandoned in *The Honourable Schoolboy*. Eventually Jerry has to acquire almost tragic status as a victim of power politics, much as Leamas does, and their deaths are closely linked to their love for a woman, both named Elizabeth (Liz in *The Spy*, Lizzie in *The Honourable Schoolboy*). As a son of Lord Westerby, a press baron who became bankrupt before he died, Jerry is entitled to the aristocratic courtesy title of "Honourable" (the Honourable Gerald Westerby), but whether he is honorable in the sense of being a man of honor is another matter altogether, although he does have a code of sorts. "Schoolboy," the nickname by which he is known in the Tuscan village where he is living when he receives what the title of chapter 2 labels his "great call" from Smiley, is also ambiguously ironical. The villagers have adopted this name because Jerry grins like a schoolboy, and it does define some of his characteristics: his youthful enthusiasm, vitality, and even naivety about a number of things. In certain ways Jerry is a throwback to the imperial past for whom espionage is "the great game," as Rudyard Kipling unforgettably called it in *Kim*, making it seem a natural extension of the playing fields of Eton.

Yet Jerry is no youngster even though he gives the impression of perpetual youth, and reviewers who placed him in his thirties were misled by his life-style and the image he projects. Having been involved in World War II as an army officer, he must be at least fifty by the mid-1970s when the novel is set, distinctly old for a schoolboy or even a playboy. Another important point about Jerry is that after the war he was rejected by the Circus as a permanent employee, flamboyance not being one of the most desirable attributes for intelligence work. He was, however, taken on as an Occasional, and it is only because Smiley discovers that Haydon has not blown the Circus Occasionals to his Soviet masters that Jerry, who knows the Far East well, is recalled from Italy to participate in Operation Dolphin. As an Occasional, Jerry can function under his own name using his status of investigative journalist as cover for his secret purpose. He can therefore exploit his conspicuousness in a way that would be absurd and dangerous for a full-time agent, although 007 Bond does it all the time—and always survives. Even so, it is dangerous enough for Jerry before he is finally killed by Fawn and the Cousins;[5] Ricardo makes two attempts on his life, and his fellow journalist Luke is murdered in the belief that he is Jerry. In a review of *The Honourable Schoolboy* Richard West, an international journalist who met le Carré in Vietnam and provided him with background information for the novel, complained that he found it "almost inconceivable that a journalist could be used for the Bond-like 'hit' operations performed by Westerby,"[6] because his cover would be quickly blown. But le Carré emphasizes that Smiley's use of Jerry is a matter of necessity rather than choice after the so-called Fall, and Mr. Tiu, Drake Ko's henchman, is suspicious of Jerry at an early stage; in the second part of the novel Jerry's cover is virtually transparent.

Another new departure in *The Honourable Schoolboy* that accords with its structural openness is the exploratory and adventurous nature of the plot, the uncertainty of precisely where Smiley and Jerry are going and what they will discover. Normally in le Carré's fiction there is a specific problem to solve or a particular aim in view from the outset, whether it is the investigation of a murder (*Call for the Dead, A Murder of Quality*), the protection of a double agent (*The Spy*), the confirmation of unsolicited intelligence (*The Looking Glass War*), the disappearance of a diplomat (*A Small Town in Germany*), or the identification of a mole (*Tinker, Tailor, Soldier, Spy*). At the beginning of *The Honourable Schoolboy*, on the other hand, there is no clear sense of direction, let alone of a goal. The Circus does not even know of the existence of the man who becomes the object of their quest, Nelson Ko. What happens is that Smiley and his Circus colleagues pick up a scent from the débâcle left by Haydon and follow the trail in the hope that it will lead them towards an intelligence coup of some kind, especially a retaliatory blow against Karla for the damage he has inflicted through Haydon. What motivates Smiley is the belief that the scent is Karla's, and his instinct is right. Nelson Ko proves to be another of Karla's moles, this time in mainland China.

This makes *The Honourable Schoolboy* more of a questing novel than *Tinker, Tailor, Soldier, Spy*, and the phrase "quest for Karla" occurs in its penultimate chapter in a passage that offers an insight into the often submerged underpinnings of myth and romance in the trilogy. Ann's description of Karla as Smiley's "black Grail" (p. 499) suggests parallels, mainly but not necessarily ironic, with the Arthurian legends; Smiley, in his ill-fitting suits rather than shining armor, being, as head of the Circus and a defender of his nation, a modern mock-heroic equivalent of the King himself, much as Leopold Bloom is of Ulysses in Joyce's novel. Smiley's grail, significantly, is not holy but virtually the opposite, black, the color of evil: Bloom's Dublin odyssey is, at one level, a grotesque parody of the Homeric original. Smiley is as haunted by his grail as the Arthurian knights were by the Holy Grail, and there are a number of references in the novel to the photograph of Karla that Smiley keeps like an icon in his office, known as the "throne-room," a phrase that sustains the regal comparison. With the exception of Peter Guillam, described as Smiley's "cup-bearer" (p. 41), another word that connotes a royal household, Smiley's inner circle at his equivalent of the Round Table consists of a truly bizarre and un-Arthurian trio: the enormous Connie Sachs, crippled with arthritis; the "Mad Jesuit" Doc di Salis, "a patchy, grubby little creature, more like Connie's monkey than her counterpart" (p. 54); and the babysitter Fawn, with his black gym shoes and his potential for vicious brutality, evidenced in Hong Kong when he breaks both arms of a Chinese boy who attempts to steal his wristwatch.

The equivalent of the knight who sets out from court in pursuit of chivalric adventure is Jerry, who actually talks about his "Galahad act" (p. 477) in coming to the rescue of Lizzie Worthington, a damsel of easy virtue in distress who in turn calls him "Galahad" (p. 492). In addition to being rather old for the part of Galahad, Jerry sometimes behaves in a far from chivalric way, as in his "burning" or blackmailing of the banker Frost, his interrogation of Charlie Marshall, and his abduction of Lizzie at gunpoint. Jerry's dangerous pursuit of Ricardo through the war-torn countries of Southeast Asia does, nevertheless, resemble a knightly journey through wastelands to locate an evil warrior. Le Carré does not exploit the collision between romance or epic and contemporary realism in the sustained and systematic way that modernist writers such as Joyce do, but he does activate certain mythic and literary archetypes in a similar way so as to create interplay between the different levels, the apparently transparent realism of the surface and deeper, underlying motifs. According to Craw his Hong Kong informant, Phoebe Wayfarer, sees the Circus as the modern equivalent of Saint George, and the mythic connotations of Smiley's first name are more obvious than ever before, including *Tinker, Tailor, Soldier, Spy* in which he appears for the first time as a kind of national savior and rescuer of Britannia.

By the standards of epic and romance Jerry and Smiley are as anti-heroic as Leopold Bloom, but like Joyce's great character, and indeed like Leamas and Leo Harting, they acquire a qualified heroic status in the morally squalid context of contemporary reality. Both Jerry and Smiley have a sense of living in a period of decadence, but in their different ways both acknowledge an old-fashioned duty to serve and defend certain values, even though this is bound to lead to unpalatable compromises and a guilty conscience. It is when talking to Jerry in London prior to his mission in Hong Kong that Smiley is most forthcoming about the need for commitment:

> A lot of people haven't these days. The will. Specially in England. A lot of people see *doubt* as a legitimate philosophical posture. They think of themselves in the middle, whereas, of course, really they're nowhere. No battle was ever won by spectators, was it? We understand that in this service. We're lucky. Our present war began in nineteen seventeen, with the Bolshevik Revolution. It hasn't changed yet.

And, Smiley, whom Jerry sees as something of a "failed priest," says of an American historian:

> He wrote of generations that are born into debtors' prisons and spend their lives buying their way to freedom. I think ours is such a generation. Don't you? I still feel strongly that I owe. Don't you? I've always been grateful to this service, that it gave me a chance to pay. Is that how *you* feel? I don't think we should be afraid of . . . devoting ourselves. (p. 106)

Much later in the novel le Carré clarifies Jerry's more intuitive and much less articulate sense of commitment vis-à-vis his fellow aristocrat Bill Haydon:

> He had never seriously doubted, in his vague way, that his country was in a state of irreversible decline, or that his own class was to blame for the mess. "We *made* Bill," ran his argument, "so it's right we should carry the brunt of his betrayal." Pay, in fact. Pay. What old George was on about. (p. 449)

Like Leamas, Jerry finally pays with his life for his decision to set individual human values above national interest and political expediency. The use of Hong Kong as a setting has a direct link with Jerry's sense of an "irreversible decline" in his country. The Crown Colony of Hong Kong is one of the few remaining outcrops of a British Empire that once spanned the globe, and because of the leasing arrangement with China dating from the very end of the nineteenth century, British Hong Kong is living on borrowed time that will run out in 1997. Hong Kong, like Gibraltar and the Falkland Islands, consequently represents one of the final flickers of British imperial power, and its continuing existence is a strange anomaly in the world today. The ironic remark that Major Masters of the Cousins makes to Jerry at the American air base in Thailand following the news that Saigon has fallen to the Viet Cong is loaded with anti-British sarcasm but roughly accords with Jerry's own sense of his country's slide from past greatness: "The United States of America has just applied to join the club of second-class powers, of which I understand your own fine nation to be chairman, president, and oldest member" (p. 436).

The Honourable Schoolboy is a true sequel to *Tinker, Tailor, Soldier, Spy* in that its main action emerges directly from its predecessor. In agreeing to take on the Circus "after the holocaust"—the discovery that most of its secrets have been betrayed by Haydon—Smiley has, in the words of Roddy Martindale, "got himself appointed captain of a wrecked ship" (p. 41). In the metaphorical parlance of the Circus the exposure of Haydon becomes known as "the fall," so that Smiley has the unenviable task of reassembling what he can of the organization in its postlapsarian state, although initially he seems to be presiding over the demolition of a ruin. Smiley has to dismiss staff, close residencies, and dismantle blown networks (those not already dismantled for him by Moscow Centre), causing him considerable pain, as when the Churayevs are shot while escaping from Russia. Even the Circus offices are partly wrecked by the "ferrets" looking for concealed bugging devices, of which they find plenty. At this dismal time Smiley and Ann become reconciled, only to become alienated again, not because of Ann's promiscuity but because of Smiley's manic commitment to his job when he finds a way of going on the offensive against Karla. There is a sense in which Smiley's preoccupation with Karla is more intense and compelling than his relationship with Ann, despite his devotion to her when they are apart. In a revealing conversation in chapter 3 with Oliver Lacon about the dismantling process, Smiley speaks of Karla only to be corrected by Lacon, not for the only time in the novel: "By Karla you mean Moscow Centre? . . . I think it safer to stay with institutions, if you don't mind. In that way we are spared the embarrassment of personalities. After all, that's what institutions are *for*, isn't it?" (p. 53). Yet Smiley's dedication to his task would not be so relentless without the element of personal combat. As Sam Collins observes when examining Smiley's photograph of Karla: "You've got some personal thing about him, haven't you?" (p, 71).

In an interesting passage at the end of chapter 5 Smiley wanders through the streets of London, looking like "the mackintosh brigade personified, cannon-fodder of the mixed-sauna parlours and the naughty bookshops" (p. 109) as he makes his way to Chelsea where Ann is living in their Bywater Street home. Outside the house he really seems like a pathetic old voyeur, especially when he catches a glimpse of Ann with another man, yet his thoughts on this foggy night are as much about Karla and his own motives for his current drive against his old foe as about his estranged wife:

> Beyond the limits of these external reasons, Smiley perceived in himself the existence of a darker motive, infinitely more obscure, one which his rational mind continued to reject. He called it Karla, and it was true that somewhere in him, like a left-over legend, there burned the embers of hatred toward the man who had set out to destroy the temples of his private faith, whatever remained of them: the service that he loved, his friends, his country, his concept of a reasonable balance in human affairs. . . . But hatred was really not an emotion he could sustain for any length of time, unless it was the obverse side of love. (p.110)

At the level of rationality Smiley is "fighting for the survival of Reasonable Man" (p. 324), to use a phrase that Connie attributes to either Steed-Asprey or Control from an earlier phase of the Circus's history; but at a deeper level Smiley is locked in a love-hate relationship with both Karla and Ann. Smiley is as unfaithful to Ann mentally as she is to him physically, and his devotion to his quest for Karla can be seen as a substitute for his unsatisfactory relationship with his wife, a sublimated love affair.

At a time when he would be expected to be entirely on the defensive and when he gives this impression to the world, Smiley sees a way of launching a counterattack by taking what are known in the argot of spying as "backbearings." If Smiley can discover, in the collective memory of the Circus, intelligence initiatives suppressed by Haydon, he might well be on the track of secret operations by Moscow Centre. Operation Dolphin stems from precisely such a discovery, Sam Collins's recollection of how Haydon had forbidden him from pursuing his investigation into the Moscow Centre "goldseam" or secret payment chain he had uncovered while working for the Circus in Vientiane, the capital of Laos. Haydon's reason was that the case was already in the hands of the Cousins, but it emerges that he has also warned off the Cousins, claiming the operation for the Circus, with the result that nothing has been done. All that Collins knows is that after making his report the massive Moscow Centre payment of twenty-five thousand US dollars a month to "a mickey-mouse aviation company called Indocharter Vientiane S.A." stopped. According to Collins, the principal personnal of Indocharter were "a wildcat Mexican pilot known round town as Tiny Ricardo on account of his considerable height," who worked for the Cousins before becoming involved in the opium trade and who is believed to have been killed in a plane crash, and "one dumb blonde for the front office" (p. 68), later identified as Lizzie Worthington, whom Collins himself recruited as an agent but who proved to be hopeless, at least in this capacity. A thorough search of the Circus records reveals that Haydon has virtually wiped the slate clean by destroying any references to Collins's inquiry. The only explanation for such a systematic elimination of the evidence by Haydon is that the Vientiane goldseam was of immense importance to Moscow Centre and that Collins was far too close for comfort.

Smiley has his lucky break, especially when Connie and her "burrowers" trace the rerouting of the goldseam. Armed with this information and what he has obtained from Collins about Indocharter, including its chain of connection to a parent company in Hong Kong called China Airsea, Smiley is ready to take the initiative by "putting in an agent" (p. 90), and dispatches Jerry to find, by fair means or foul, the exact terminus of the goldseam in Hong Kong. Jerry's successful "burning" of Frost in chapter 6, before Smiley has obtained official permission to use an agent, establishes that the Moscow Centre payments are held in trust by Drake Ko, the chairman and managing director of none other than China Airsea and a leading figure in the life of the Colony who has been honored by the Queen with an OBE (Order of the British Empire) for social and charitable services.

One of the most important differences between Smiley's roles in *Tinker, Tailor, Soldier, Spy* and *The Honourable Schoolboy* is that in the earlier novel he functions as a kind of private investigator for the government, virtually free from bureaucratic control and political pressure. As head of the largely discredited Circus in *The Honourable Schoolboy,* on the other hand, he has to fight institutional battles from a position of weakness, as well as advance Operation Dolphin, even if this means jumping the gun, as in his employment of Jerry before obtaining permission to put in an agent. Of the two major hurdles in Smiley's path, one is entirely of Whitehall's creation, the Intelligence Steering Group, while the other and more intractable one is the interest of the Cousins. Chapter 8 provides a detailed account of Smiley's success in getting his own way against the odds at a crucial meeting of the Steering Group by playing his not particularly strong cards in a most skillful way. Smiley takes advantage of the internal divisions between Enderby's Foreign Office contingent and Wilbraham's so-called Colonialists, and uses the veiled threat of direct American involvement in a British territory if the Circus is not allowed to proceed. The irony of the situation is that Smiley has more in common with the old-fashioned and staunchly anti-American Wilbraham, who would prefer to abort the Circus's plans, than with those who are prepared to back him, the much more suave and devious group led by Saul Enderby, "a great supporter of the American hard line" (p. 167). Le Carré's subtle and detailed treatment in this chapter of the maneuvers of senior officials at the heart of the British Establishment is enhanced by details of another kind that ironically undermine the façade of elegance and sophistication cultivated by the Foreign Office: the poorly designed catering trays that allow custard to flow into the meat; the leaking paper teacups; the broken extractor fans for which parts have been ordered nearly a year previously.

For Smiley the breakthrough achieved on the basis of Collins's information is a Circus success and its follow-up should be left in his hands. Enderby and Lacon, however, are eager to involve the Americans, even to leave it largely to them, since Dolphin is a marvelous opportunity to heal the wounds to the "special relationship" between the intelligence services of the two nations that were caused by Haydon's partial conversion of the Circus into a branch of Moscow Centre. For them Dolphin is part of a political game, not part of the quest for Karla that it is for Smiley; indeed for Enderby it is a way of ingratiating himself with the Americans and of advancing his own career. Even before Smiley has sent Jerry to Hong Kong, he is under pressure from Lacon at least to collaborate with the Cousins. Smiley is determined to resist this pressure and in chapter 12, the final chapter of the first of the novel's two parts, defends his position in a meeting with two senior American officials, Martello, representing the Cousins, and Sol Eckland, a member of the Drug Enforcement Administration in hot pursuit of Drake Ko as a drugs racketeer. Just as there is a conflict of interests within the British camp at the meeting of the Steering Group, there is tension between the two Americans with their different concerns. The insensitive Sol, who is prepared to ride roughshod over anything in his fanatical drive against narcotics, belongs to the species known as "the ugly American." Smiley has to stand his ground and insist on the formal contract between the two countries that in British territory all American agencies will observe "a complete hands-off in exchange for a complete sight of the product" (p. 271), although all he wins is the promise of a short stay of action by Sol's Drug Enforcement Administration. It is Smiley's fate to be caught in any crossfire around, so that in Whitehall, for example, "the Wilbraham set branded him as anti-Colonial and pro-American, while Enderby's men accused him of ultra-conservatism in the handling of the special relationship" (p. 393).

Superficially, *The Honourable Schoolboy* might be interpreted as anti-American in the way that Graham Greene's *The Quiet American* is, and le Carré satirizes not only the American love of jargon and unplain English ("exfiltration assignment" [p. 50] for "escape," for example) but also the embarrassingly clumsy naivety that often underlies America's condescending "big brother" attitude towards other countries. Yet le Carré balances such ridicule with his criticism of British attitudes and conduct, such as the public school ethos pervading the Civil Service and especially obvious in the Intelligence Steering Group. In describing the regular London meetings between the Circus and the Cousins before "the fall," le Carré says that "if it was the American turn to play host" the Circus representatives "would be shepherded to a vast roof-top bar, known within the Circus as 'the planetarium,' to be regaled with dry martinis and a view of West London they could not otherwise have afforded." The British equivalent to this typically American delight in (to British eyes) vulgar ostentation is penny-pinching tawdriness and patronizing hypocrisy, which leaves a nastier taste in the mouth—literally as well as metaphorically—than the Americans' conspicuous generosity: "If it was the British turn, then a trestle-table was set up in the rumpus room, and a darned damask table-cloth spread over it, and the American delegates were invited to pay homage to the last bastion of clubland spying, and incidentally the birthplace of their own service, while they sipped South African sherry disguised by cut-glass decanters on the grounds that they wouldn't know the difference" (p. 257). Mutual trust is not a feature of the special relationship between these "old friends," since at their convivial meetings they are spying on each other—in the nicest possible way. They are obeying the "oldest maxim of the trade, Karla's favourite," as Connie calls it: "Spy on your friends today, they're certain to be your enemies tomorrow" (p. 309). The reference to the English "birthplace" of the American service has a precise historical analogue: during World War II, President Roosevelt's new secret service, the Office of Strategic Services (OSS) modeled itself closely on the British Secret Intelligence Service (MI6).

In depriving Smiley of Nelson Ko virtually at his moment of triumph in the penultimate chaper, with what can only be called a piece of unashamed body-snatching banditry, the Cousins are guilty of a morally outrageous act since it is in total violation of the assurances given to Smiley. The Cousins seize Nelson Ko because they clearly regard him as far too valuable to be left to their British allies. As di Salis explains to members of the Circus as early as chapter 14, Nelson should be able to provide vastly more information than the Cousins could obtain after spending "hundreds of millions in research, overflights, satellites, listening devices, and God knows what" (p. 311). Yet the Cousins' perfidy is made possible only by the greater perfidy of Lacon, Enderby, and Collins in betraying Smiley's operation to Martello from its early stages and consequently undermining his authority.

When Smiley, on the verge of leaving for Hong Kong with his operations party in chapter 18, officially briefs Martello on all aspects of the Dolphin case at the instigation of Enderby and Lacon, Guillam intuits that Martello already knows everything. In Hong Kong itself, where the Cousins are gradually usurping Smiley's power and increasingly involving themselves, Guillam "became with every moment more convinced that he was looking at a spider's web, and that only George Smiley, obsessed by the promise of the case and the image of Karla, was myopic enough, and trusting enough—and, in his own paradoxical way, innocent enough—to bumble straight into the middle of it" (p. 487). It is in these closing stages that Smiley might tentatively also be called an "honourable schoolboy." Outwardly at least, he is trusting and innocent enough to uphold an essentially aristocratic notion of honor that means nothing to what Guillam sees as "a bunch of wolves" led by Martello, whose crudely simplistic view of history as either "conspiracy" or "fuck-up" (p. 266) has no place for honor.

Convinced that Smiley is likely to produce "fuck-up," Martello opts for "conspiracy"—in this case, conspiracy against Smiley, who consciously refuses to believe it and rejects Guillam's warnings: "I shall not tolerate your Byzantine notions of a palace plot. These people are our hosts and our Allies. We have a written agreement with them. We have quite enough to worry about already without grotesque and—I may tell you honestly—paranoid fancies" (p. 501). Jerry's return to Hong Kong for Lizzie's sake in defiance of Circus orders could pose a threat to the success of the operation and therefore presents Martello with a ready-made excuse for direct action by the Cousins, but even ignoring Jerry's "Galahad act" there is nothing grotesque, paranoid, or fanciful in Guillam's "fancies." Indeed Smiley's confessional letter to Ann, quoted only on the final page of the novel, suggests that at least deep down Smiley himself was not unaware of the possibility of a conspiracy against him by his own side, since a theory of universal conspiracy is the most appropriate way of apprehending the entire human world, even if this was not always the case:

> So far as I can remember of my youth, I chose the secret road because it seemed to lead straightest and furthest toward my country's goal. The enemy in those days was someone we could point at and read about in the papers. Today, all I know is that I have learned to interpret the whole of life in terms of conspiracy. That is the sword I have lived by, and as I look round me now I see it is the sword I shall die by as well. These people terrify me, but I am one of them. If they stab me in the back, then at least that is the judgment of my peers. (p. 532)

By a mixture of dedicated research, the "burning" of Frost, patient interviewing, imaginative interpretation of information obtained from Martello and Sol, and inspired guesswork, Smiley has deduced the solution to the mystery at the heart of Operation Dolphin by the end of the first part of *The Honourable Schoolboy*. The Moscow Centre payments to Drake Ko are really for his brother Nelson's invaluable work as a mole within the top levels of the Chinese Communist hierarchy. After being purged in what Connie calls "the Great Beastly Cultural Revolution of the mid-sixties" (p. 256), Nelson has recently been rehabilitated and has been able to resume his work for Karla. Furthermore Drake Ko is determined to rescue his much-loved brother from mainland China, and the "unspecified load in payment" (p. 266) that Ricardo was supposed to pick up for Tiu in China after an illegal flight over the border to deliver drugs was Nelson himself. In the second part of the novel, "Shaking the Tree," more information about these issues emerges, including di Salis's detailed statement in chapter 14 about Nelson's career and value as an intelligence source, Ricardo's account to Jerry in chapter 17 of his double-crossing of Tiu over the secret flight, and the network of relationships involving Drake Ko, Tiu, Ricardo, Charlie Marshall, Lizzie, and Collins (under his work name of Mellon), but this only confirms that Smiley has grasped the essentials long before.

By the end of "Winding the Clock" Smiley is sufficiently confident to do what is called "reversing the controls" with the intention of "shaking Ko's tree" (p. 278). This means a complete change of tactics, from discreet, invisible investigation to the application of direct pressure on Drake Ko by revealing to him that his secrets are under scrutiny. The aim is to panic Ko into initiating action of some kind, especially a second attempt to bring Nelson to Hong Kong. Smiley's first move is to unleash Jerry on Lizzie in his role as an investigative jounalist, and through her he immediately reaches Tiu. Later, Smiley sends Jerry in pursuit of Ricardo as a way of maintaining his squeeze on Ko, and instructs Sam Collins, now in Hong Kong, to "go in" (p. 396). What Smiley cannot foresee is exactly what the shaking of the tree will produce. He is leaving behind the orderly processes of thought, in which he is king, for the unpredictable ones of action, in which he has to rely on others. Above all, Smiley could hardly predict the effect that Lizzie has on Jerry—"the human factor," to borrow the title of Graham Greene's fine novel about an English double agent caught between human loyalty to a Communist friend and duty to his country and service. Jerry falls completely for Lizzie, and as the novel moves to its climax his infatuation with her and consequent desire to save her from the web of intrigue she is caught up in pull against and eventually overcome his commitment to the Circus.

Once Smiley reverses the controls, the tone of the novel changes. In "Winding the Clock" everything seems under control, and although there are references to the fighting in Southeast Asia, even the most "violent" action, Jerry's blackmailing of Frost, is not physical. In "Shaking the Tree," on the other hand, the world suddenly becomes much more dangerous, uncontrollable, and uncertain, and is liable to erupt into violence: Frost's horribly mutilated corpse (chapter 14); Luke shot dead in mistake for Jerry (chapter 18); Ricardo's two attempts at murdering Jerry (chapters 16 and 17) before Jerry is finally killed (chapter 21); Jerry forcing the drug addict Charlie Marshall to "catch cold turkey" (chapter 16, p. 413); Fawn's vicious assault on a boy pickpocket (chapter 19) and his attack on Jerry (chapter 20); Jerry's armed abduction of Lizzie (chapter 19) and his attack on Tiu (chapter 21); the Cousins' violent seizure of Nelson Ko (chapter 21). This microcosmic violence involving some of the main characters is placed against a background of macrocosmic violence involving Southeast Asia. Jerry's to-and-fro journey through four countries in the region has been accused of being journalistic padding, included neither to advance the narrative nor for artistic reasons but to display the knowledge le Carré acquired during his own travels. This is grossly unfair. These chapters do include vivid reporting, but as in Conrad and Greene the detail is not there solely for its own sake. The muddled battles that are being fought in the main plot (including Smiley vs. Karla, Smiley vs. Drake Ko, the Circus vs. the Cousins, the Circus vs. the Foreign Office) belong to a world where conflict and confusion are rife, where to use Matthew Arnold's marvelous image at the end of his great poem "Dover Beach:"

> And we are here as on a darkling plain
> Swept with confused alarms of struggle and flight,
> Where ignorant armies clash by night.

Images of destruction and desolation pervade this part of *The Honourable Schoolboy*—Phnom Penh is "a city about to be given back to the jungle" (p. 389)—but as elsewhere in the novel the realism is close to surrealism. Some of the descriptions of Hong Kong in the first part exhibit this tendency, such as "the Scottish inn with kilted Chinese Scots" and "the Tudor pub in the unfinished high-rise building . . . where genuine, sour-faced English wenches in period décolleté served genuine English beer at twenty degrees below its English temperature, while outside in the lobby, sweating coolies in yellow helmets toiled round the clock to finish off the elevators" (p. 204). Altogether more grotesque is the private party that Jerry gate-crashes in pursuit of Lizzie towards the end of the novel:

> The pyramid of champagne glasses was six feet tall, with black satin steps so that the waiters could take them from the top. In sunken ice coffins lay magnums awaiting burial. There was a wheelbarrow full of cooked lobsters and a wedding cake of pâté de foie gras, with "Maison Flaubert" done in aspic on the top. (p. 466)

But it is during Jerry's wanderings that le Carré most forcefully portrays the surreality of reality, as in part of the description of Ricardo's house with this incongruous Buñuel-like juxtaposition of weaponry (imitation fruit) and religion (plastic variety): "Grenades lay about like fruit, in clusters of three and four, and on the hideous walnut cocktail cabinet under a plastic effigy of the Madonna lay a selection of pistols and automatics for all occasions" (p. 411). Then there is the Thai Colonel who can blandly transform his cold-blooded killing of one of his own men into a propaganda exercise on behalf of democracy: "You got to win the hearts and minds of the people" (p.407).

The account of Jerry's visit to the battle front outside Phnom Penh, accompanied by two Americans, Keller and Lorraine, and of their silent encounter with a Khmer Rouge roadblock during a downpour, is decidedly eerie, not least because the "blue-eyed and flaxen and Aryan" Lorraine reveals an alarming blend of perplexed innocence and voyeuristic exhilaration—she is a photographer—as she makes her way with difficulty over the deeply rutted ground in her short skirt: "The girl was looking excitedly across the river, smiling" (p. 344). Perhaps most bizarre of all is the elegant dinner party given by a British diplomat that Jerry attends in Phnom Penh, a city under siege and about to fall to the Khmer Rouge. Despite rocket attacks, bombing, and firing, the dinner, complete with silver card holders for placing the guests at table, a silver menu holder promising "le roast beef à l'anglaise" (p. 350), and silver candlesticks, continues as if the entire world were at peace with itself, although the dining-room ceiling is concrete to withstand blast. It is difficult to know whether this extraordinary exhibition of sangfroid and the stiff upper lip is a manifestation of thick-skinned, dim-witted insensitivity or courageous defiance and a refusal to be cowed.

By using a much larger canvas than usual, le Carré gives some of his main preoccupations, such as the nature of betrayal and the ethics of deception in both public and private life, a new dimension. In the increasingly nightmarish world that le Carré creates as the novel develops, the unavoidable contradictions and unresolvable conflicts of life take on tragic overtones. According to a Russian aphorism quoted by Connie, "There'll be no war. . . . But in the struggle for peace not a single stone will be left standing." Smiley consciously lives with the paradox of having to be "inhuman in defence of our humanity . . . harsh in defence of compassion . . . single-minded in defence of our disparity" (p. 461). Having authorized the "burning" of Frost, Smiley acknowledges his own degree of responsibility for Frost's horrible murder even though he did not remotely consider that the blackmailing would have such a consequence. Indeed Smiley's conscience can cause him agonies of self-doubt about his own motives. When Martello urges him to pull out all the stops to apprehend Jerry and Lizzie in chapter 21, Smiley's sympathy momentarily goes out to the lovers, whose cause "Ann would warmly have espoused," and he questions himself as to whether "his striving had become nothing other than a private journey among the beasts and villains of his own insufficiency, in which he ruthlessly involved simplistic minds like Jerry's" (p. 499).

For much of the novel the gregarious, happy-go-lucky adventurer Jerry is sharply contrasted with the introspective, intellectual loner,

Smiley, but after he has committed himself to Lizzie and returned to Hong Kong in defiance of Circus instructions, Jerry grows in stature as he achieves a new and more profound understanding of what is involved. At the beginning of the novel when summoned by Smiley, Jerry discards the girl he is living with in Italy and heads for London. Faced with the choice between love and honor, so familiar to heroes in tragic drama of the sixteenth and seventeenth centuries, Jerry unhesitatingly decides on honor. His attitude, virtually that of a correctly programmed automaton, is summed up in his words to Smiley: "You point me and I'll march. . . . Tell me the shots, I'll play them" (p. 106). At the end of the novel he reverses his own controls by rejecting honor for love and asserting his moral autonomy. He is no less committed than before, but the nature of his commitment has changed. After having an apocalyptic vision of Hong Kong's last day as a colony, which widens to become a vision of "one vanishing world; here, Phnom Penh, Saigon, London—a world on loan, with the creditors standing at the door, and Jerry himself, in some unfathomable way, a part of the debt that was owed" (pp. 488–89), Jerry now questions Smiley's speech to him in chapter 5 about being grateful for the chance to pay. In retrospect Smiley's words strike Jerry as verging on self-indulgence since "the paying is actually done by the other poor sods," including the two men murdered in Hong Kong after being unwittingly caught up in Operation Dolphin: "He'd mention that to George . . . about the selfless and devoted way in which we sacrifice other people, such as Luke and Frost and Lizzie. George would have a perfectly good answer, of course. Reasonable. Measured. Apologetic. George saw the bigger picture. Understood the imperatives. Of course he did. He was an owl" (p. 489). The staccato phrasing of these words of reassurance suggests skepticism rather than conviction on Jerry's part.

Jerry's love for Lizzie opens his eyes to the human implications of what is going on rather than their political and intelligence significance: in *The Spy* Liz produces a comparable response in Leamas. When Jerry contemplates the plan to seize Nelson Ko after Drake has arranged his escape from China by exactly the same route that Drake took in 1951, Jerry thinks of Nelson as a human being, not as a "great prize" (p. 490), "the biggest catch" (p. 498) of Martello's career, and imagines the unenviable future awaiting Nelson: "after the years of his debriefing—two, three even; he had heard some ran for five—Nelson would become one more Wandering Jew of the spy-trade, to be hidden, and moved again, and hidden, to be loved not even by those to whom he had betrayed his trust" (p. 490). In making his extraordinary approach to Drake Ko as he awaits Nelson's arrival, Jerry's primary aim is to safeguard Lizzie, for whom he is willing to subvert the Circus's scheme; but his warning to Drake about the imminent danger to Nelson is in keeping with his newfound priorities. When the Cousins' helicopters arrive to capture Nelson at the moment he is reunited with his brother after more than twenty years of separation, thus preempting the Circus's own plans, Jerry desperately tries to help the brothers against impossible odds, "not for Nelson's sake, still less for Drake's; but for what linked them, and for what linked him to Lizzie" (p. 524).

The link is nothing less than love, and it is literally love that Jerry dies for when he is shot from one of the helicopters, which descend in the night like the agents of a malign deity to discharge not men but "a dark swarm." The final tableau of chapter 21, of "Drake Ko's hopeless, choking grief against the victorious armadas of the West, which had stolen his brother and left their hard-pressed soldier dead at his feet" is as bleak as that of *The Spy* with Liz and Leamas dead. The values of the heart stand no chance against the forces of ruthless inhumanity inseparable from modern power politics. It is only at this point that the full significance of the novel's four-line epigraph from one of Auden's most famous poems, "September 1, 1939," becomes clear. Auden's words, "Those to whom evil is done / Do evil in return," evoke a world of perpetual conflict and retaliation, and are as appropriate to the world le Carré writes about as to the outbreak of World War II; this, says Auden, is "what all schoolchildren learn," and le Carré's "schoolboy" could be included in their number. In order to "show an affirming flame," Auden offers an essentially Christian solution to the vicious circle of evil in the most-quoted line of the poem (though not quoted by le Carré): "We must love one another or die." Le Carré implicitly rewrites this line pessimistically as: "If we love one another, we die." For Jerry, as for Leamas, the discovery of love is not an alternative to death but its concomitant.

In each of the three novels constituting *The Quest for Karla*, Smiley finally achieves what appears to be a brilliant success, but for different reasons there is another side to the coin of success. His exposure of Haydon as a mole in *Tinker, Tailor, Soldier, Spy* might be thought of as an unqualified triumph, but in a completely irrational though emotionally understandable way, Smiley is subsequently thought of as damaging, even betraying, the Circus by bringing Haydon's treachery into the open, thus calling in question the notions of loyalty and duty in an unacceptably disturbing way. Even though it is Haydon who has done the damage and the betraying, there is a suggestion that it would have been better if the mole had never been discovered, on the grounds that ignorance is bliss. The sense of anticlimax is much more conspicuous in *The Honourable Schoolboy* because the Cousins scoop Smiley when they seize Nelson Ko at the very end of the penultimate chapter. The final chapter opens with the Circus's initially euphoric "mood of wild triumph" (p. 524) when news arrives that Nelson has been safely "landed" or "bagged," but this quickly evaporates as full realization of what has happened sinks in. What follows at the Circus is an extraordinarily quiet and singularly bloodless palace revolution, with Smiley's old order being replaced by Enderby's American-approved new one, "a younger and more vigorous service, with closer links to Whitehall" (p. 527). Smiley chooses not to resist but to acquiesce philosophically as he fades back into the retirement from which he emerged at the beginning of *Tinker, Tailor, Soldier, Spy,* his quest for Karla still unfinished.

It was with *The Honourable Schoolboy* that le Carré finally convinced some influential members of the English literary establishment that he was more than a superior thriller writer, although this patronizing attitude remains remarkably resistant to change. In a review of *Smiley's People* one of the most distinguished of English literary journalists, Michael Ratcliffe, admitted that until the end of 1979 he had read very little le Carré and that the television version of *Tinker, Tailor, Soldier, Spy* only served to endorse his lack of interest. Nevertheless, "lightning conversion" occurred when he tried *The Honourable Schoolboy,* which "for its energy, compassion, rich and overwhelming sweep of characters and action . . . was simply one of the finest English novels of the Seventies."[7] In praising *Smiley's People* too, Ratcliffe argued that "the Circus novels are composing a kind of roman-fleuve in which themes of loyalty, betrayal, innocence, memory and time recur at regular intervals like *Leitmotiven,*" and compared le Carré to Anthony Powell, whose twelve volume roman-fleuve, *A Dance to the Music of Time,* is one of the monuments of postwar English fiction. The late Lord Snow (the novelist C. P. Snow), himself the author of a roman-fleuve, *Strangers and Brothers,* also used his review of *Smiley's People* as an opportunity to rescue le Carré from the literary condescension that has damned him with faint praise as excellent of his kind, the kind being lightweight entertainers. For Snow, le Carré is "one of the best of contemporary novelists":

> It is time we broke out of our pigeon-holes and our petit-maître confines, and became as sensible as our Victorian predecessors, who wrote better novels than we do. It wouldn't have occurred to them not to recognise Wilkie Collins as a fellow-master. It is a sign of literary narrowness, and probably decay, when one finds lists of the newly dominant novelists of the 1970s and doesn't see the name of Le Carré.[8]

In championing le Carré at this time as a "serious novelist . . . passionately curious about people and their peculiarities" who has "turned the novel of action into a novel of character and motivation," the famous poet, novelist and critic A. Alvarez also attacked the "tiresome intellectual snobbery which fixes a gulf between strong plot and psychological depth."[9] For Alvarez this is "a spurious distinction, and we have the novels of Walter Scott, Conrad, Hammett and Greene . . . to prove it," and now, he would add, those of le Carré as well.

9

Ahab Chasing His Big White Whale: *Smiley's People* (1980)

In real life it is said that spies never make comebacks. Once out they are out for good. In le Carré's world, however, Smiley possesses an almost supernatural ability to return and return again from retirement. At the end of *The Honourable Schoolboy* he makes his third departure from the Circus—the first occurs in *Call for the Dead* and the second is described retrospectively in *Tinker, Tailor, Soldier, Spy*—so the possibility of another resurrection would seem remote, although not as remote as Sherlock Holmes's miraculous recovery after his apparent death in the Reichenbach Falls incident with Moriarty. Yet Smiley's quest for his "black Grail" is not much further advanced at the end of *The Honourable Schoolboy* than it was at the beginning. As in *Tinker, Tailor, Soldier, Spy* he deprives Karla of one of his most productive moles, therefore achieving another victory over his adversary, but he has still not found a way of grappling with Karla except at arm's length. To use the language of chess, he has taken some of his opponent's important pieces but is a long way from checkmate.

Smiley's People, the only novel by le Carré to include Smiley's or anybody else's name in its title, describes the final phase of the quest, the conquest itself—Smiley's triumph over his Moriarty, George's defeat of his dragon. Smiley at last locates the sole weakness in his antagonist's defense and is able to exploit this in an endgame he is bound to win. The triumph and the victory are, nevertheless, seriously qualified. Smiley's quest ends not with simple affirmation of unambiguous, permanent truths but with a resigned acceptance of the paradoxical contradictoriness of human experience, the impossibility of certainty. In an interview with Byron Rogers shortly before the television version of *Smiley's People* was broadcast in Britain, le Carré said that "the central theme" of the novel was clear even before he began work on it: "This was to be Smiley's confrontation with Karla that would destroy them both, Smiley by an act of professional absolutism, Karla by a lapse into humanity. It was to be a moral Reichenbach Falls with no happy moment when Smiley returns to his bee-keeping."[1]

Karla's weakness turns out to be his love for his daughter, and the trail of murder and mystery that Smiley successfully pursues in *Smiley's People* leads not to top-secret affairs of state or something similar, as it would in conventional spy fiction, but to a father and his mentally ill child. *The Honourable Schoolboy* is similar in this respect, because what Smiley and Jerry discover at the end of their research and adventure is not some diabolical plot hatched by a Soviet arch-fiend, but a man attempting to be reunited with the brother he loves. Like *The Honourable Schoolboy* and unlike *Tinker, Tailor, Soldier, Spy*, *Smiley's People* is characterized by an open plot of exploratory adventure, not a closed investigation. Smiley's entry into the novel just after the killing of his former agent General Vladimir might suggest that a murder inquiry is going to play an important part, but this is merely a starting point for Smiley on an uncertain path in the direction of Karla.

As in *The Honourable Schoolboy* there are three openings in *Smiley's People*: Ostrakova in Paris in chapter 1, Villem in Hamburg in chapter 2, and Smiley on Hampstead Heath in London in chapter 3, the only link between them being Vladimir, who is referred to in the first two chapters and whose murdered body provides the focal point in the third chapter. However, the narrative structure of *Smiley's People* is more straightforward than that of *The Honourable Schoolboy* in several ways. *Smiley's People* does not contain a double narrative, and after the opening two chapters Smiley is the central consciousness and is only rarely offstage. Working from a few clues—a minicab receipt, a high telephone bill, a missing cigarette packet, Ostrakova's second letter to Vladimir—Smiley painstakingly tries to discover what Vladimir was attempting to communicate to him about Karla on the day of his death; and after seeking out Connie Sachs in chapter 14 in order to pick her brains, as he did in *Tinker, Tailor, Soldier, Spy,* Smiley continues his inquiries in Germany, where, with no equivalent to Jerry Westerby to assist him, he has to be his own agent in the field. He is then in a position to take the initiative against Karla in Switzerland. In *The Honourable Schoolboy* le Carré uses a narrative frame in an elaborate and systematic way to create a sense of distance between the reader and the events described. In *Smiley's People* there is nothing comparable to the sustained application of this technique, although there are occasional reminders, such as the section in chapter 19 opening: "Again there is mystery about Smiley's decision not to reply to this question."[2]

In one way or another the past often plays an important part in le Carré's fiction. In *Call for the Dead* the appearance of Dieter Frey suddenly brings the past into conflict with the present for Smiley, while in *The Looking Glass War* the Department has locked itself in its past and does not want to escape, and in *A Small Town in Germany* the past threatens to return, history to repeat itself. The trilogy as a whole is full of research and inquiries into the past as a way of coming to grips with the present, but it is in *Smiley's People* that the past manifests itself most strongly. Smiley himself, recalled from retirement for what must surely be his last case, with its roots in an earlier period of Circus history, appears as a figure from the past with a long memory. When he visits Vladimir's small apartment at the opening of chapter 7, he vividly recalls the time many years before when he took the General there on a flat-hunting expedition in London following his defection from Russia. At the opening of chapter 16 when Smiley revisits Hamburg after a long absence, his memory goes even further back to his boyhood recollections of the city, as well as wartime and postwar ones. Yet in *Smiley's People* the past does not exist only as memory but thrusts itself dramatically into the present.

The first chapter, in which a middle-aged Russian woman living in Paris, Maria Ostrakova, is approached by Oleg Kirov, one of Karla's agents, ostensibly with the aim of reuniting her with her daughter Alexandra, whom she has not seen for twenty years, is full of references to her past life in the Soviet Union: her husband who defected to the West in 1950; her subsequent detention in a labor camp; her relationship with a Jewish dissident, Glickman, who fathered Alexandra; her reunion with her seriously ill husband in the West in 1956 on condition that Alexandra remained in Russia. Kirov, who is preparing a "legend" or cover story for Karla's daughter Tatiana as Alexandra Ostrakova, brings the past alive for Maria Ostrakova and opens many old wounds, especially as she rightly suspects that the Soviets are exploiting her maternal feelings for their own ends and are substituting another young woman for the real Alexandra. By turning in desperation to someone she has only heard of, General Vladimir, she unwittingly stirs up the past in a potentially dangerous way, as she discovers when Soviet agents attempt to kill her in Paris. The letter Vladimir receives from Ostrakova brings the past alive even more spectacularly for him, because he recognizes its significance in a way that she cannot. The letter is the first step on the road to Karla's downfall, and before he is killed by Karla's agents in an effort to close that road, Vladimir is in no doubt about the momentous nature of what he is in the process of uncovering. Mikhel, an associate of the General's and a fellow emigré, tells Smiley that Vladimir, in an unusually excited state, said: "In all my life this is my most important mission. It reaches far into our past" (p. 125).

The past involves the Russian annexation of the three independent Baltic republics, Estonia, Latvia, and Lithuania, in 1940 when the Soviet Union was still at peace with Nazi Germany following the 1939 nonaggression pact between the two totalitarian countries. As an Estonian dedicated to Communism, Vladimir had fought with the Red Army against Hitler during World War II, but became completely disillusioned with the Soviet régime after the war when his homeland was ruthlessly repressed by Stalin. Vladimir's response was to offer his services to the Circus as a mole, and in Smiley's words, "for three long years, Vladimir was the best source we ever had on Soviet capabilities and intentions—and at the height of the cold war" (p. 55). After defecting to the West, luckily in time to avoid being blown by Haydon, Vladimir continued his war against the Soviet Union as an exile in Paris and London, working with émigré organizations for the liberation of the former Baltic republics, "a lost cause" (Smiley's phrase, p. 56) if ever there was one. It is so often the fate of political exiles to look back, to inhabit an irrecoverable past. When Smiley visits a center of the Baltic independence movement, the Free Baltic Library near the British Museum in the central London district of Bloomsbury, in order to interview Mikhel after Vladimir's murder, he virtually steps back in time to enter "this haunted backwater from the fifties, once a rallying point of the so-called Bloomsbury Irregulars" (p. 120). The "burning" of Kirov by Vladimir's associate, Otto Leipzig, is partly an act of revenge for Kirov's betrayal of a dissident Estonian group to the Soviet secret police in the past.

Vladimir's urgent phone calls to the Circus in an attempt to reach

Max (Smiley's code name) almost literally sound like a voice from the past to Mostyn, the young man who takes them. For one thing Smiley is no longer a member of the Circus, having retired three years earlier after Operation Dolphin; and when Mostyn checks on Vladimir, he discovers him listed as "ex-agent, ex-Soviet General, ex-leader of the Riga Group" (p. 59), more or less an ex-man and obviously an historical relic in the eyes of the Circus. It is because this figure from the past is murdered in Moscow Centre style, soon after his emergency phone calls requesting an urgent meeting using maximum security methods known as Moscow Rules, that the Circus summons its own figure from the past, Smiley, to cap whatever undesirable wells have suddenly begun to gush in the Circus's backyard. Because of his great knowledge of Vladimir's world, Smiley is, as it were, raised from the dead, or at least from the London Library where he is working on a monograph on the German baroque poet Opitz, to brush over the traces so as to prevent any adverse publicity and potential scandal from being laid at the door of the Circus. In instructing Smiley to "pour oil on the waters, not muddy them" (p. 68), Oliver Lacon appeals to his loyalty and sense of duty, appeals that tend to backfire in the case of Smiley because of the restless questioning of "that part of himself which sometimes seemed to be a spectator to the rest" and which knows from bitter experience in public and private life that, in Ann's words, "there is no loyalty without betrayal" (p. 66). It is one of the ironies of *Smiley's People* that, in Smiley's hands, what is meant to be a small piece of tidying-up rapidly develops into a most ambitious operation. No sooner does Smiley receive his brief from Lacon than he surreptitiously learns from Mostyn that the Circus is already busy cleaning up—by erasing from the tapes of Vladimir's telephone messages any reference to "the Sandman" (Karla) and Vladimir's "two proofs" (p. 69). From this point Smiley, haunted by Vladimir's erased words, is in the grip of his quest. Contrary to Lacon's wishes, Smiley is fanning, not dousing, the flames.

The tension between Smiley and Lacon is that between an individualist, often uneasy within an institution, and a bureaucrat, primarily concerned with preserving the institution. Smiley concludes: "I invested my life in institutions . . . and all I am left with is myself" (p. 156). The tension is comparable to that between Smiley and Maston in le Carré's first novel, and similar oppositions are common in his fiction (the individualists Leo Harting and Alan Turner are at odds with the Embassy Establishment in *A Small Town in Germany*), although sometimes they develop instead of being present from the early stages

(Leamas in *The Spy*, Avery in *The Looking Glass War*, Jerry in *The Honourable Schoolboy* begin as good servants of their organizations but undergo a change). In *Smiley's People* Smiley is committed to "his lonely quest" (p. 147), Lacon, to appeasing his political masters. However compromised his values are in a world of contradictions, Smiley still upholds moral and political principles, whereas "sophistry was Lacon's element. He was born to it, he breathed it, he could fly and swim in it, nobody in Whitehall was better at it" (p. 65). Much the same could be said of Saul Enderby, the current head of the Circus, who took over from Smiley at the end of *The Honourable Schoolboy*. Enderby is extremely eager to secure Karla's defection as long as there is no risk to himself; but whereas Smiley's quest for his "black Grail" has a quasi-mystical dimension, Enderby's cautious, unofficial backing of Smiley's scheme, to which he gives his "totally deniable blessing" (p. 285), is motivated by his awareness of the enhanced prestige and power he will enjoy as a result: "I *want* the American Cousins to eat out of my hand for years to come" (p. 281).

In defense of Lacon and Enderby it must be said that they have had to adapt to important changes in political policy during the period since Smiley's retirement after Operation Dolphin. Le Carré nowhere states that a Labour Government is in office at this time, but the hints are so very broad as to be unmistakable, the best example being Lacon's description to Smiley in chapter 4 of the attitude towards intelligence work of his "new masters" in Westminister:

> You should *hear* the way they talk about the Circus! I'm their dog's-body, damn it; I *know*, get it every day! Gibes. Suspicion. Mistrust at every turn, even from Ministers who should know better. As if the Circus were some rogue animal outside their comprehension. As if British Intelligence were a sort of wholly owned subsidiary of the Conservative Party. Not their ally at all but some autonomous viper in their Socialist nest. (p. 51)

Much later, in chapter 19, Enderby puts the same case to Smiley with even less respect for his political overlords. Labour governed Britain between 1974 and 1979, and if the action of *Smiley's People* takes place three years after that of *The Honourable Schoolboy*, it presumably begins in August 1978, although le Carré does not specify the year. Just as Guillam has to explain the new lateralist structure of the Circus to Smiley at the beginning of *Tinker, Tailor, Soldier, Spy*, Lacon has to clarify the even greater changes that have been made under the Labour Government, such as the high-powered supervisory committee known facetiously as "the Wise Men" and described by Lauder

Strickland as a "bunch of left-wing flannel merchants" (p. 51). After the so-called Fall, Smiley's exposure of Haydon's treachery, the Circus has been extremely vulnerable to attack and in no position to resist political pressure to dilute or even terminate many of its activities. During the 1970s, especially during the Labour administration, "détente" became the modish word to define a supposedly more amicable relationship with the Soviet Union, which was advocating "peaceful coexistence"; in le Carré's novel, the Wise Men, espousing a softly, softly approach to the Kremlin, are anxious to sever any Circus ties with people or movements that might be thought of as anti-détente, such as Vladimir's Estonian group. On this occasion, Smiley, a paradoxical amalgam of rebellious liberalism and conformist conservatism, finds his conservative instincts deeply offended. One cannot help thinking that he would agree with a remark made by an Israeli Prime Minister, Golda Meir: "Why use a fancy French word when there is a perfectly serviceable English one: Cold War?" Like "détente," "peaceful coexistence" was merely a modish euphemism for "Cold War," used dishonestly by politicians to suggest that the Cold War was over.

In an important passage of self-analysis at the end of chapter 12, Smiley recalls the "verbal antics" of politicians and civil servants throughout his long career, and concludes skeptically that, despite the enormous importance attached to "supposedly great changes in Whitehall doctrine," they are little more than games with jargon and amount to "another reason for doing nothing":

> He had been the witness, or victim—or even reluctant prophet—of such spurious cults as lateralism, parallelism, separatism, operational devolution, and now, if he remembered Lacon's most recent meanderings correctly, of integration. Each new fashion had been hailed as a panacea. . . . Each had gone out with a whimper, leaving behind it the familar English muddle, of which, more and more, in retrospect, he saw himself as a lifelong moderator. (p. 156)

As described in chapter 20, Smiley's visits to the Circus after an absence of three years only serve to reinforce his convictions about the essential stasis of English society: that beneath all the superficial changes, which attract attention to themselves and create the illusion of movement, there is little or no real change deep down. In one paragraph the word "same" occurs prominently in three consecutive sentences. Much earlier in the novel when Smiley goes to Vladimir's flat for the first time in many years, he has an identical experience of sameness: "There was a smell of curry and cheap fat frying, and disinfectant. There was a smell of too many people with not much money jammed into too little air. He remembered that too. Nothing had changed" (p. 79). Smiley's historical perspective is evident throughout the trilogy, not to mention *Call for the Dead*, but especially in *Smiley's People* he is reaching the stage of summing up a lifetime's experience. When he takes what is likely to be his final leave of the Circus, he gazes at the building "much as old men will look at the houses where they were born, the schools where they were educated, and the churches where they were married" (p. 291).

Most of le Carré's novels, even his earliest ones, might be considered to be novels of middle age, in that the central characters (Smiley, Leamas, Jerry) and the majority of those surrounding them fit into that category, but in *Smiley's People* middle age is giving way to old age. Smiley's people are getting on in years; the former policeman Mendel, Smiley's loyal friend since *Call for the Dead*, is referred to as "old Mendel," and even Peter Guillam, whom Percy Alleline repeatedly labels "young" in *Tinker, Tailor, Soldier, Spy*, is "close on fifty" although "he fought it every inch of the way" (p. 261). For Smiley the murder of Vladimir, himself an old man, is a reminder "that his own existence too was dwindling; that he was living against the odds" (p. 42). On his visit to Ann in Cornwall in chapter 20, a couple of lines from Rupert Brooke's *1914* sonnets (lines used as the epigraph to part 3 of *The Looking Glass War*) come into Smiley's mind as he watches children in the sea, "To turn as swimmers into cleanness leaping, / Glad from a world grown old and cold and weary" (p. 296), and he acknowledges the appropriateness of the final phrase to himself. Karla, too, is aging, and when Smiley imagines his crossing to the West he sees "Karla's hopeless old man's run" (p. 384). It is above all through the bronchitic and badly crippled figure of Connie Sachs in chapters 14 and 15 that the physical decline of the elderly is most graphically conveyed. Her condition has deteriorated markedly since *The Honourable Schoolboy*, and although she remains a treasure house of information, a research library on legs, she tells Smiley that "it's death, that's what I'm suffering from. The systematic encroachment of the big D" (p. 185). The valedictory mood pervading *Smiley's People* is strongest in moments such as Smiley's departure from Connie, probably a final farewell, when she appears to doze off, perhaps "in order to avoid the pain of saying goodbye" (p. 213).

Because *Smiley's People* describes the successful accomplishment of a quest, the elements of myth and romance usually beneath the surface of le Carré's fiction are more conspicuous than ever before, including *The Honourable Schoolboy*, and le Carré uncharacteristically draws attention to them at times, instead of undermining or disguising them with irony. Enderby's tentative suggestions for analogues to Smiley's preoccupation with Karla, "So what's *your* name, George? Sherlock Holmes dogging his poor old Moriarty? Captain Ahab chasing his big white whale?" (p. 268), provide literary parallels in which similar conventions of romance are used by Conan Doyle and Melville. Le Carré later drives the parallels home when Sam Collins describes Karla as "sitting in Moscow waiting for Holmes or Captain Ahab to catch up with him" (p. 279) and when Enderby imagines Smiley and Karla "stuck on your ledge on the Reichenbach Falls" (p. 283). Lacon may tell Smiley, "We are *pragmatists*, George. We *adapt*. We are *not* keepers of some sacred flame" (p. 56); but Smiley is as much a man with a mission as Holmes or Ahab and he is the keeper of "some sacred flame," even if it is one within himself. In *The Honourable Schoolboy* Smiley's uncanny power in masterminding an operation on the other side of the world from his London office occasionally brings Prospero in Shakespeare's *The Tempest* to mind, with a frequently airborne Jerry performing some on-the-spot mischief in the manner of Ariel, but Smiley's power has to encompass not an island but a planet. In the circumstances it is not surprising that Smiley's Ariel breaks loose from his master's control and that other forces exploit Smiley's success in shaking the tree. In *The Honourable Schoolboy* Smiley has to pursue his quest from within a bureaucracy, with all the disadvantages this imposes, whereas in *Smiley's People*, as in *Tinker, Tailor, Soldier, Spy*, he is a much freer agent, working like a private detective rather than a police officer. Furthermore he has the advantage of functioning in the arena he knows intimately: Northern Europe. In *The Honourable Schoolboy* Smiley's action is limited to shaking the tree in the hope that this will produce the desired result; consequently a number of unforeseen things happen, such as the murders of Frost and Luke, for which Smiley must bear some of the responsibility. In *Smiley's People*, like *Tinker, Tailor, Soldier, Spy*, Smiley is much more in control and is able to spin a web in which he knows he will catch his victim. The difference lies in the victims. If Smiley is an enchanter or sorcerer, so is Karla, whereas Haydon, for all his treachery, is but a sorcerer's apprentice.

Karla's schizophrenic daughter, Tatiana (disguised as Alexandra), sees her father in folkloric or fairy-tale terms, which the nursing sisters in the clinic dismiss as examples of her dementia, but her apparent ravings are remarkably close to the truth:

> Alexandra had spun these tales before. How her father was a secret prince more powerful than the Czar. How he ruled at night, as the owls

> rule while the hawks are at rest. How his secret eyes followed her wherever she went, how his secret ears heard every word she spoke. And how, one night, hearing her mother praying in her sleep, he sent his men for her and they took her into the snow and she was never seen again: not even by God, He was looking for her still. (p. 326)

Karla has indeed disposed of the woman he loved, his mistress and Tatiana's mother, because she rebelled against orthodoxy; and as head of the elite Thirteenth Intelligence Directorate of Moscow Centre, he possesses something like supernatural power. The code name for Karla used by General Vladimir, "the Sandman," comes from a German fairy tale about a supernatural being who has the power of putting to sleep anyone he comes close to—in Karla's case "sleep" is, of course, a euphemism for "death." Tatiana is the girl for whom "the Sandman is making a legend" (p. 180) in order to safeguard her in the Swiss clinic where she is receiving medical treatment, but Vladimir's cryptic phraseology, meaning that Karla is preparing a cover story, is resonant with overtones of magic and romance. Even Tatiana's name inevitably recalls the queen of the fairies in *A Midsummer Night's Dream*, Titania. Anton Grigoriev's account of his visit to the Thirteenth Directorate in chapter 25 presents Karla as someone so out of the ordinary as to be a mystery, a quasi-religious and almost omnipotent figure, puritanical to the point of hair-shirt asceticism. Grigoriev calls him both "monk" (p. 348) and "priest" (p. 350), whose office is not "large and splendid . . . as became a senior official and a great Soviet fighter" but "a room so barren it would have done duty for a prison cell, with a bare wood desk at the centre, and a hard chair for a visitor to sit on" (pp. 349–50).

The element of magic or enchantment is most evident in the Swiss section of the novel occupying most of its final quarter, although le Carré's presentation of Otto Leipzig in the earlier part deserves a mention. With his "arched eyebrows and a grooved face and flicked-up horns of black hair above his pointed ears," this small elflike character is actually described in chapter 1 as "a little hobgoblin of a fellow" (p. 22) and in chapter 12 as "a little imp of a fellow" (pp. 148–49), and to Ostrakova he is "the magician" or Vladimir's "magic friend." It is thanks to Otto's "burning" of Kirov in Hamburg that Smiley discovers the greatest secret of his rival enchanter in Moscow Centre—the concealment of his ill and therefore vulnerable daughter Tatiana in Switzerland; the acquisition of this knowledge gives Smiley the power to vanquish Karla. In the Swiss chapters Smiley, with the help of Toby Esterhase's "bizarre army of discarded specialists—the pavement artists, the sound-thieves, the drivers, the photographers" gathered from "the byways of Europe's seedier cities" (p. 287)—virtually casts a spell to entrap the Soviet Counsellor Grigoriev, who provides Smiley with a direct route to Karla and therefore the means to entrap him too. Le Carré describes the "burning" of Grigoriev in Berne as "one of those rare operations where luck, timing, and preparation come together in a perfect marriage" (p. 326)—an almost magical achievement.

Another echo of romance conventions in this part of the novel is the confinement of the mentally ill Tatiana in an institution in Switzerland run by an outlandish "interdenominational Christian theosophist" community (p. 369), which brings to mind the heroines of Gothic romances imprisoned in remote castles in the Alps, especially as the building "might have been a castle, or one of those small farmsteads that sit on hilltops in the Swiss wine country, with turrets, and moats with covered bridges leading to inner courtyards" (pp. 368–69). In an interesting review that unfortunately degenerates into a bogus attempt to subject le Carré's unconscious to Jungian analysis on the evidence of the novel, Christopher Booker suggests that Tatiana is a version of the imprisoned princess or "anima" figure in "Overcoming the Monster" myths, just as Ostrakova, Vladimir, and Karla are, respectively, "Mother," "Father," and "shadow" figures.[3] When, in the closing pages, Karla makes his way to the West via a Berlin crossing point, Smiley sees him "about to cut himself off from the black castle behind him" (p. 383); this startling phrase again recalls the world of romance literature such as Spenser's *Faerie Queene*, and suggests that Karla is leaving a stronghold of evil, not just East Berlin. Despite the differences this episode has obvious affinities with the opening and the ending of *The Spy*. It is at this point that the cigarette lighter given to Smiley by Ann and obtained from him by Karla in Delhi, as described in *Tinker, Tailor, Soldier, Spy*, appears most clearly as a talisman in the romance tradition. Coming face to face with Smiley for the first time in nearly twenty-five years, Karla drops the lighter at Smiley's feet: "He heard the ring of something metal falling onto the icy cobble, and knew it was Ann's cigarette-lighter, but nobody else seemed to notice it" (p. 386). A talisman is usually a small precious object credited with magical or protective powers, and in allowing Karla to keep the lighter carrying an inscription from Ann and therefore an emblem of their relationship, Smiley was placing in his possession something that could be interpreted as a talisman. Now that Smiley has fulfilled his destiny in decisively winning the struggle between them, Karla discards the lighter like a talisman that has lost its power: it is his way of acknowledging defeat. Significantly, Smiley does not bother to retrieve this strange symbol of the bond between them as it lies "glinting like fool's gold on the cobble" (p. 387). Ann's gold lighter no longer has value for Smiley: once it could be valued as gold but now only as "fool's gold."

Smiley's decision not to pick up the "talisman" can be interpreted in at least two ways, one concerning Ann and the other Karla. Smiley seems to be acknowledging that in his relationship with Ann he has been nothing if not a fool; at the end of *Smiley's People*—unlike *Call for the Dead, Tinker, Tailor, Soldier, Spy,* and *The Honourable Schoolboy*—there is no suggestion of Smiley either pursuing or being reunited with Ann. Indeed when Ann pursues him in chapter 12, he resists her telephone appeals because of the primacy of his quest, like a knight in courtly romance rejecting the temptation of sensuality embodied in a tantalizing though probably treacherous lady. Nevertheless in chapter 20, before leaving for Switzerland, Smiley makes a special journey to Cornwall solely to see "his bitch goddess" (p. 292), as Enderby calls Ann.[4] This, strangely enough, is the only face-to-face encounter between Smiley and Ann in any of le Carré's novels featuring Smiley, and therefore assumes considerable importance in the trilogy. The imagery of decay, disintegration, and even death dominating le Carré's description of the Sercomb estate can be interpreted as emblematic of their relationship at the personal level, and of the condition of the English aristocracy at the public level:

> The house stood on a hill, in a coppice of bare elms still waiting for the blight. It was granite and very big, and crumbling, with a crowd of gables that clustered like torn black tents above the tree-tops. Acres of smashed greenhouses led to it; collapsed stables and an untended kitchen garden lay below it in the valley. . . . The drive was very pitted; stubs of felled trees lay like yellow tombstones either side. (p. 292)

With its paradoxes and oxymorons, reminiscent of the love poetry of Petrarch and his numerous Renaissance progeny—"He loved her, he was indifferent to her . . . She was all he wanted, she was nothing . . . she was remote to him, he knew her entirely" (p. 295)—the episode is inevitably inconclusive, and le Carré ironically follows it with Lacon and Smiley's rather ridiculous "seminar on marriage" (p. 297) in which Lacon seeks what he believes to be expert advice about his broken marriage. It is not long after this meeting with Ann that Smiley comes face-to-face for only the second time in his life with the one person who might be called Ann's rival, Karla. The oddity that the man known only as Karla employs a female cover name is commented on elsewhere in the trilogy, but nowhere are the sexual implications of the name more evident than in the last part of *Smiley's People;* the use of Karla rather than, say, Karl does make a subtle difference. Smiley's quest for the remote and inaccessible Karla, whose seductive power Smiley often finds stronger than Ann's, can be interpreted as compensation for his failure in love.

The novel, indeed the trilogy, concludes with the relationship between Smiley and Karla, and by leaving his lighter where Karla has dropped it, Smiley is registering a sense of hollowness in his victory. "George. . . . All your life. Fantastic!" (p. 387), exclaims Toby after Karla's defection, and Guillam says, "George, you won" (p. 388), to which Smiley makes the very qualified reply, "Did I? . . . Yes. Yes, well, I suppose I did," the final words of the novel and the trilogy. Smiley's victory is not that of Saint George or Spenser's Red Cross Knight over their dragons, of good over evil, of light over darkness; he is too aware of his own guilt for that. As so often in le Carré's fiction, crucial events take place at night in a world of shadows, where there can be no clear distinction between black and white, only degrees of darkness and shades of gray. Smiley enters *Smiley's People* during the night of Vladimir's murder in chapter 3, and the concluding encounter between Smiley and Karla is also at night, the symbolic domain of both men. As becomes increasingly clear in *Smiley's People*, Smiley's quest for Karla is, in a sense, a quest for himself, for self-definition. When he confronts Karla, he is not looking so much at his enemy as at his double, a mirror image, a kind of Doppelgänger as in legend and romance. During Smiley's visit to Connie, she tells him: "Twin cities, we used to say you were, you and Karla, two halves of the same apple" (p. 211).

In consulting his old Circus files on Karla in chapter 20, Smiley finds that he is journeying into himself as much as into the man he is hunting: "He read as far into his own past as into Karla's, and sometimes it seemed to him that the one life was merely the complement to the other; that they were causes of the same incurable malady" (p. 290). Somewhat earlier, at the end of chapter 17, Smiley's analysis of Karla as "two Karlas" could be mistaken for a transferred self-analysis; "Smiley" could easily be substituted for "Karla":

> There is Karla the professional, so self-possessed that he could allow, if need be, ten years for an operation to bear fruit . . . Karla the old spy, the pragmatist, ready to trade a dozen losses for one great win. And there is this other Karla, Karla of the heart after all, of the one great love, the Karla flawed by humanity. (pp. 252–53)

Karla's Achilles heel is his love for his daughter and his determination to do everything he can for her, including smuggling her to the West for treatment, even though this means grossly abusing his professional powers, putting himself in a most precarious position, and sanctioning murders to protect both Tatiana and himself. In order to conceal the fact that he is cheating and defrauding Moscow Centre, Karla has to resort to low-grade and unintelligent operators, Kirov and Grigoriev, both of whom are very easily compromised into betraying vital information. As Smiley closes in on Karla and feels that he holds the advantage for the first time in their long struggle, he becomes increasingly conscious of Karla's "human face" and of the resemblance between them:

> It was no brute whom Smiley was pursuing with such mastery, no unqualified fanatic after all, no automaton. It was a man; and one whose downfall, if Smiley chose to bring it about, would be caused by nothing more sinister than excessive love, a weakness with which Smiley himself from his own tangled life, was eminently familiar. (p. 364)

If Smiley's victory leaves a somewhat nasty taste in the mouth, including his own, it is because it depends entirely on ruthlessly exploiting rather than respecting the human factor, Karla's love for his daughter. In a context of nonviolent warfare between East and West where fair play is an impossible luxury, to hit one's opponent below the belt is unexceptional and often necessary, however reprehensible in strictly moral terms. This is what Smiley does, just as Karla did when he encouraged Haydon to have an affair with Ann, Smiley's Achilles heel, in order to confuse Smiley's reactions and consequently deflect him from the activities of the Circus mole—this emerges in Haydon's final confession to Smiley in *Tinker, Tailor, Soldier, Spy*. Indeed Toby Esterhase initially interprets Smiley's continuing pursuit of Karla as a determination to obtain personal revenge for his sexual humiliation: "So okay, Ann gave you a bad time with Bill Haydon. So there's Karla, and Karla was Bill's big daddy in Moscow. George, I mean this gets very crude, know what I mean?" (p. 173). Be that as it may, Smiley lives with the uncomfortable paradox that to defend the moral scheme he believes in he must resort to expediency and opportunism, as his uneasy conscience at the end makes clear. To succeed, he must sell part of his soul to the devil. Smiley's most vivid experience of this contradictory condition occurs when he watches Karla about to cross into West Berlin, and recognizes that he and his supposed archenemy are not polarized opposites but mutually compromised occupants of the same piece of ground:

> He looked across the river into the darkness again, and an unholy vertigo seized him as the very evil he had fought against seemed to reach out and possess him and claim him despite his striving, calling him a traitor also; mocking him, yet at the same time applauding his betrayal. On Karla has descended the curse of Smiley's compassion; on Smiley the curse of Karla's fanaticism. I have destroyed him with the weapons I abhorred, and they are his. We have crossed each other's frontiers, we are the no-men of this no-man's-land. (p. 384)

As Connie tells Smiley much earlier in the novel, "no one knows where the lines are" in the Cold War with "half-angels fighting half-devils" (p. 207).

Karla's "human face" may be revealed in *Smiley's People*, but his real identity is still a mystery, as though he has the power magically to retain an inviolable secret to the very end of Smiley's quest. In modern spy fiction, as in real-life intelligence work, the use of cryptonyms, work names, and false identities is routine, but in le Carré's work before *The Quest for Karla* there are not many instances, *The Looking Glass War* providing most of them. Taylor is in Finland as Malherbe, Haldane is known to Leiser as Captain Hawkins, and Leiser sets out on his mission as Hartbeck. In the trilogy examples are more abundant, especially in *Smiley's People*, where the quantitative increase produces a qualitative change, reinforcing the element of romance enchantment. In *Tinker, Tailor, Soldier, Spy* Haydon is mole Gerald, Prideaux is also Ellis, Viktorov is Polyakov in London, Karla (itself a cryptonym) is Gerstmann in Delhi, and Smiley uses both Barraclough and Carmichael. In *The Honourable Schoolboy* Collins is also Mellon, Lizzie Worthington passes as Liese Worth in Hong Kong, and Smiley uses Standfast and Oates. In *Smiley's People* the list is appreciably longer; there is an unprecedented fluidity in names and identities, especially in Smiley's case, though as with Lizzie-Liese in *The Honourable Schoolboy* not all are for intelligence reasons. Vladimir, originally named Voldemar, is both Miller and Gregory; Esterhase is both Benati and Hector; Kirov's real name is Kursky; Grigoriev is also Glaser; Tatiana is Alexandra; Villem is William; Karla is often called "the Sandman," and Otto, "the magician"; while Smiley is Max, Angel, Standfast, Lorimer, Barraclough, and Lachmann. It is Smiley's protean ability to assume different guises, and to adopt or discard them almost at will to suit his circumstances, as in his hurried abandonment of Standfast in Germany, that helps to enhance his status as an enchanter, like Merlin in the Arthurian legends who can magically transform himself into all sorts of things. The code name for an intelligence source in *Tinker, Tailor, Soldier, Spy* is Merlin, again suggesting that le Carré was unconsciously, if not consciously, incorporating Arthurian elements into his trilogy.

It used to be thought that romance and realism were strongly opposed literary modes, but beneath the surface of much realistic fiction, conventions of romance can be discerned, however heavily disguised. Even hard-boiled, private-eye fiction, with its tough, naturalistic exterior, often draws on the same archetypes as stories of knightly adventure. To emphasize romance elements in *Smiley's People* (and in the trilogy as a whole) is not to suggest that le Carré is sacrificing realism and verisimilitude. On the contrary, le Carré's greater attention to detail, his filling out of characters, and his more expansive approach to narrative in the trilogy compared with, say, *The Spy* gives these novels a greater sense of ordinary, everyday reality than his early ones, with their more selective and stylized methods. The Swiss section can be discussed in romance terms with Smiley as the enchanter, but it is also remarkable for its wealth of realistic detail. The care with which le Carré gradually builds up to the "burning" of Grigoriev and the subsequent victory over Karla corresponds to the elaborate research and planning necessary for the successful execution of the plan by Smiley, Esterhase, and their numerous helpers. Incidentally, Switzerland is a country that le Carré knows well, and the Swiss chapters allow him to poke fun at some aspects of this supposedly model democratic republic: the incongruous "modern Swiss antique" café, which reminds Smiley of "Bavarian beer cellars on the fifteenth floor" in Hong Kong (pp. 313–14); the equally incongruous plastic flowers in a vase of water; the police, whose clutches should be carefully avoided, according to Toby Esterhase: "thank God the Swiss are only neutral, know what I mean?" (p. 328).

Another outstanding example of the fusion of romance and realism in the novel is the first part of chapter 17 describing Smiley's lone journey in pursuit of Otto Leipzig to the remote and bizarre "water camp," once a military installation on the Baltic coast and now a blend of holiday camp and refuge for social dropouts. This is one of the most haunting passages in the novel, perhaps in le Carré's entire oeuvre, and its power arises from the way in which the underlying romance motif of quest is given precise, realistic embodiment, even though it also verges on surreal nightmare. In romance terms the journey is of a solitary adventurer into unknown and possibly hostile territory where various dangers may lie between him and his goal. Smiley drives into an eerie part of the North German coast very close to the border between East and West, which could be a contemporary equivalent of the mythic wasteland. He learns that he has been preceded by other visitors looking for Otto, and when he finds Otto's mutilated corpse on his ransacked houseboat and examines Otto's equally ripped-apart car, his apprehensions about the purpose of that earlier visit prove to be well founded. Other incidents and details contribute to the sinister atmosphere of menace: the grotesque moment when Smiley pulls in a fishing line with an old gym shoe on the end, to the chorus of laughter from the crowd of spectators on the shore; the woman justifying the indifference of the camp people to what happened on Otto's boat by claiming that the visitors were police and that "when police go about their business, it is the duty of the citizen to keep his trap shut"; the old man apparently excusing the destruction of Otto's car—"He was scum . . . They all are. Look at them. Polacks, criminals, subhumans" (p. 243); the two boys systematically smashing the trunk lid of Smiley's hired car "till it lay like a crude parcel on the floor" (p. 244) and then trying to charge him for repairs. As Smiley leaves the site with considerable relief, memories of his experiences in the nightmare Germany of the Nazis return to him, and he feels that he has just revisited the past or, more disturbingly, that beneath the surface things have not changed very much:

> He had left Germany before, he had come and gone illicitly, he had hunted while on the run, and though he was old now and in a different Germany, he felt as if he had been returned to the wild. He had no way of knowing whether anybody from the water camp had telephoned the police, but he took it for an accomplished fact. The boat was open and its secret out. Those who had looked away would now be the first to come forward as good citizens. He had seen that before as well. (p. 245)

There is an obvious parallel here with Leo Harting's sense in *A Small Town in Germany* that the supposedly eradicated forces of Nazism in German society are still alive and well. As elsewhere in *Smiley's People* there is a frightening sense of the present being in the grip of an ugly past; Smiley's quest comes to an uneasy end, but its outcome cannot cancel out or redeem that past.

10

A Country Not Ours to Give: *The Little Drummer Girl* (1983)

For a writer to discard a fictional world he has sustained over a series of novels might be thought to be traumatic, but le Carré's own remarks in his televised interview with Melvyn Bragg in 1983 suggest that after completing *Smiley's People* he abandoned Smiley and the Circus with relief rather than regret. Le Carré's devoted readers, faced with the disappearance of comfortingly familiar characters, places, and struggles, may well feel differently, but when a novelist stays on well-defined paths for too long, his work is liable to atrophy and the opening up of new territory can become increasingly difficult for him. Not that le Carré was in a creative rut with *The Quest for Karla*; but had the series expanded beyond a trilogy it might well have begun to show signs of fatigue. Speaking of Smiley before the publication of *The Little Drummer Girl*, le Carré told his *Newsweek* interviewers that after the trilogy "I wanted to leave myself without him as a prop, and give myself the opportunity to write about the new generation, younger people, modern problems."[1] Coming immediately after three closely related novels, *The Little Drummer Girl* is bound at first sight to seem a radical departure, but it is a less self-conscious attempt by le Carré to expand his literary frontiers than *The Naive and Sentimental Lover* was in 1971. In that novel he jettisoned the elements of espionage and detection he had used in remarkably varied ways in his first five novels.

In *The Little Drummer Girl*, on the other hand, he not only adheres to the conception of spy fiction he developed in the trilogy, but introduces in a new guise a number of familiar preoccupations and methods.

The most immediately startling innovation is signaled by the title, with its playfully ironic transformation of the popular modern Christmas song, "The Little Drummer Boy." Le Carré's choice of title has precisely the same effect as *The Honourable Schoolboy* in giving prominence to a particular individual, but *The Little Drummer Girl* is his first novel to have a woman as its central character, and although other viewpoints are prominent at times, that of Charmian (Charlie) is the one the reader experiences most fully. Women do have important parts to play in some of the earlier novels, including Elsa in *Call for the Dead*, Liz in *The Spy*, Lizzie and Connie in *The Honourable Schoolboy*, and Ostrakova in *Smiley's People*, but none of these occupies the center of the stage in the way that the major male characters do. In one sense Ann Smiley is as much a series character as her husband, but in another sense she is an absentee from the Smiley novels since she usually features as a part of George's consciousness rather than as a dramatically realized individual. Even in le Carré's only straight novel about love and human relationships, *The Naive and Sentimental Lover*, the main female characters, Sandra and Helen, are overshadowed by their male counterparts, Aldo and Shamus, and Shamus's impact on Aldo is the main trigger of the narrative.

In a largely enthusiastic review of *The Little Drummer Girl* one of the few women ever to write on le Carré, the British novelist Sally Emerson, argues that "like Smiley, John le Carré is not good on sex and love and women,"[2] a view that some critics have expressed in the past. In another very favorable review Julian Symons makes a similar point when he states that "erotic feeling plays a large part in Charlie's make-up, but le Carré is a markedly unerotic writer, and we are sometimes told what we should be shown."[3] By choosing to concentrate on the predominantly masculine world of intelligence and diplomacy, le Carré has usually avoided a searching analysis of emotional relationships between the sexes, nowhere more obviously than in his treatment of George and Ann Smiley. When interviewed in 1974 by Michael Dean, le Carré called *The Spy* "a very romantic story: two people fall in love,"[4] and the same could presumably be said about *The Honourable Schoolboy*; but although symbolically crucial the relationships between Leamas and Liz and between Jerry and Lizzie are not presented in depth. In another televised interview, this time with Melvyn Bragg in 1976, le Carré said that "one of the greatest realities is sex, but we almost never succeed in betraying our sexuality to one another fully";[5] if this great reality is usually repressed in life, it has been repressed, in another way, just as much in his fiction.

In building his new novel around "the little drummer girl," a phrase carrying complex, even contradictory, connotations of innocence, militarism, and mechanical toys, le Carré seems to have accepted the challenge not only of doing something different but also of attempting what has sometimes been thought to be beyond his reach. Charlie is based to some extent on le Carré's half-sister Charlotte Cornwell, a well-known English actress who has worked with the Royal Shakespeare Company; le Carré's Proust-like use of the normally masculine name Charlie for a woman reverses his procedure in the trilogy, in which the feminine form Karla (Karl is equivalent to Charles) is applied to a man. The first name of the fictitious Charlie (Charmian), who is in her late twenties, closely resembles that of her real-life model; and like Charlotte Cornwell, Charlie is a vivid redhead, an actress, and initially a political radical, sympathetic to extremist movements. Her nickname, Charlie the Red, therefore carries two meanings, and recalls the nickname of another redheaded radical, Daniel Cohn-Bendit, one of the leaders of the student revolution in France in 1968, known as Danny le Rouge. During her twenties Charlotte Cornwell was attracted to the far left for a time, as many young British actors and actresses of the past fifteen years have been; the acting profession has been one of the mainstays of the small Workers' Revolutionary Party during this period, one of its leading figures being an even better-known redheaded actress with an uncannily appropriate surname, Vanessa Redgrave. These parallels do not mean that Charlie is, as it were, Charlotte Cornwell, since the differences are as important as the resemblances; for example, Charlie's career as an actress is far from successful and she seems unlikely to break away from small, second-rate, touring companies. Le Carré's presentation of the renowned journalist Dick Hughes as Craw in *The Honourable Schoolboy* may be closer to the original than Charlie is to Charlotte, but it is interesting that in order to create a woman as central character for the first time, le Carré should have turned to a near relative for inspiration and drawn so much from life in order to delineate a convincing female protagonist.

In parting company with Smiley, le Carré also drops the Cold War as the context for the action of his new novel, choosing instead the much more volatile and violent Middle Eastern conflict between Israel and the Arab world, especially the Palestinians. This is a completely new departure for le Carré, who spent several months carrying out research for the novel in Israel and Lebanon, much as he did for *The Honourable Schoolboy* in Southeast Asia. Like the earlier novel *The Little Drummer Girl* contains a foreword in which le Carré acknowledges his indebtedness to the many people who helped him. In this foreword le Carré takes pains to appear impartial, and although he mentions his Israeli hosts and informants before his Palestinian ones, the opening words of the foreword ("Many Palestinians and Israelis gave me their help and time in the writing of this book") put the Palestinians first. Le Carré's "special gratitude" to the former chief of Israeli military intelligence, General Shlomo Gazit, is carefully balanced by his tribute to the Palestinian military commander at Sidon, Salah Ta'amari, not only for his courage but "for having shown me the Palestinian heart."

A superficial reading of the novel might suggest that le Carré is adopting a decidedly pro-Israeli stance, or alternatively a decidedly pro-Palestinian one, and he has been accused of both of these by different commentators, but the foreword is not an exercise in disinformation, an attempt to camouflage political bias by hypocritical gestures of open-minded and even-handed neutrality. Le Carré is preeminently the novelist who has raised the spy novel to the level of tragedy, and it is precisely because he sees the long-drawn-out Israeli-Palestinian conflict as genuinely tragic in its irreconcilability that he has made it the subject of this long, spacious novel, which is as replete with detail as the preceding trilogy. The tragedy lies in the paradox that both Israelis and Palestinians can legitimately claim to have right and justice on their side, with the result that a fair and just solution is apparently impossible and human suffering is perpetuated indefinitely. To right the appalling wrong done to the European Jews during World War II, another appalling wrong has been done to the Palestinians. Throughout the novel the tragic irony is obvious in the way both Israelis and Palestinians defend their actions by identical appeals to the metaphysical abstraction of justice. Yet as le Carré himself acknowledged in his television interview with Melvyn Bragg when *The Little Drummer Girl* was published, the ironies proliferate further, since the blame for the prolonged Middle Eastern conflict cannot be laid solely at the doors of the Israelis and the Palestinians:

> There is a terrible historical irony in the fact that, because very properly and far too late, the Jews engaged our Western consciences, we gave them a country which was not ours to give. We in fact obliged the Palestinians to pay the price for the Western conscience. It was not the

> Palestinians who persecuted the Jews; it was us, us Westerners. It was us Brits for not letting them in; it was the Americans for not letting them in; it was a whole mucky Western conspiracy of which the Germans were the spearhead, but we are not without blame in the matter.[6]

In the novel le Carré presents a not dissimilar view in a perplexingly oblique way when the Israeli agent Gadi Becker, alias Joseph, adopts the voice of a young Palestinian terrorist, Salim alias Yanuka alias Michel, in order to present the Palestinian viewpoint to Charlie:

> Yet who has the simple courage to tell out loud the cruellest joke in history: that thirty years of Israel have turned the Palestinians into the new Jews of the earth? You know how the Zionists described my country before they seized it? "A land without a people for a people without a land." *We did not exist!* In their minds, the Zionists had already committed genocide; all that remained for them was the fact. And you, the British, were the architects of this great vision. You know how Israel was born? A European power made a present of an Arab territory to a Jewish lobby. And did not consult a single inhabitant of the territory concerned. And that power was Britain.[7]

The way in which an Israeli patriot can authentically and convincingly mimic a Palestinian patriot is disturbingly ironic, because it indicates how similar they are in some ways: Becker actually tells Charlie before she goes to Lebanon that she will find the Palestinians "an easy people to love" (p. 327). The Palestinians in *The Little Drummer Girl* repeatedly insist that they are not anti-Semitic, an attitude they attribute to Christian Europe, but anti-Zionist, although in practice the distinction is hard to maintain.

Towards the end of the novel the tragic irony of the political situation manifests itself in the predicament of Professor Minkel, a liberal Israeli intellectual who is critical of current Israeli policy and defends Palestinian rights, yet who finds himself the intended victim of a Palestinian bomb because he is regarded as "a dangerous moderate, capable of diluting the pure wine of their cause" (p. 373). When moderation is dangerous, equitable solutions are the sheerest fantasies. While preparing the device with which he intends to assassinate Minkel, the Palestinian bomb-maker Khalil tells Charlie: "They say Minkel's a nice person. Maybe he is. When I read about him, I too said to myself—this old fellow Minkel, maybe he's got some courage to say those things. Maybe I would respect him. I can respect my enemy. I can honour him" (p. 398). Khalil's behavior consequently seems totally irrational, but as Charlie comes to realize by the end of the novel, the irrationality belongs to the whole situation, with both sides hopelessly trapped in mutual hatred and fear, and obsessed with doing "back to the bastards what the bastards did to me. To redress injustice. With injustice. Until all the just are blown to smithereens, and justice is finally free to pick herself out of the rubble and walk the unpopulated streets" (p. 417). Justifying his plan to blow up "a nice person," Khalil stresses to Charlie the Palestinian need for revenge and retaliation: "Do the Zionists think of all the nice people when they bomb us? I don't think so. When they napalm our villages, kill our women? This I doubt very much. I do not think the terrorist Israeli pilot, sitting up there, says to himself, 'Those poor civilians, those innocent victims' " (p. 398).

The Israeli-Palestinian conflict is seldom far from the headlines and is too well known to require documentation here, especially as the novel contains reminders of such crucial political realities and historical events as the British Mandate over Palestine before the creation of Israel in 1948, the Israeli involvement in the Suez Crisis of 1956, the Six Day War of 1967, and the Yom Kippur War of 1973. *The Little Drummer Girl* is set in the period before the Israelis launched their blitzkrieg in June 1982 in a determined effort to rid Lebanon of the Palestinian Liberation Organization (PLO), although near the end of the novel there is a reference to this full-scale offensive, which led to the partial occupation of Lebanon by both Israel and Syria. Le Carré had been working on the novel for a couple of years before the Israeli invasion of 1982 precipitated the national agony Lebanon has endured since then, so he cannot be accused of opportunistically exploiting the current phase of the Palestinian problem, but as with some of his earlier books the publication of *The Little Drummer Girl* at the beginning of 1983 proved to be most timely, giving the novel the same kind of urgent topicality *The Spy* possessed in 1963. Le Carré was in the Middle East in June 1982 and wrote an article about his experiences, "Memories of a Vanished Land," for one of the British quality Sunday newspapers, *The Observer*, in which he fiercely criticized the Israeli action:

> The attack was a monstrosity, launched on speciously assembled grounds, against a people who on the Israelis' own admission constitute no serious military threat. It is as if we British had lost our temper with the IRA and decided to punish the entire Irish people once and for all—convincing ourselves at the same time that when we had done so, we would hear no more of their troubles.
>
> Too many Israelis, in their claustrophobia, have persuaded themselves that every Palestinian man and woman and child is by definition a military target, and that Israel will not be safe until the pack of them are

> swept away. It is the most savage irony that Begin and his generals cannot see how close they are to inflicting upon another people the disgraceful criteria once inflicted upon themselves.[8]

Since then le Carré has made further public statements about Israeli policy under Menachem Begin and his defense minister, General Ariel Sharon, following the invasion. In his 1983 interview with Melvyn Bragg, le Carré repeated his charge that the Israeli government was committing "a modern monstrosity" in the name of security and that the persecution of the Jews did not give Begin the license to "draw his own borders, annexe chunks of territory, turf out more people or subjugate them." Speaking of his meeting with the PLO leader, Yasser Arafat, le Carré said that he "found him very interesting, very touching, very genuine . . . a much maligned man . . . extremely moderate," and went on to say that

> by exploring the roots of Palestinian anger one gets closer to understanding the acts of violence. If you are a displaced people, and you've got to make the world listen—that is the Palestinian argument—if you've been driven from camp to camp, if you've had the living daylights persecuted out of you by your own people, by the Israelis, but above all by your brother Arabs, I can understand that you would turn to violence.[9]

In the novel this understanding is most fully embodied in Khalil, who, like his friend and associate Tayeh, has suffered greatly. Le Carré is not, of course, condoning Palestinian terrorism, which he deplores as much as he deplores Israeli militarism, but he is able to enter imaginatively into both points of view. There is no reason to doubt le Carré's sincerity when he told Bragg, "I was determined to balance the story as perfectly as I knew how." Fully aware that in writing the novel he was walking a tightrope over a minefield, le Carré made Charlie, neither Jew nor Palestinian though involved with both, the central consciousness, so that balance would emerge through her ambivalent perception.

After visiting Yasser Arafat's temporary PLO headquarters in Tunisia not long after the publication of the novel, le Carré wrote two more articles for *The Observer*: "Exiles in the White Hotel" (26 June 1983), about the PLO leadership after its withdrawal from Beirut, and "The Betrayal" (3 July 1983), a report based on the terrible experiences of one Palestinian family in Beirut during the summer and autumn of 1982 following the Israeli invasion of Lebanon. Le Carré clearly endorses Faisal's eye-witness account, which incorporates the appalling massacres of noncombatant Palestinians, including women, children, and medical staff, at the refugee camps of Sabra and Chatila by

Lebanese Christian militia while the Israelis turned a not-so-blind eye. What particularly horrified le Carré was the way in which the Israeli Army intimidated young Palestinian children into providing information about their relatives, betraying them without understanding the meaning of "betrayal." "The Betrayal" is deeply critical of current Israeli policy and methods, and extremely sympathetic towards ordinary Palestinians. Exactly the same response is evident at the opening of chapter 3 of the novel, about a typical example of indiscriminate Israeli retaliation: "Israeli jets bombed the crowded Palestinian quarter of Beirut, in what was afterwards declared to be an effort to destroy the leadership, though there were no leaders among the several hundred dead—unless of course they were the leaders of tomorrow, for many were children" (p. 48). Similar passages occur later in the novel.

It is not altogether surprising that at publication le Carré felt that the novel might offend Jewish readers, and at least one reviewer, David Pryce-Jones, saw it as almost hysterically pro-Palestinian and anti-Israeli ("the Palestinians are good, the Israelis are bad").[10] Yet one should never forget D. H. Lawrence's sage advice to trust the tale, not the teller. Le Carré's state of mind after the 1982 invasion is not the same thing as the work of the imagination he had been writing during the previous two or three years. *The Little Drummer Girl* is neither investigative journalism nor documentary history but a fiction built on the archetypal romance narrative of quest. Le Carré's statement to *Newsweek* is virtually an admission of this: "I began with the traditional Jewish hero looking for the Palestinian 'baddie.' " He goes on to say that from this starting point he wanted, in his usual way, to raise "more ambiguous moral preoccupations," and to give the novel "an unashamed educational purpose" since "what has happened, and how the Palestinian problem occurred, is something most Western readers don't know about."[11] Le Carré does present moral ambiguities of considerable tortuousness, but the thrust of the quest narrative is such that a number of reviewers, including John Wyver, did indeed take the Israelis to be heroes and the Palestinians to be villains: "to this reviewer it seemed straightforwardly pro-Israeli. The voices of the recruiting agents are voices of calm, order, reason and sophisticated common-sense. The few Palestinian voices are all strident, instinctive, spattered with jargon."[12] Both Wyver and Pryce-Jones have political axes to grind, so that their opinions are suspect, but what is interesting is that the novel has produced such flatly contradictory interpretations (as opposed to evaluations).

All of le Carré's novels since the unanimously praised *The Spy* have met with a mixed reception, in the sense that some reviewers have thought better of them than others, but no British critic has, for example, ever suggested that because le Carré is critical of aspects of Britain he is pro-Soviet or pro-Communist. By leaving Smiley and the Cold War for the much hotter Middle East, le Carré has manifestly presented his readers with a greater problem in distinguishing between imaginative fiction and current affairs, and Christopher Hitchens's review in *The Literary Review* (July 1983) is not untypical in considering how factually reliable or unreliable *The Little Drummer Girl* is in all its details, as though it is to be judged as reportage. It is therefore necessary to emphasize the status of *The Little Drummer Girl* as fiction and as art, which, as Picasso never tired of reminding us, is a lie that reveals the truth. What le Carré is writing about is the human condition, and in doing so he adheres to the realistic convention of taking his metaphors from the world immediately around him, just as an Augustan writer such as Pope did in *The Dunciad*, rather than from the past or classical mythology as many Romantics did. The Israeli-Palestinian conflict can therefore be seen as the vehicle for le Carré's moral vision, just as the Cold War is in several earlier novels, rather than as the novel's so-called content. The final stages of the struggle for Indian independence from British rule functions in a similar way in a major work of contemporary English fiction, Paul Scott's *The Raj Quartet*, dealing with the last years of the Raj between 1942 and 1947.

One reason for the difficulty of interpretation is the increasing subtlety of le Carré's narrative technique with his expansive approach to fiction since the early 1970s, so that he requires much more concentrated effort than conventional thriller writers do, and is therefore liable to be misread. He presents rather than tells, working through suggestions and implications for the reader to interpret, as opposed to explicit statement. In this respect *The Little Drummer Girl* is his most ambitious and subtle novel to date. More crucially, the obvious imbalance in the narrative, with the Israelis receiving far more attention than the Palestinians, has naively been assumed to indicate an imbalance of attitude on le Carré's part, usually in favor of the Israelis, although the emphasis on them has also been seen as a ploy for systematic denigration. Le Carré has chosen to approach the Israeli-Palestinian issue by describing a most ingenious operation by Israeli Inttelligence, involving Charlie as a double agent, to destroy a highly successful Palestinian cell carrying out an anti-Israeli bombing campaign in Europe. Until Charlie arrives in Beirut in chapter 21, three-quarters of the way through the novel, the narrative focuses on the Israeli pursuers rather than the Palestinians and their European accomplices, and although le Carré presents the principal Israeli characters sympathetically, careful reading indicates just how equivocal he is towards the Israeli cause, long before he describes Charlie's encounter with the reality of Palestinian suffering. This account is plainly based on le Carré's own experiences of the violence and the camps in Lebanon. Nevertheless the long chapter 21, in which he achieves a successful fusion of vivid reporting, narrative development, and psychological crisis (in Charlie's case), is the only one really devoted to the Palestinians in the Middle East, since chapter 23, also set in Lebanon, is about Charlie's experiences at an international training camp for terrorists.

Another factor contributing to the pro-Israeli and anti-Palestinian interpretation of the novel is le Carré's manifestly unsympathetic treatment of the European terrorists on whom the Palestinian bombing campaign depends for support. These include the Italian "apostle of the peaceful solution" (p. 230), Albert Rossino alias Luigi alias Mario; the Swiss "humanist lawyer" (p. 422) Anton Mesterbein; and the sadistic German woman Astrid Berger, alias Helga alias Edda alias Maria Brinkhausen "alias you name it" (p. 292), who likes to threaten Charlie with unspecified punishment. Indeed the only Palestinians presented in Europe are the two brothers Salim and Khalil, the latter of whom does not appear until the closing chapters. This late entry by the principal target of the Israeli quest is reminiscent of the even later ones made by Leo Harting in *A Small Town in Germany*, Nelson Ko in *The Honourable Schoolboy*, and Karla in *Smiley's People*, all prime objects of quest in their respective novels.

Le Carré does not attempt to present any of the European terrorists in depth or with subtlety, preferring satirical irony or even straightforward ridicule to depict their addiction to sex, violence, and drugs. Of the promiscuous Dutch "bomber girl" Larsen, the Israeli agent Shimon Litvak says: "She drugs so hard you get stoned just standing over her" (p. 250). Although Litvak, who repeatedly calls her a "half-wit," is a prejudiced observer, le Carré's handling of, for example, Mario and Helga in Verona's bourgeois house, which they have systematically wrecked to make Verona "free" and a member of "the masses," is equally sarcastic; the irony as the lovers noisily reach orgasm within Charlie's hearing is especially bitter: "Helga and Mario were advancing the revolution without her assistance" (p. 381). Le Carré's hostility to these terrorist playboys and playgirls, mainly from the prosperous, middle-class intelligentsia, may appear to rub off on the Palestinian cause, irrevocably tarnishing it, but he is careful to distinguish between the two. The sympathetically portrayed Palestinian commander, Captain Tayeh, has no illusions about some of their European supporters, as he tells Charlie in Lebanon: "Some of the scum we get, they want to blow the whole world up. . . . They are scum, those people. Helga—Mr. Mesterbein—necessary scum" (p. 333). Khalil makes a similar point to Charlie: "We have many friends in Germany. But not because they love Palestine. Only because they hate Jews" (p. 399). He also deplores the attitude and conduct of some of his European accomplices, who "when they kill . . . laugh and triumph . . . Got drunk, tore their clothes off like animals" (p. 412).

It is easy to understand le Carré's decision to cast *The Little Drummer Girl* in the form of an anti-Palestinian mission by Israeli intelligence. For one thing the novel, as a story of pursuit, conforms to the underlying pattern of the majority of his previous books, including the three novels in the trilogy, and in every case he concentrates on the pursuers, not the pursued (however admirable, as in the case of Leo Harting in *A Small Town in Germany*, the pursued may be). Furthermore the questors, like their fictional predecessors, notably Smiley, are members of an intelligence organization; le Carré can therefore continue his exploration of themes that have always fascinated him, including the relationship between intelligence work and the political cause it serves, the suppression of morality in the name of national interest, and the discrepancy between defensible ends and indefensible means. A novelist with a particular interest in intelligence is bound to be familar with the renowned Israeli equivalent of the CIA, the Mossad (Institution for Intelligence and Special Assignments), one of the finest intelligence services in the world and certainly the best belonging to a small country, since security and survival are synonymous for Israel; in writing about the Middle East, he would consequently be attracted by the fictional possibilities afforded by the Mossad's already well-documented exploits and achievements. In comparison with the Mossad, Arab intelligence organizations are notoriously inefficient. The very accessibility of information about Israel, including its intelligence services, made it much easier for le Carré, as a writer aiming at plausibility, to give narrative prominence to Israeli rather than Palestinian characters. While researching for the novel in the Middle East, le Carré encountered no obstacles in obtaining what he wanted to know from the Israeli authorities, who were most cooperative, as he explained to Melvyn Bragg. But like most investigators he found it much harder to penetrate Palestinian layers of defense and secrecy, although he eventually succeeded in collecting sufficient first-hand material to make the Lebanese section of the novel vividly evocative as reportage and tragically intense within the imaginative framework of the novel.

Had le Carré attempted to write the book differently, concentrating on the Palestinians, he might well have found it extremely difficult to achieve verisimilitude and psychological conviction. Only in one previous novel, *The Honourable Schoolboy,* had he attempted to create non-European (or non-Western) characters, and he never focuses for long on any of the Asians. By surrounding Charlie with a group of Westernized Israelis, most of whom are in fact Europeans rather than sabras, le Carré has sidestepped a major hurdle inherent in his choice of subject: entering into the non-European mind. Furthermore much of the novel is set in Europe, especially England and Germany, rather than the Middle East, so that le Carré is again on artistic terra firma. The opening of the novel in the main residential zone for foreign diplomats in Bonn recalls *A Small Town in Germany,* as do le Carré's treatment of the unnamed high-ranking Silesian policeman in chapter 1, whose right-wing speech reminds another German of the Führer himself, and his reference to the "stultifying insensitivity" of the Bavarian police in housing its flying squad in the barracks of the former Nazi concentration camp at Dachau. Le Carré's caution could be interpreted as artistic cowardice, but it is also artistic common sense. Readers who agree with Robert Browning's dramatis persona Andrea del Sarto that "a man's reach should exceed his grasp" may well feel, however, that le Carré's failure to develop the Palestinian side more is a weakness. What is crucial is not to take this *artistic* decision as evidence of *moral* and *political* bias on le Carré's part.

The political context of the operation masterminded by Marty Kurtz in *The Little Drummer Girl* corresponds to that of the early 1980s: the threat of a full-scale Israeli offensive against the Palestinians in Lebanon by Begin's right-wing Likud government. Indeed Kurtz—the name inevitably recalls Conrad's extraordinary character of that name in *Heart of Darkness*—is partly motivated by his desire to prevent such an invasion; he hopes that success in putting an end to a particularly effective Palestinian bombing campaign in Europe will not only ensure his own professional survival but also help to hold Israeli militarism in check by removing a major irritant, which is provoking retaliation. Following a Palestinian bombing in Aachen and an Israeli reprisal raid on a camp in Lebanon to assuage "mounting popular fury," Charlie reads a chilling newspaper interview with an Israeli general "who promised to solve the Palestinian problem 'from the roots up' " (p. 260), a phrase disturbingly reminiscent of the Nazi policy of a final solution to the Jewish problem. Kurtz's aim is to "take the enemy from inside his house, rather than beat him down with tanks and artillery from the front, which was increasingly the inclination in Jerusalem" (p. 27). By eventually eliminating the bomber and his aides, Kurtz achieves one of his goals, but this microcosmic victory has no effect on the macrocosm of Israeli policy. The Israeli military juggernaut rolls into Lebanon, the crude might of overkill rather than sophisticated subtlety being the order of the day, so that Kurtz's success is, in a larger context, a failure. The ambiguity is characteristic of le Carré, especially in all the Smiley novels, where apparent success is always heavily qualified.

This similarity is one of several between *The Little Drummer Girl* and the Smiley novels, notably the trilogy, and in some respects Kurtz is an Israeli version of Smiley. Even physically they resemble each other in their inelegance: "squat and Slav and strong . . . with a barrel chest and a wrestler's wide stride" (p. 14), Kurtz is roughly the same shape as the short, round Smiley, also described as "squat" in the second paragraph of *Call for the Dead.* Well into middle age—as a child during World War II he was destined for extermination by the Nazis but survived—Kurtz is something of a maverick outsider in Israeli Intelligence, and although part of him is deeply patriotic, another part of him is just as deeply at odds with institutional orthodoxy and the Establishment. Much the same can be said of Smiley. Substitute "England" for "Israel," and the positives for which Kurtz fights—"For love of Israel. For peace. For moderation"—are also Smiley's. Similarly, Kurtz's exasperated contempt for his political and administrative masters—"If we don't take the enemy from inside his own camp, those clowns in the Knesset and Defence will blow up the whole of civilisation in their hunt for him" (p. 28)—recalls Smiley's, although it is marked by aggressive outspokenness rather than English restraint.

In order to obtain official approval for his operation from a "steering committee of nervous politicians and war-hungry generals" (p. 30), Kurtz has to indulge in devious political maneuvering, just as Smiley does in *The Honourable Schoolboy* to receive the backing of the

Intelligence Steering Group. Again like Smiley, Kurtz belongs to the old order and is consequently very different from the new men with their new methods who are taking over the power structure:

> He was not a sabra; he lacked the élitist background from the kibbutzim, the universities, and the crack regiments that, to his dismay, increasingly supplied the narrowing aristocracy of his service. He was out of tune with their polygraphs, their computers, and their ever-growing faith in American-style power-plays, applied psychology, and crisis management. He loved the diaspora and made it his speciality at a time when most Israelis were zealously and self-consciously refurbishing their identity as Orientals. (p. 28)

Both men have an ambivalent relationship with their country and their service, and Kurtz seems to be as much at home outside Israel as in it. He certainly adopts and discards aliases with the same ease displayed by Smiley in *Smiley's People*, appearing as Schulmann, Gold, Raphael, and Spielberg. As in *Smiley's People*, in which Smiley has to assemble a group of ex-Circus employees in Switzerland to create his trap for Karla, Kurtz has to enlist what le Carré calls his "private army" (p. 32) in order to launch his operation.

The most important member of the team, Gadi Becker, is an Israeli hero and a much more romantic figure than Kurtz himself: Jerry Westerby bears a similar relationship to Smiley in *The Honourable Schoolboy*. Although the parallel is far from exact since their characters are so different, both Jerry and Becker are sent in to the field alone by their respective operational chiefs to perform an essential task, in Becker's case the first stage of Charlie's "wooing" by Israeli Intelligence. There is nothing schoolboyish about Becker, however, for whom intelligence work has lost the glamorous appeal it once had, so that in this respect he is the opposite of the immature Jerry, who yearns for adventure. Initially reluctant to have anything to do with Kurtz's scheme, Becker has to be won over, though in a less startling manner than Charlie.

Becker—in Israeli eyes "the great Becker" (p. 224) and nicknamed "the Steppenwolf" (p. 267)—is, significantly, a man who has fought courageously for Israel since his youth in a number of capacities during a period of twenty-five years, but is now tired of the continuous fighting and killing and retaliations, and, like Kurtz, has no enthusiasm for any Israeli military intervention against the Palestinians. When Charlie asks him what he has fought for in the past, he replies: " 'In '56 I wanted to be a hero, in '67 for peace. And in '73'—he seemed to find it harder to remember—'for Israel' " (p. 218); but when she inquires about his reason for fighting this time, he remains silent. It is as though he is no longer fighting *for* something in a positive sense, but in a more negative way to prevent something worse happening. Confronted with Charlie's passionate accusation, "The Israelis can hack the Palestinians to pieces any time. But a couple of rabbis knocked off in Frankfurt or whatever—I mean that's real grade-one prime-beef international disaster, isn't it?", Becker replies that "they are all disasters" (p. 191). Although disillusioned and sceptical, he accepts Kurtz's view that a limited operation involving a few specific violent actions is preferable to the full-scale violence that is otherwise likely to be unleashed. Kurtz's anti-Palestinian operation is, paradoxically, intended to help ordinary Palestinians. Nevertheless a world in which political murder is an instrument for keeping the peace and "for moderation" is plainly one on the brink of madness, if it has not actually gone over the edge. Kurtz's confident justification of killing only "those who break completely the human bond" (p. 107) is dangerously ambivalent because it begs the question of what "the human bond" is: Khalil's announcement to Charlie, "Zionists kill for fear and for hate . . . Palestinians for love and justice" (p. 399), may be more extreme but is the same kind of self-righteous rhetoric, which can lend respectability to any atrocity.

Because the Palestinian terrorist he wants to dispose of takes highly sophisticated security precautions, Kurtz knows that he has virtually no hope of catching him unless he employs a devious, roundabout route. Unlike "a lot of people in Jerusalem" who "would prefer to charge the windmills of Lebanon than fight the enemy with their heads" (p. 39), as Kurtz tells his right-hand man, Shimon Litvak, he wants to fight with his head. Against an invisible enemy like Khalil, a direct or frontal attack is impossible; so in order to make Khalil visible, Kurtz has to follow his own prescription: "You want to crack the terror target these days . . . you practically have to build yourself your own terrorist first" (p. 203). The scheme Kurtz puts into effect is extraordinarily elaborate, full of risks and uncertainties, requires meticulous attention to every detail, and does involve building himself a terrorist, Charlie. Kurtz's dictum is that "to catch a lion, you first must tether the goat" (p. 36), the lion being Khalil and the goat his younger brother Salim (Yanuka, Michel), ostensibly a student in Munich, but secretly involved in the bombing campaign. One prong of Kurtz's plan is to kidnap Yanuka (the Israeli name for Salim) while he is driving a car packed with explosives from Turkey to Germany for his brother, interrogate him so as to extract as much information as possible, and then kill him in what appears to be an accidental explosion. The Israeli choice of an apartment in Munich's Olympic Village, built for the 1972 Games, as a temporary prison and condemned cell for Yanuka carries a retributive sting, because the eleven Israeli athletes massacred during those Games by members of Black September, a Palestinian group committed to violence, were seized at the Village.

Kurtz's other prong, which has to be synchronized with the first, is much more difficult and chancy, and is dependent on extensive, preliminary research and on correctly predicting the behavior of individuals and groups. It involves selecting a pro-Palestinian sympathizer of revolutionary tendencies, who would be acceptable to Khalil as a terrorist recruit and who would also be capable of conversion to the Israeli cause. Khalil relies on young European women, such as the Dutch "little bomber girl" who plants the bomb at Bad Godesberg. As a young Englishwoman, a political activist with Baader-Meinhof leanings, a skilled actress, and a person whose life, both intellectual and emotional, is in disarray and who is therefore looking for a purpose, Charlie fits the bill. Becker's initial role is to lure Charlie to a Greek villa, where she is subjected to a crash-recruitment session by Kurtz, provided by Israeli Intelligence with a completely fabricated record of a passionate love-and-politics affair with Salim, whom she calls Michel, and released with the certainty that sooner or later Khalil's organization will contact her, allowing her to enter it as a double agent and lead the Israelis to Khalil himself. Like *The Honourable Schoolboy, The Little Drummer Girl* is divided into two parts, the first, "The Preparation," corresponding to "Winding the Clock" in the earlier novel, and the second, "The Prize," corresponding to "Shaking the Tree."

Stripped to a bare outline Kurtz's scheme may seem highly improbable, and le Carré has been accused of uncharacteristically shaping his novel around an implausible plot, but we must remember that le Carré is not an intelligence officer planning an operation, but a novelist creating a fiction in which the demands of realism have to be accommodated within the artist's overriding need to project his vision of the human condition as well as the requirements of form. There is no contradiction here because art, by definition, is not life, and realism is always relative, not absolute. In *The Little Drummer Girl* the issue is much the same as in *The Spy*, which also involves an intelligence outfit placing an agent in the heart of the enemy camp: not whether Israeli Intelligence would have countenanced an operation like Kurtz's, but whether le Carré gives conviction to his imaginary operation.

Nevertheless le Carré has the advantage that Israeli Intelligence is well known to be far less conservative than its British counterpart, and to have undertaken highly imaginative and spectacularly daring missions.[12] In the novel as in reality the Israeli criterion is success, not caution. Le Carré fusion of realism and romance in *The Little Drummer Girl*, as in the Smiley trilogy (even though the romance elements are less conspicuous than in *Smiley's People* where Smiley emerges as an enchanter in his pursuit of Karla), is paradoxically truer to life than drab realism would have been. Israeli Intelligence has often given the impression of achieving the impossible with ease, as though it is run by men with supernatural powers, and its amazing successes have given it a magical aura. The great military successes in the 1967 and 1973 wars would have been impossible without superb intelligence work, even though the outbreak of the Yom Kippur War did catch Israel on the wrong foot, and the now almost mythical raid on Entebbe airport in Uganda to free Jewish hostages in 1976 also combined extraordinary intelligence and military capability; two feature films about the Entebbe incident were made. The notorious ineptitude displayed by the Israelis in assassinating the wrong Palestinian in the Norwegian town of Lillehammer in 1973, followed by the arrest and trial of six Israeli agents, is an exception that proves the rule.

In creating an imaginary operation in which all the gambles finally pay off, le Carré is not indulging in far-fetched fantasy, because the Israeli historical record, on which he draws, frequently reads like adventure fiction, and is sometimes so bizarre that if presented as fiction it would be thought totally incredible. Le Carré lends realism to Kurtz's operation by describing its processes in so much detail, including fall-back arrangements and emergency procedures, and by showing that Kurtz is fully aware of all the risks and short cuts he takes, but at the same time Kurtz and Becker do seem to wield magical power because everything they attempt goes to plan. Becker virtually casts a spell over Charlie, who rapidly succumbs to Kurtz's persuasion in his biggest gamble of all, but one he is convinced will work despite considerable skepticism among members of his own group. Kurtz, Becker, and their associates are always in the right place at the right time. They are able to exert influence and control events in different countries through such senior officials as Dr. Alexis of the West German Ministry of the Interior and Commander Picton of British counterintelligence. Luck is always on their side, as in their advance identification of the time, place, and target of Khalil's bomb attack against Professor Minkel in Freiburg-im-Breisgau, involving Charlie. And the elaborate web they spin catches their enemies much as they had hoped. In a mainly adverse review of *The Little Drummer Girl* the distinguished critic Anthony Quinton describes it pejoratively as "a romance" and likens it to the work of Mary Stewart;[14] but in failing to take account of the positive way in which le Carré exploits romance conventions, Quinton reveals himself to be fundamentally out of sympathy with le Carré's fiction, especially as it has developed during the last ten years. At the end of a perceptive review of the novel, in which he analyzes some structural constants of le Carré's fiction, Peter S. Prescott presents a contrary view: "That he writes romances . . . in no way lessens his claim to a place in our literature. Stories precede literature and remain fiction's essential element still."[15]

The quasi-magical powers of the Israelis pervade the novel, and even when Charlie is amongst the Palestinians in Lebanon and apparently completely out of touch with Kurtz's group, she encounters sprigs of white heather, a reassuring sign that the Israelis are still with her. In chapter 11 when Paul Alexis, who is sympathetic to Israel and willing to cooperate with Kurtz, thinks that Kurtz is making impossible demands on him, he says: "Am I a conjurer—an alchemist—that I make such wonderful pieces of information out of stones? What are they thinking about in Jerusalem—that a *coordinator* is suddenly a magic man?" (p. 201). The effect of these words is to suggest that even though Alexis is not a conjurer, alchemist, or magic man, Kurtz is. Just before this passage, Kurtz has, as if by magic, been providing Alexis with a mass of information about the Bad Godesberg bombing described in chapter 1, which the German authorities have been investigating for some time without getting anywhere at all. Kurtz has, in fact, obtained his information from the interrogation of Yanuka. Earlier (chapter 4) Kurtz and Litvak, posing as Gold and Karman, virtually magic a store of invaluable material concerning Charlie from her theatrical agent, Ned Quilley, by means of a convincing confidence trick.

Becker's appearances can also seem almost magical on occasion, notably at the church hall in Peckham where Charlie flees when she discovers her flat being pulled apart by the British security service and feels she is on the run (chapter 19), and again near the end when his timely arrival at the house where Charlie and Khalil are saves her life (chapter 26). In the early section of the novel set on the Greek island of Mykonos and the mainland of Greece, Becker, traveling as Peter Richthoven but labeled with the Biblical name of Joseph by Charlie and her friends, works a form of enchantment over them by his mere presence. Charlie in particular finds him hypnotic. Even the presence of Charlie's "rackety troupe of young British acting people" on

Mykonos is "a miracle to all of them" (p. 48); if they knew that Israeli Intelligence was ultimately responsible, rather than their supposed benefactor, a wealthy City company with an interest in supporting small theater companies, they would regard it as even more miraculous. Kurtz decides to arrange the troupe's visit to Greece because the "magic of her situation" (p. 143) will make Charlie more vulnerable to Becker's approach and his own powers of persuasion. Another "miracle" (p. 56) is the urgent cable to Charlie's current lover, Alastair, summoning him home, ostensibly from his agent but again arranged by Israeli Intelligence to remove Alastair from the scene and allow Becker to isolate Charlie from the others. The episode in which the anarchistic Alastair panics after losing his air ticket, passport, wallet, credit card, and "almost everything else that a good anarchist might reasonably regard as the disposable trash of the enslaved society" makes Becker (Joseph) positively genie-like, because he arrives with all the missing documents, "quite from where, nobody seemed to know—as Pauly put it, somebody just rubbed the lamp" (p. 58).

From the first, Charlie senses something disturbingly strange and powerfully alluring about Joseph that is not simply sexual: she "knew he was a ghost" (p. 50) and feels that "he's come to collect my soul" (p. 52). Later, after she abandons her friends in Piraeus (the port near Athens) to join Joseph, he actually describes himself as her "personal Mephistopheles" (p. 88). The way in which she is wafted away from her friends and virtually delivered to Joseph by one of Kurtz's agents, Raoul, is itself almost magical—or an example of superb Israeli foresight and planning. When Joseph takes Charlie to the Acropolis at dusk, it is, for her, like entering a fairy-tale world of romantic enchantment, which evaporates with her realization that the sound of a car horn is a signal to Joseph; she then feels like Cinderella as the clock strikes twelve: "The coach has turned into a pumpkin" (p. 95). Yet the magic is not over: the pumpkin, as it were, turns into Yanuka's Mercedes, awaiting them on their descent. Subsequently, in helping Charlie to create imaginatively the details of her fictitious affair with the Palestinian she knows as Michel, Joseph tells her to think of Michel as "your magician," another enchanter, but when, apparently speaking as Michel, he talks of "the magic of being with me" (p. 149), the ambiguity is a reminder that Joseph is engaged in creating in reality something comparable to the magic of the theater, a convincing illusion.

Pervading the novel is the metaphor of the theater, the entire Israeli operation being conceived as a play performed in what le Carré calls "the theatre of the real" or "the theatre of deeds." He is here revitalizing a metaphor that Shakespeare and his poetic and dramatic contemporaries were particularly fond of, the most familiar example being Jacques's seven-ages-of-man speech in *As You Like It*, which opens: "All the world's a stage, / And all the men and women merely players." There is, of course, nothing entertaining about the Israeli "play," as Kurtz explains to Charlie:

> We are not speaking of some enchanted forest. When the lights go down on the stage, it will be nighttime in the street. When the actors laugh they will be happy, and when they weep they will very likely be bereaved and broken-hearted. And if they get hurt—and they will, Charlie—they will surely not be in a position, when the curtain falls, to jump up and run for the last bus home. (p. 108)

Words and phrases associated with drama, such as "script," "lines," "dialogue," "audition," "début," "role," "performance," "exit," "first night," "curtain up," "lightning change between scenes," and "between acts," are appropriated to describe the action in the theater of the real, and even the victim of the Israeli "plot," Khalil, speaks in such terms when he is justifying Palestinian terrorism to Charlie: "Terror is theatre. We inspire, we frighten, we awaken indignation, anger, love. We enlighten. The theatre also. The guerrilla is the great actor of the world" (p. 398).

Before she becomes involved with the Israelis, Charlie thinks theatrically about Joseph, the mysterious stranger haunting the beach on Mykonos, whom she remembers attending some of her company's productions in England: "Who writes his lines and gives him his directions? He was on stage for her, just as she had been for him in England. He was a trouper like herself" (p. 53). Her intuition is correct; Joseph is already playing his part in the theater of the real, which Kurtz invites her to enter, following her virtual abduction by Joseph in Greece. Kurtz's proposal that Charlie work for the Israelis is initially couched in the language of theater, appropriately enough since being an agent, especially a double agent, involves complex role-playing: he offers her "an acting job" (p. 106) in which "we handle the plot, Joseph does the dialogue. With a lot of help from you" (p. 107). It is not, however, the Israelis but the Palestinians who provide Charlie with all the aliases she acquires: Joan, Fräulein Palme, Comrade Leila, Imogen Baastrup, and Margaret.

From Kurtz's research into Charlie's background, he knows that she has adopted a persona and created a role for herself offstage as much as she does onstage, but he also knows that her real-life part is confused and unsatisfactory, and he is convinced that if he offers her a much better part she will be won over, as indeed she is. One of the most astonishing pieces of "theater" staged by the Israelis is Kurtz's exercise in interrogation and persuasion in chapters 6 and 7, a major crux of the novel, especially as le Carré takes a considerable risk in depicting Kurtz's "one devil of a gamble" (p. 143) as close to a walk-over. Reluctantly delivered on stage by Joseph in the Greek villa, Charlie finds herself a participant in a duologue with Kurtz, while Joseph and other members of the Israeli team provide the audience. Before this encounter, when Kurtz and Litvak act out their parts as Gold and Karman in the London office of Ned Quilley's theatrical agency, Ned says a number of things about actors, specifically Charlie, that point forward to the Israeli gamble over converting her. Claiming that "on stage they acted out all the agonies of man, and off stage were hollow vessels waiting to be filled," Ned states that actors "don't have *opinions* . . . They have moods. Fads. Poses. Twenty-four-hour passions. There's a lot wrong with the world, dammit. Actors are absolute suckers for dramatic solutions. For all I know, by the time you get her out there, she'll be Born Again!" (p. 79). It is because he is convinced that Charlie is "waiting to be filled" and is capable of being "Born Again" that Kurtz has singled her out; he later describes Joseph as "her saviour" (p. 140), thus maintaining the religious parallel.

Le Carré presents Charlie as a classic example of a middle-class rebel of her generation with a strong moral conscience, who is reacting against the complacent inertia, apathy, and "repressive tolerance" (to use her own Meinhof-like oxymoron) of her background and searching for a purpose and direction in her life. She rejects the conformity of English society, but like all rebellious, idealistic nonconformists she is, as Kurtz recognizes, searching for "a better conformity" (p. 108), and this is what he offers her along with a moral anchor and a mission. Previously, as one of Ned's "suckers for dramatic solutions," Charlie has found her "better conformity" in left-wing political activism and sexual promiscuity. Kurtz's task is to break her down so that he can build her anew: to show her the partly phoney image she has created for herself, shatter it, and create another in its place.

Charlie's rebellion has been directed against bourgeois England as embodied in her parents, whom she sees as unreal figures in a waste-land, members of the living dead populating her country. She sees herself as a representative product of such a society, one of the "rich English suburban kids from Nowheresville" who "had no traditions, no faith, no self-awareness, no nothing (p. 114) and who inhabit the vacuum left by the disappearance of faith in a post-Christian era. Although Charlie might be considered an unreliable witness at this stage, her view of England as moribund and exhausted resembles that presented in other le Carré novels, and is endorsed by Rachel, an English Jewess who has become an Israeli agent, and by Charlie herself after her transformation by Kurtz and Joseph. Of her fifteen years in the Midlands town of Macclesfield before emigrating to Israel, Rachel says: "It's death . . . All that class and coldness and hypocrisy. I think it's the unhappiest place on earth" (p. 138); and when the operation takes her to London she "kicked against the very idea of coming back to England at all, and had made an ostentatious point of not travelling on a British passport" (p. 266).

Charlie's own return to London from Salzburg, after driving the Mercedes from Greece to Austria, is characterized by "the smell of English sadness that had greeted her even on the runway, reminding her of what it was that had turned her towards radical solutions in the first place: the malign sloth of authority, the caged despair of the losers. There was a luggage handlers' go-slow and a rail strike; the women's lavatory was like a taste of prison" (p. 246). Although she has now made a new commitment, her experience of living in England still provides overwhelming "support for her identity as the radical committed to the violent path" (p. 258). Reading the quality Sunday newspapers, she marvels "at the self-regarding irrelevance of the ruling English mind"; shopping, she is struck by "the hopeless faces of the shoppers shuffling like manacled slaves through the neon-lit supermarket." Indeed everything from "shiny banks with their air of secular worship and their righteous martinets of managers" to "betting shops" contributes to her vision of London as "an unemptied dustbin of discarded hopes and disappointed souls."

What Kurtz knows before his interrogation of Charlie is that her quest for a faith has led her to fabricate a false adolescence, an "ingenious fiction" (p. 136) involving her reviled parents, in order to give credence to the strength of her revolt. Her faith is therefore partly built on a well-concealed lie, which is the weapon Kurtz uses to break her. She is irritated when he teases her about the inconsistency of her philosophical position, accusing her of being "peaceably unaligned" and belonging to "the extreme centre" (p. 129) because the logic of her politics demands not words but violent actions, which she disavows. But what strikes home devastatingly is not Kurtz's fun at her parrotlike regurgitation of left-wing clichés, but his exposure of the deep, virtually buried, psychological reasons from her adolescence that underlie much of her behavior. Kurtz seems to know her better than she knows herself, and sees through her façade to the inner emptiness behind it. Here he is more like a Freudian analyst than an interrogator, because what he does is to bring to the surface submerged secrets and fantasies, at first causing her humiliation and precipitating her explosion of violent outrage against Joseph. The process of self-discovery is painful for her but also liberating, since she can admit to herself that she has been "a stupid little fool of a radical actress who made up feeble versions of herself as she went along, who had denied her father and mother and embraced a half-cock faith she hadn't the courage to renounce" (p.137).

Having stripped her of the inauthentic role she has assiduously created for herself in life, Kurtz rescues her by making her feel wanted, cared for, useful, despite all her past failings: "After all her drifting, their straight line. After all her guilt and concealment, their acceptance. After all her words, their action. . . . She was a featherweight . . . theirs was the commanding wind" (p.138). There is, of course, nothing altruistic about Kurtz's cure, which is a form of brainwashing: he dispossesses her of one identity in order to possess her for his own purposes in the theater of the real. She is to be a little drummer girl for the Israelis, marching to Kurtz's tune and pretending to be another little bomber girl for the Palestinians; one of le Carré's discarded working titles for the novel was *The Piper and the Tune*. By this time Charlie has become emotionally dependent on Joseph, and although part of him disapproves of the coldly calculated ploy he has used to entrap her, the Israeli "play" demands that he continue to exploit her potential for love. The entire "seduction" of Charlie is a sophisticated piece of manipulation, as opposed to crude coercion, because Kurtz wants to make Charlie feel she has volunteered to play the part he has prepared for her in the theater of the real. As he says, "if you are proposing marriage to a lady, it is wiser not to rape her first" (p. 142), and he speaks honestly enough to Charlie when he tells her, "We want to share with you, to make use of you" (p. 136), but a more cynical awareness of what he is doing is evident in his remark to Litvak, "Tonight she lies for herself, tomorrow she lies for us" (p. 117). From being a self-deceiver harming only herself, she will become a deceiver of others in the Israeli cause.

The idea of taking possession of someone is so antipathetic to the underlying ideology of Western democracy and bourgeois individualism that several reviewers questioned the ability of Kurtz and Becker to do so in the case of Charlie; but far from being a throwback to medieval superstition, psychological possession is a widespread phenomenon in recent history, at both mass and individual levels. People have been brainwashed and "turned" with frightening ease, especially but not only in totalitarian countries. A particularly well-known American case was that of Patty Hearst, and more to the point several young British actresses have commented on how rapidly they succumbed to a form of possession by ideologues of what in England is known as the loony left. Interviewed by Hugh McIlvanney just before *The Little Drummer Girl* was published, le Carré, apparently recalling his own experience in intelligence work, said:

> If I had met Charlie in the circumstances defined in the book I could have recruited her. The factor of the lability of loyalty, its flexibility, was working for the Israelis when they moved in on her. And they played on her actress's nature. They offered her reality, which all actors yearn for. They offered her love and money, too. They completed her life for her.[16]

To be of service to Kurtz, Charlie has to create a new identity based on the fiction that she is Michel's devoted lover and protegée as a potential terrorist, and it is partly because of her involvement in radical politics that she is able to develop this so convincingly. At the opening of the novel she actually is a potential terrorist who in the right circumstances might have been persuaded to serve the Palestinians. To the consternation of some of his colleagues, Kurtz has chosen to build his own terrorist from Charlie rather than, for example, an Israeli girl agent, precisely because of the significant overlap between what she is and the role he wants her to perform. Chapters 8, 10, and 12 describe what might be called Charlie's first rehearsals at the hands of her director, coactor, and script writer, Joseph, who, by adopting the persona of Michel, helps to "make the fiction" (p. 155) of her love affair down to the last detail so that her cover story will be watertight when eventually put to the test. Indeed when it is tested by two European members of Khalil's terrorist cell, Helga and Mesterbein, Helga's suspicious comment, "she could lie easily, such an actress. . . . A woman so trained to pretend, how can one believe anything, actually?" (p. 274), is more accurate than she realizes.

On their brief journey together in Greece before Charlie drives Michel's Mercedes to Austria on her own, Joseph and Charlie have to encompass two forms of fiction: they have to establish a credible past for Michel and Charlie while simultaneously acting out the imaginary relationship in the present. For Charlie the experience of being with an Israeli intelligence officer reproducing the arguments and rhetoric of a Palestinian terrorist with considerable authority is inevitably confusing because of the ambiguity of his identity, and consequently of her own. Where does the fiction begin and where does it end? Is she with Joseph or Michel? Is she on the Israeli or the Palestinian side? At times she is not sure whether Joseph is speaking in his own voice or that of Michel, so that she sees herself as "the twice-promised girl" whose emotional attachment to Joseph is being transferred in the fiction to Michel: she feels that Joseph has "pimped me for his phantom in the theatre of the real" (p. 190), a phrase that foreshadows the denouement of Kurtz's "play" in the penultimate chapter. *The Twice Promised Girl* was another of le Carré's discarded working titles.

Charlie's simple appeal to Joseph during their fiction-making, "Who the hell are you? What do you *feel* inside all those barbed-wire entanglements?" (p. 192), is a response to her increasing difficulty in holding on to reality, especially her own selfhood. What she does not know is that Joseph, so confident and in control on the surface, cannot answer because he is also suffering a crisis over his identity, and her question subsequently forces him to acknowledge this to himself as he stares into a mirror and sees not so much his reflection as his double:

> I *feel* as if I am looking at a dead friend, hoping he will come alive. I *feel* as if I am searching for my old hopes in someone else, without success. I *feel* that I am an actor, as you are, surrounding myself with versions of my identity because the original somehow went missing along the road. But in truth I feel nothing, because real feeling is subversive and contrary to military discipline. Therefore, I do not feel, but I fight and therefore I exist. (p. 194)

Joseph's commitment to his role as Israeli agent in the theater of the real is an attempt to escape from the human and moral dilemmas confronting him as a result of being sucked into Kurtz's operation. His resort to the phrase, "I fight and therefore I exist," is deeply ironic in context, because not long before, while impersonating Michel in order to accustom Charlie to standard Palestinian arguments, he has been sarcastically ridiculing these famous words of one of Israel's founders and prime ministers, David Ben-Gurion, "a peace-loving, patriotic, idealistic Zionist, who has killed many British and many Palestinians by terrorist methods, but because he is a Zionist he is not a terrorist but a hero and a patriot" (p. 185). Joseph's apparent identification with Michel at times like this is as disturbing for the reader as it is for Charlie. Playing the part of an enemy whose violent death he acquiesces in, Joseph becomes a walking contradiction, and his human side, which can see the situation whole, is in conflict with his professional side, which has to see through partisan blinkers. This is why he is such an isolated figure, detached even from the Israeli team he belongs to. Although he manipulates Charlie, he himself has been pressured by Kurtz into the role of manipulator, something part of him resents because of the duplicity involved in exploiting her potential for love.

By choosing, or being persuaded, to act in the theater of the real, Charlie finds herself inhabiting a world of contradictions and paradoxes where the clear distinction possible in the ordinary theater between actress and role no longer applies. Her sense of identity is blurred and eroded, partly because she has to play two opposing roles at the same time, Israeli agent and Palestinian activist, and partly because her deepest self is involved in both roles. Back in England after what might be called her conversion and her brief but necessary encounter with the real Michel in his Munich prison where he is kept drugged, the boundary between fact and fiction is increasingly tenuous. Although Charlie can detach herself sufficiently to recognize "a certain madness" in maintaining the pretense that she is Michel's lover, even going into mourning for him after she hears of his death, she has come to accept "that without the madness there was no sanity; there was the rôle, or there was nothing" (p. 304). Her one fixed star, her only constant in the topsy-turvy world she has entered, is Joseph himself, whom she loves; and because Joseph has created Michel for her, her devotion to Michel is an expression of her love for Joseph. Fact becomes fiction, and fiction, fact—except for the evening they spend together in the London church hall before Charlie goes to Beirut, making love for the first time. This is "outside the script" (p. 313), a time out of time, a reality beyond the theater of the real, where they can briefly be themselves, so that "their whole shared fiction was nothing but foreplay for this night of fact" (p. 314).

When Charlie first arrives in Lebanon, she discovers that it is Joseph, paradoxically, who has enabled her to respond so warmly to the Palestinians and has "opened her heart to their tragedy" (p. 328). Indeed she is very conscious of the similarities between the Israelis and the Palestinians, and Captain Tayeh reminds her of Joseph because he also speaks "from pains she had not experienced, from a viewpoint she had yet to learn" (p. 333). Living with the Palestinians she is gradually "educated to tragedy," feels herself "to be part of a monstrous injustice" (p. 337), and as a result of identifying with them, her fictional commitment to Michel becomes more real than her actual commitment to Joseph. The contradiction between the duplicity that has brought her to the Palestinians and her genuine concern for them is most naked when she meets Michel's sister Fatmeh and speaks of him "from the heart, from her wounded memory." In one way Charlie is an imposter guilty of a most objectionable deceit, but le Carré says, "She was an impostor to nobody, not even to herself" (p. 340), indicating that she has entered so far into her role as Michel's "grieving, outraged widow" (p. 361) that the role is playing her. Consequently, when Tayeh asks her an unexpected and potentially disastrous question about Joseph, she unhesitatingly provides him with an appropriate pro-Palestinian response and is not in the least nonplussed: "Was the actress in her dead at last? Or was she so reconciled with the theatre of the real that the difference between life and art had disappeared? None of her repertoire occurred to her; she had no sense of selecting her performance" (p. 367). Shortly before this she is true to her zealous revolutionary persona in reporting one of her fellow recruits at the terrorist training camp to Tayeh for counterrevolutionary attitudes, a betrayal of a confidence that the old Charlie would have considered highly immoral.

After her training she flies to Zurich from Beirut as "Tayeh's soldier" who has "come to enlist in the army of her dead lover's brother" (p. 374). Yet the skeptical Litvak is wrong in assuming that she has genuinely joined the Palestinians and rejected the Israelis. Her secret signals to the Israelis confirm her loyalty, even though she denies to herself what she is doing when she makes contact with Rachel at Zurich airport. Becker's diagnosis, that "part of her has gone over, part has stayed. . . . That is what we asked of her" (p. 383), is far more sophisticated than Litvak's. Charlie is doing exactly what Joseph instructed her to do when he told her in London to "stay with the logic of the fiction" (p. 306), merging herself with her role no matter where that should lead her. By staying with the fiction, Charlie has effectively ceased to be a moral agent and has acted as an automaton, just as the Israelis required. Her premonition on Mykonos that Joseph has "come to collect my soul" and his subsequent joke about being her "personal Mephistopheles" prove to be close to the truth.

The fiction leads Charlie to Kahlil, whose death at the hands of the Israelis is the final multifaceted betrayal in a chain of betrayals and manipulations orchestrated by Kurtz. Not only does Charlie betray Khalil, but in doing so she is conscious of betraying herself and of being betrayed by Joseph. From the outset the entire operation has its own logic, which is largely divorced from ethical considerations, and makes use of confidence tricks and other deceptions—theft, the threat of blackmail, kidnapping, and assassination. Necessity demands that

Yanuka and the Dutch girl be blown up together in a fake accident, and although both victims are themselves killers, the cold-blooded ruthlessness of the Israelis is only marginally mitigated by their brief consideration of more humane yet counterproductive alternatives. At the opening of the final chapter the killings of all Khalil's European accomplices is reported, the Israelis obviously having made a clean sweep, which does not, however, prevent a Lebanese bloodbath. All the Palestinian places Charlie visited in Lebanon and many of the people, including Tayeh and Fatmeh (the last of six brothers and sisters to die at the hands of Israel), are "sanitised," "eradicated," or "destroyed" (p. 425). Yet the gulf separating expediency from morality is nowhere so anguished as in Charlie's experience as a "little bomber girl" for Khalil after her return to Europe from Lebanon.

At Zurich, on her way to participate in the Freiburg bombing, she remembers Fatmeh's parting words as they kissed goodbye in Lebanon, "Give my love to Khalil" (p. 374), yet it is death, not love, that Charlie is bringing him. And it is precisely at the point where she is to become the agent of death that the full horror of the accumulation of deception and betrayal registers, causing Charlie herself to crack under the strain. Having delivered the bomb to Minkel and simultaneously played her part in the Israeli-German trick to convince Khalil that the attack has been successful, Charlie cannot face the prospect of returning to Khalil and continuing the pretense, especially as she knows that they will make love to celebrate what Khalil calls "a great victory" (p. 411). Feeling completely drained of courage and incapable of continuing, she pleads with Joseph not to make her rejoin Khalil, but he insists. His dismissal of her distraught appeal, "He wants a wedding night, Jose. Doesn't that stir you slightly?" (p. 409), has the effect of killing something in her, so that she goes to her night of love and death with Khalil as a whore as well as a decoy, believing that she is back where she started with her inner emptiness: "She was without love and without value to herself . . . and the whole rotten world could screw her" (p. 410). The man she has committed herself to entirely now truly acts like a pimp, prostituting her not for money but for Israel. Love is no match for national expediency, as Leamas discovers at the end of *The Spy*. When Joseph bursts into the house where Charlie and Khalil spend their one night together and shoots Khalil, he might almost be a jealous husband murdering his wife's lover after discovering them in flagrante delicto, but it is he himself who has forced her into Khalil's arms. Morally, she feels totally degraded, as degraded as she thinks Joseph is, and sees herself in him as Khalil's killer.

Le Carré's handling of irony is particularly effective in Charlie's final scene with Khalil. When she cries, he regards it as a grief-stricken reaction to her first bombing assignment; but she is weeping for him, and for her own treacherous self. Khalil takes her outburst, "They're pigs. . . . Ruthless, murderous," as one of self-justification, referring to the supposed victims of the bomb, but she is really thinking about the very-much-alive Israelis closing in on the real victim, Khalil. What makes the irony particularly galling is Khalil's abundant trust in Charlie, whom he regards not only as a comrade-in-arms but as "one of us . . . our sister . . . part of a great family" (p. 414). By taking the sexual initiative at a time when she wants "to smash herself" (p. 415), Charlie is desperately attempting to annihilate her identity in eroticism and to commit herself to a grotesquely compensatory act of solidarity with the man she is deceiving. Under orders from Joseph to activate the homing device concealed in her clock radio when Khalil is asleep, she tries hard to keep him awake so that she will not be responsible for raising the curtain for the final scene. It is Khalil himself who does that when he discovers the device, but his last words before he is killed, "And you are the same English who gave away my country" (p. 420), link her responsibility for betraying an individual Palestinian to the Israelis with a much larger historical process: in Palestinian eyes, the betrayal of the entire Palestinian people by Britain after the Balfour Declaration of 1917 (named after the current Foreign Secretary), which promised support for a Jewish homeland in Palestine. For Khalil, as he dies, Charlie is nothing less than an embodiment of Perfidious Albion.

The theme of betrayal preoccupies le Carré as much as it did Conrad. Throughout le Carré's oeuvre there is an irreconcilable and therefore tragic conflict between personal loyalty and political necessity, between morality and expediency. Even his only "domestic" novel, *The Naive and Sentimental Lover,* is about deception and betrayal. For le Carré human life is irreducibly paradoxical: victory at one level requires defeat at another; success is inevitably characterized by failure; to achieve a desirable objective, something else of value must be sacrificed; good ends may well demand unpleasant means, and good means are likely to produce the wrong ends. Above all, the values of the heart, of love, are extremely vulnerable in a world dominated by power struggles, whether between nations, groups, or even individuals. Smiley's dilemma over Dieter, both friend and enemy, in le Carré's very first novel is insoluble: whatever Smiley does involves a betrayal. In *The Spy* individual loyalties are ruthlessly exploited by the Circus for national advantage in the Cold War struggle. Probably not since *The Spy* has le Carré pursued the theme of betrayal so wholeheartedly as in *The Little Drummer Girl,* in which the Israeli road to Khalil is paved with double standards.

In both novels, significantly, an intelligence organization uses an idealistic woman in a completely immoral way to achieve its goal, and Liz and Charlie further resemble each other in having espoused left-wing politics as a secular faith. Feminists could rightly make much of the callous male exploitation of both Liz and Charlie, especially as it is their potential for love and sympathy that is being manipulated so objectionably and destructively. The fact that the Palestinians also exploit women, such as the Dutch girl Larsen and, at least in intention, Charlie herself, in no way detracts from what the Israelis make Charlie endure. Admittedly, Kurtz gives her the chance to drop out of the operation more than once, but she is too addicted to both Joseph and her role in the theater of the real to deprive herself of what has become necessary. It is also true that Becker has to be pressured by Kurtz into undertaking the initial "seduction" of Charlie and the subsequent stage management, but although deeply divided he does exactly what is required of him. There is a crucial difference between Leamas and Joseph here. Whereas Leamas is as much a victim of the Circus's scheme as Liz and can in no way be held responsible for her exploitation, Joseph has complete knowledge of the operation from the start and, despite his misgivings, is as culpable as Kurtz for what is done to Charlie. The surprise ending, with Charlie and Joseph reunited, may consequently seem untypically optimistic and sentimental, although S. S. Prawer, in a lengthy review of *Smiley's People,* argued that the author himself, not only some of his characters as in the past, was now revealing a "sentimental streak,"[17] and in his otherwise commendatory review of *Smiley's People* A. Alvarez accused le Carré of tending to sentimentalize the women.[18]

During the operation, Joseph repeatedly assures Charlie that when it is over the Israelis will pick up all the pieces and put her world together again. But, like Humpty Dumpty, people are not easily reassembled after they have been smashed. Charlie's life since meeting Joseph cannot be unlived: her experiences cannot be erased nor can her profound sense of having become one of the living dead be easily cured. In the final chapter Charlie resumes her career in the ordinary theater, and it is while she is on stage, ironically, that she experiences the sensation of reentering the theater of the real when she sees Joseph in the audience, a reminder of how her involvement with the Israelis began. The fragile barriers between her inner and outer worlds dissolve, but despite le Carré's heavy qualifications the image with which the novel ends, of Charlie and Joseph "locked together" (p. 430), carries distinctly positive connotations of love conquering all. If this ending seems facile and inappropriate, it is partly because it can be taken as a vindication of Joseph and therefore, however mistakenly, of the Israeli position too. Perhaps what le Carré is suggesting here is that there is a stage beyond disaster and tragedy, at least for the survivors, and that, in the words of the old saying, "where there's life there's hope." Unlike Liz and Leamas, or Leo Harting, or Jerry Westerby, Charlie and Joseph do come out of the ordeal alive, even though as late as the last sentence but two of the novel Charlie repeatedly insists that she is dead. But le Carré's attempts to avoid a sentimental ending—for example, by ingeniously revitalizing a cliché in "he wanted her dead or alive" (p. 430)—is not wholly successful because this separation of the private world of human relationships from the public world of politics flies in the face of the reality depicted in the novel and in le Carré's fiction as a whole. For individuals to triumph over society, even in this limited way, is bound to strike a false note in a novel giving such conviction to the conspiratorial view of life and to the inexorable betrayal of love.

The Little Drummer Girl is likely to remain a much more controversial novel than most of le Carré's because its relative openness as a text, combined with a subject provoking violent controversy, makes the reader's role more complex and difficult than in the Smiley and Cold War novels. When a novel produces such diametrically opposed readings as *The Little Drummer Girl*, one is inclined to think that there is something seriously wrong with the book, or that external factors make it difficult for the novel to be appraised dispassionately. If the recent phase of the Israeli-Palestinian problem has given the novel an exceptional immediacy and urgency, it has also blurred its status as imaginative reality, not documentary truth. As time passes, it will become easier to see *The Little Drummer Girl* steadily and to see it whole, and the way we view it now may well be modified by le Carré's as yet unwritten fiction, just as the trilogy opened some readers' eyes to aspects of his novels of the 1960s. It is a commonplace that poets often produce their best work when young, whereas novelists usually produce theirs in middle age, and two of the founding fathers of the English novel, Defoe and Richardson, did not begin publishing fiction until they were over fifty. Le Carré is now in his early fifties, perhaps only halfway through his writing career, and has said that there are a number of books he is keen to write. At this stage any assessment of his work is inevitably provisional, but of the many postwar writers who have been attracted by the possibilities of spy fiction, he is far and away the one most deserving of serious attention. It is symptomatic of the contemporary literary scene that this enormously popular writer, who has stretched the imaginations of millions of readers while giving them pleasure, has been largely ignored by the academic establishment.[19]

Notes

Chapter 1

1. "The case of the hot writer," *New York Times Magazine*, 8 September 1974, p. 66.
2. Stefan Kanfer with Dean Fischer, "The Spy Who Came in for the Gold," *Time*, 3 October 1977, p. 52.
3. "The Secret World of John le Carré," *The Observer*, 3 February 1980, p. 35.
4. Ibid.
5. "Closing the File," *Radio Times*, 18–24 September 1982, p. 91.
6. "The Secret World of John le Carré," p. 35.
7. "Hard Cash and le Carré," in "Goings On," *Sunday Times*, 11 September 1977, p. 35.
8. "Tinker, Tailor, Soldier, Novelist," *The Times*, 6 September 1982, p. 7.
9. "Le Carré Interview," *The Times*, 10 September 1982, p. 9.
10. "The Secret World of John le Carré," p. 33.
11. Unpublished broadcast on ITV's *South Bank Show*, 27 March 1983.
12. "The Secret World of John le Carré," p. 33.
13. Ibid.
14. Ibid.
15. Ibid., p. 35. See also "The Real Smiley," in "The Times Diary," *The Times*, 27 October 1982, p. 10. In a strongly worded letter to *The Times*, "Unlicensed to Quote," 17 March 1981, p. 13, le Carré completely rejected the journalistic speculation, widely publicized in 1979, that Smiley was based on Sir Maurice Oldfield, a very distinguished figure in British Intelligence and Head of MI6 from 1973 to 1978: "I never heard of Sir Maurice, either by name or in any other way, until long after the name and character of George Smiley were in print."
16. Ibid.
17. "Hong Kong Was a 'Halfway House,' " *Newsagent and Bookshop*, 30 November 1978, p. 22.
18. Tim Heald, "The Lively Arts," *Radio Times*, 24–30 September 1977, p. 10.
19. "The Secret World of John le Carré," p. 35.
20. Ibid.
21. "The Case of the Hot Writer," p. 59.
22. "A Stellar Spymaster Returns," *Newsweek*, 7 March 1983, pp. 40–45.
23. *South Bank Show*.
24. Chapter 16 in *Bloody Murder: From the Detective Story to the Crime Novel* (London: Faber and Faber, 1972).
25. In *The Mystery Story*, edited by John Ball (San Diego: University of California, 1976; Harmondsworth: Penguin Books, 1978).
26. *Who's Who in Spy Fiction* (London: Elm Tree Books, 1977), p. 2.
27. Ibid., p. 3.
28. "The Spy Who Came in for the Gold," p. 49.
29. "Criminal Activities," *New Review*, 1, no. 4 (July 1974), p. 60.
30. "Hong Kong Was a 'Halfway House,' " p. 22.
31. "The Things a Spy Can Do—John le Carré Talking," *The Listener*, 22 January 1976, p. 90.
32. "The Case of the Hot Writer," p. 55.
33. *Tinker, Tailor, Soldier, Spy* (New York: Bantam Books, 1975), p. 187.

34. *The Literature of War* (London: Macmillan, 1978), p. 136.
35. "Between Two Worlds: The Novels of John le Carré," *South Atlantic Quarterly*, 79, no. 1 (Winter 1980), p. 17.
36. "John le Carré and England: A Spy-Eye's View," *Modern Fiction Studies*, 29, no. 3 (Autumn 1983), pp. 569–82. See also Richard W. Noland, "The Spy Fiction of John le Carré," *Clues* (now called *Ford Truck Times*), 1, no. 2 (1980), pp. 54–70. A copy of Noland's enthusiastic but balanced article did not reach the author until this book was in production, but it is one of the very few attempts to examine as a whole le Carré's contribution to spy fiction. It covers seven of the nine novels published at the time, omitting only *A Murder of Quality* and *The Naive and Sentimental Lover* as not being relevant to this theme, and contains some shrewd insights, especially into le Carré's treatment of postimperial England. After the present study had gone to press, the first full-length critical survey of spy fiction was published: John Atkins's *The British Spy Novel: Styles in Treachery* (London: John Calder; New York: Riverrun Press, 1984). This important though flawed study contains two short chapters on le Carré's fiction as well as incidental comment elsewhere.
37. When this book was in production, new information was released about the Anglo-American plan to precipitate a crisis in Albania by means of a coordinated resistance movement in 1949. The aim was to take the country out of Stalin's Communist empire, but the joint MI6-CIA scheme was a total failure because it was betrayed to Soviet Intelligence by Kim Philby, who as a senior MI6 official was actually in charge of the flow of information between MI6 and the CIA. The name of the man chosen to lead the British effort was none other than Smiley (Colonel David, not George), a professional soldier with the prestigious Royal Horse Guards who had been involved in secret work during World War II. Although le Carré's Smiley has nothing in common with the real-life Smiley except for his involvement in secret service operations, the name Smiley does have associations with British Intelligence in fact as well as in fiction.

Chapter 2

1. *Bloody Murder*, p. 233.
2. "Criminal Activities," p. 60.
3. "The Spy in Fact and Fiction," in *The Mystery Story*, p. 216 (Penguin).
4. Quoted in *Who's Who in Spy Fiction*, p. 109.
5. "John le Carré—The Writer Who Came in from the Cold," *The Listener*, 5 September 1974, p. 307.
6. "To Russia, with Greetings," *Encounter*, 26, no. 5 (May 1966), p. 6.
7. *Call for the Dead* (New York: Bantam Books, 1979), p. 1.
8. The American paperback here reads "We Never Close," which makes more sense to a non-British reader, although the chapter title is "We Never Closed," as in the British editions. Le Carré is alluding to a well-known phrase employed by a famous London theater for many years after World War II to advertise itself as the one that never closed during the Nazi blitz of the city.
9. "The Secret World of John le Carré," p. 33.
10. "Introduction," in *Poetry of the Thirties* (Harmondsworth: Penguin Books, 1964), especially p. 14.
11. "The Secret World of John le Carré," p. 33.
12. Ibid., p. 35.
13. Ibid., p. 33.
14. "The Things a Spy Can Do—John le Carré Talking," p. 90.
15. "Hong Kong Was a 'Halfway House,' " p. 23.
16. "A Stellar Spymaster Returns," p. 45.

17. Considering that le Carré is more precise about dates and times in this novel than in any other ("The post arrived at exactly 8.35. By 9.30 she was walking briskly down the drive, booted and spurred. She made straight for the railway station and caught the 9.52 to Victoria" [pp. 115–16]) it is perhaps surprising that he does not specify the year, and his chronology is not impeccable. The day on which Smiley begins his investigation into Fennan's death, "Wednesday, 4th January" (p. 8), fits 1961, not 1960, the year consistent with some internal evidence. The Fennans first met Dieter "in January, 1955" (p. 99), which is "five years ago" (p. 95), suggesting that the action opens in January 1960. Furthermore, when 4 January is a Wednesday, 15 February must also be a Wednesday, but the denouement at the Sheridan Theatre, Hammersmith takes place on "Thursday, 15th February" (p. 145), which fits 1962. These discrepancies are only observable with a microscope, but they may suggest that le Carré was less interested in the mechanics of the case, as a Golden Age crime novelist would have been, than in its human and political dimensions.
18. *Thrillers* (London: Edward Arnold, 1978), p. 40.
19. "At Last, It's Smiley," *Telegraph Sunday Magazine*, 21 October 1979, p. 108.

Chapter 3

1. *A Murder of Quality* (New York: Bantam Books, 1980), p. 27.
2. "The Decline and Fall of George Smiley: John le Carré and English Decency," *Southwest Review*, 66, no. 4 (Autumn 1981), pp. 377, 378.
3. The foreword is in the British paperback (Harmondsworth: Penguin Books, 1964), p. 7.
4. Quoted in *Who's Who in Spy Fiction*, p. 108.

Chapter 4

1. "To Russia, with Greetings," p. 3.
2. Ibid., p. 6.
3. "Criminal Activities," p. 60.
4. Quoted in Hugh Trevor-Roper, *The Philby Affair* (London: William Kimber, 1968), p. 61.
5. "The Secret World of John le Carré," p. 33.
6. "The Things a Spy Can Do—John le Carré Talking," p. 90.
7. "Le Carré's Circus: Lamplighters, Moles and Others of That Ilk," *The Listener*, 13 September 1979, p. 340.
8. *The Spy Who Came in from the Cold* (New York: Bantam Books, 1975), p. 17.
9. *The Literature of War*, p. 146.
10. "John le Carré: Murder and Loyalty," *New Republic*, 31 July 1976, p. 24.
11. "To Russia, with Greetings," p. 5.
12. Ibid.

Chapter 5

1. "John le Carré—The Writer Who Came in from the Cold," p. 307.
2. "To Russia, with Greetings," pp. 5–6.
3. "John le Carré: Murder and Loyalty," p. 23.
4. *The Looking Glass War* (New York: Bantam Books, 1975), p. 22.

5. *Anatomy of the Spy Thriller* (Montreal: McGill-Queen's University Press, 1977), pp. 47–54.
6. *Philby* (London: Sphere Books, 1977), p. 33.
7. "Hong Kong Was a 'Halfway House,' " p. 23.
8. *Philby*, pp. 29–30.
9. *My Silent War* (London: Granada, 1969), p. 23.
10. *The Looking-Glass War* (London: Pan Books, 1966), p. 22.
11. Ibid., p. 7.
12. *MI5* (London: Bodley Head, 1981), p. 78. The other two books are: *A Matter of Trust: MI5, 1945–72* (London: Weidenfeld and Nicolson, 1982) and *MI6: British Secret Intelligence Service Operations, 1909–45* (London: Weidenfeld and Nicolson, 1983). With Richard Deacon, West has also published *Spy!* (London: BBC, 1980), based on a television series.
13. *South Bank Show.*

Chapter 6

1. *A Small Town in Germany* (New York: Dell, 1969), p. 16.
2. "From Bonn, a Literary Bundle," *The Times*, 2 November 1968, p. 22.
3. *Requiem for a Nun* (London: Chatto and Windus, 1953), p. 85.

Chapter 7

1. "What Ritual Is Being Observed Tonight?", *Saturday Evening Post*, 2 November 1968, p. 64.
2. "Le Carré's Circus: Lamplighters, Moles and Others of That Ilk," p. 339.
3. Quoted in "Points from Publishers," *The Bookseller*, 11 September 1971, p. 1566.
4. *The Naive and Sentimental Lover* (New York: Bantam Books, 1978), p. 253.
5. *The Little Drummer Girl* (New York: Alfred A. Knopf, 1983), p. 8.
6. *The Honourable Schoolboy* (New York: Bantam Books, 1978), p. 18.
7. "Life without Roots," *The Times*, 4 July 1974, p. 10.
8. "Tinker, Tailor, Soldier, Novelist," p. 7.
9. "Le Carré's Circus: Lamplighters, Moles and Others of That Ilk," p. 339.
10. *Tinker, Tailor, Soldier, Spy* (New York: Bantam Books, 1975), p. 215. The American edition contains 39 chapters, the British edition only 38, but there is no substantive difference. The last few pages of chapter 38 in the British version are grouped as a separate chapter in the American version.
11. "National Myths," *Encounter*, 54, no. 6 (June 1980), p. 58.
12. *South Bank Show.*
13. "At Last, It's Smiley," pp. 108, 111. The television serialization of *Tinker, Tailor, Soldier, Spy* prompted a strange correspondence in *The Guardian* in October and November 1979 concerning the identity of the mole. On 7 November le Carré made his own ironic contribution to this bizarre and facetious speculation under the heading, "Tinker, Tailor and the Mole that never was" (p. 14).
14. "Hard Cash and le Carré," p. 35. In an interview with Godfrey Hodgson published in the following month, le Carré made the same point: "I have come to think of *Tinker, Tailor* and this book [*The Honourable Schoolboy*] and the next two—as I think it will be—as a single continuing novel" ("The Secret Life of John le Carré," *Washington Post Book World*, 9 October 1977, p. E1).
15. "Le Carré's Circus: Lamplighters, Moles and Others of That Ilk," p. 339.
16. "The Things a Spy Can Do—John le Carré Talking," p. 90.
17. "The Spy Who Came in for the Gold," p. 51.

18. *After Long Silence* (London: Collins, 1983), p. 62.
19. "The Secret World of John le Carré," p. 33.
20. *Philby*, p. 29.
21. *The Real Spy World* (London: Weidenfeld and Nicolson, 1974), p. 29.
22. *The Philby Affair*, p. 60.
23. *Philby*, pp. 41–42.
24. "It Was a Man," *New Statesman*, 8 February 1980, p. 209.
25. "Triple Agents?", *London Magazine*, 14, no. 4 (October/November 1974), p. 75.
26. *The Literature of War*, p. 150.
27. *Anatomy of the Spy Thriller*, p. 212.
28. *Philby*, p. 35.
29. Ibid., p. 31.
30. "National Myths," p. 58.
31. "John le Carré: Murder and Loyalty," p. 25.
32. "Between Two Worlds: The Novels of John le Carré," pp. 28, 33.

Chapter 8

1. *The Honourable Schoolboy* (New York: Bantam Books, 1978), p. 67.
2. "Hong Kong Was a 'Halfway House,' " p. 22.
3. "Triple Agents?", pp. 73–77.
4. During World War II a man with a most unusual name very similar to that of le Carré's fictional character was a member of MI6: Charles de Salis. See Nigel West, *MI6: British Secret Intelligence Service Operations, 1909–45*, p. 133.
5. The assumption that Fawn shoots Jerry from one of the Cousins' helicopters seems safe enough, but le Carré's description of Jerry's killer is slightly tinged with ambiguity: "A single figure remained in the open doorway, looking down, and perhaps it was Fawn, for he looked dark and mad" (p. 524). But if the "single figure" is not Fawn, it is difficult to see why le Carré mentions him by name.
6. "Local Colour," *The Spectator*, 10 September 1977, p. 20.
7. "George's Black Grail," *The Times*, 7 February 1980, p. 12.
8. "Estonian Connection," *Financial Times*, 2 February 1980, p. 10.
9. "Half-angels versus Half-devils," *The Observer*, 3 February 1980, p. 39.

Chapter 9

1. "Closing the File," p. 90.
2. *Smiley's People* (New York: Bantam Books, 1980), p. 125.
3. "Spymasters and Spy-monsters," *The Spectator*, 9 February 1980, pp. 16–17.
4. In *A Murder of Quality* Ann's childhood is associated with Carne in Dorset, but in *Smiley's People* it is linked with what she calls "Harry's Cornish Heap" (p. 292) near Penzance in Cornwall. An interesting feature of *Smiley's People* is that three of its settings, Hampstead, rural Cornwall near Penzance, and the Berne region of Switzerland, correspond to the three places where le Carré himself has homes and spends most of his time.

Chapter 10

1. "A Stellar Spymaster Returns," p. 44.
2. "Recent Fiction," *Illustrated London News*, May 1983, p. 76.
3. "A Book to Be Buried with," *Sunday Times*, 27 March 1983, p. 42.

4. "John le Carré—The Writer Who Came in from the Cold," p. 307.
5. "The Things a Spy Can Do—John le Carré Talking," p. 90.
6. *South Bank Show.*
7. *The Little Drummer Girl* (New York: Alfred A. Knopf, 1983), p. 181.
8. "Memories of a Vanished Land," *The Observer*, 13 June 1982, p. 10.
9. *South Bank Show.*
10. "Drumming up Hatred," *The Spectator*, 16 April 1983, p. 9.
11. "A Stellar Spymaster Returns," p. 41.
12. "Fiction," *City Limits*, 1 April 1983, p. 22.
13. Two recent histories of Israeli Intelligence are Dennis Eisenberg, Uri Dan, and Eli Landau's *The Mossad: Israel's Secret Intelligence Service* (New York and London: Paddington Press, 1978) and Stewart Steven's *The Spymasters of Israel* (London: Hodder and Stoughton, 1981).
14. "Romance of a Charlie," *The Times*, 31 March 1983, p. 13.
15. "In the Theater of the Real," *Newsweek*, 7 March 1983, p. 43.
16. "The Secret Life of John le Carré," *Observer Magazine*, 6 March 1983, p. 21.
17. "The Circus and its Conscience," *Times Literary Supplement*, 8 February 1980, p. 131.
18. "Half-angels versus Half-devils," p. 39.
19. When this book was in production, an interview-article by Norman Moss about le Carré's model for Charlie, his half-sister Charlotte Cornwell (see p. 183), appeared in the *Telegraph Sunday Magazine* (15 July 1984). The title, "Charlie: Fact and Fiction," indicates that it is partly about the relationship between Charlotte Cornwell and the fictional Charlie. For the student of le Carré the most interesting revelation concerns the impact Charlotte's performance as Rosalind in *As You Like It* had on le Carré when he saw a Royal Shakespeare Company production of the play in Padstow. Moss quotes le Carré as saying: "I began the story thinking I would write about a boy, between 19 and 25, who got caught up in a terrorist movement. . . . It was when I went away from that performance in Padstow that I decided that it was going to be a girl. And Charlotte was there as a starting point" (p. 17). At the beginning of the novel Charlie is learning the part of Rosalind for a forthcoming tour of *As You Like It.* Moss also notes that when le Carré "was writing *The Little Drummer Girl* Charlotte briefed him on an actress's life, and also went over it chapter by chapter."

Bibliography

1. *Works by John le Carré*

A. NOVELS

(Dates are of first editions. Details of editions quoted in this book are contained in the Notes.)

Call for the Dead. London: Victor Gollancz, 1961; New York: Walker, 1962. Published as *The Deadly Affair*; Harmondsworth: Penguin Books, 1966.

A Murder of Quality. London: Victor Gollancz, 1962; New York: Walker, 1963.

The Spy Who Came in from the Cold. London: Victor Gollancz, 1963; New York, Coward-McCann, 1964.

The Looking-Glass War. London: William Heinemann; New York: Coward-McCann, 1965. (*The Looking Glass War* in the USA.)

A Small Town in Germany. London: William Heinemann; New York: Coward-McCann, 1968.

The Naive and Sentimental Lover. London: Hodder and Stoughton, 1971; New York: Alfred A. Knopf, 1972.

Tinker Tailor Soldier Spy. London: Hodder and Stoughton; New York: Alfred A. Knopf, 1974. (*Tinker, Tailor, Soldier, Spy* in the USA.)

The Honourable Schoolboy. London: Hodder and Stoughton; New York: Alfred A. Knopf, 1977.

Smiley's People. London: Hodder and Stoughton; New York: Alfred A. Knopf, 1980. In 1979 a limited fine edition, privately printed for members of the First Edition Society, was issued by the Franklin Library.

The Little Drummer Girl. London: Hodder and Stoughton; New York: Alfred A. Knopf, 1983.

B. SHORT STORIES

"Dare I Weep, Dare I Mourn?", *Saturday Evening Post*, 28 January 1967, pp. 54, 56, 60.

"What Ritual Is Being Observed Tonight?", *Saturday Evening Post*, 2 November 1968, pp. 60–62, 64–65.

C. MISCELLANEOUS NON-FICTION

"To Russia, with Greetings," *Encounter*, 26, no. 5 (May 1966), pp. 3–6.

"The Spy to End Spies," *Encounter*, 27, no. 5 (November 1966), pp. 88–89;

review of *The Case of Richard Sorge* by Frederick William Deakin and Richard Storry.

"Introduction," in Bruce Page, David Leitch, and Phillip Knightley, *Philby: The Spy Who Betrayed a Generation*. London: André Deutsch, 1968. Revised edition, Harmondsworth: Penguin Books, 1969.

"At Last, It's Smiley," *Telegraph Sunday Magazine*, 21 October 1979, pp. 105, 108, 111, 114.

"Introduction," in Don McCullin, *Hearts of Darkness*. London: Secker and Warburg, 1980. A version of this essay appeared as "McCullin's World," *Sunday Times Magazine*, 26 October 1980, pp. 50–51, 53, 55, 57–58, 61.

"Memories of a Vanished Land," *The Observer*, 13 June 1982, pp. 9–10.

"Exiles in the White Hotel," *The Observer*, 26 June 1983, pp. 25–26.

"The Betrayal," *The Observer*, 3 July 1983, pp. 23–24.

"Hughes of Hong Kong," *Sunday Times*, 8 January 1984, p. 9.

D. LETTERS TO THE PRESS

"Tinker, Tailor and the Mole that never was," *The Guardian*, November 1979, p. 14.

"Unlicensed to Quote," *The Times*, 17 March 1981, p. 13.

"World Service," *The Times*, 1 July 1981, p. 15.

"Optical Illusion," *The Times*, 22 March 1982, p. 11.

2. *Major Interviews and Profiles*

Interview with Michael Dean, "John le Carré—The Writer Who Came in from the Cold," *The Listener*, 5 September 1974, pp. 306–7.

James Cameron, "The Case of the Hot Writer," *New York Times Magazine*, 8 September 1974, pp. 55, 57, 59, 61, 64, 66, 68.

Interview with Melvyn Bragg, "The Things a Spy Can Do—John le Carré Talking," *The Listener*, 22 January 1976, p. 90.

Stefan Kanfer with Dean Fischer, "The Spy Who Came in for the Gold," *Time*, 3 October 1977, pp. 48–53.

Interview with Godfrey Hodgson, 'The Secret Life of John le Carré," *Washington Post Book World*, 9 October 1977, pp. E1, E6.

Interview with Michael Barber, "Hong Kong Was a 'Halfway House,' " *Newsagent and Bookshop*, 30 November 1978, pp. 22–23.

Interview with Paul Vaughan, "Le Carré's Circus: Lamplighters, Moles and Others of That Ilk," *The Listener*, 13 September 1979, pp. 339–40.

Interview with Miriam Gross, "The Secret World of John le Carré," *The Observer*, 3 February 1980, pp. 33, 35.

Nicholas Wapshott, "Tinker, Tailor, Soldier, Novelist," *The Times*, 6 September 1982, p. 7.

Hugh McIlvanney, "The Secret Life of John le Carré," *Observer Magazine*, 6 March 1983, pp. 18–19, 21–22.

Alexis Gelber with Edward Behr, "A Stellar Spymaster Returns," *Newsweek*, 7 March 1983, pp. 40–41, 43–45 (incorporates Peter S. Prescott's review of *The Little Drummer Girl* on pp. 42–43).

3. *Selected Criticism on John le Carré*

(A number of reviews of individual novels are cited in the Notes but are not included here.)

Atkins, John. "The World of John le Carré" and "Le Carré's People," Chapters 16 and 17 in *The British Spy Novel: Styles in Treachery*. London: John Calder; New York: Riverrun Press, 1984.

Barzun, Jacques. "Meditations on the Literature of Spying," *American Scholar*, 34 (1965), pp. 167–78.

Gadney, Reg. "Triple Agents?", *London Magazine*, 14, no. 4 (October/November 1974), pp. 73–77.

Grella, George. "John le Carré: Murder and Loyalty," *New Republic*, 31 July 1976, pp. 23–25.

Halperin, John. "Between Two Worlds: The Novels of John le Carré," *South Atlantic Quarterly*, 79, no. 1 (Winter 1980), pp. 17–37.

Jeffares, A. Norman. "John le Carré," in *Contemporary Novelists*, ed. James Vinson. Third edition, London: Macmillan, 1982, pp. 381–82.

McCormick, Donald. "John le Carré," in *Who's Who in Spy Fiction*. London: Elm Tree Books, 1977, pp. 108–12.

Monaghan, David. "John le Carré and England: A Spy-Eye's View," *Modern Fiction Studies*, 29, no. 3 (Autumn 1983), pp. 569–82.

Noland, Richard W. "The Spy Fiction of John le Carré," *Clues* (now called *Ford Truck Times*, 1, no. 2 (1980), pp. 54–70.

Rothberg, Abraham. "The Decline and Fall of George Smiley," *Southwest Review*, 66, no. 4 (Autumn 1981), pp. 377–92.

Rutherford, Andrew. "The Spy as Hero: Le Carré and the Cold War," Chapter 6 in *The Literature of War: Five Studies in Heroic Virtue*. London: Macmillan, 1978.

Symons, Julian. "Criminal Activities," *New Review*, 1, no. 4 (July 1974), pp. 60–62.

Index

Allingham, Margery, 14
Alvarez, A., 163, 210
Ambler, Eric, 10
Apostles, The, 122
Arafat, Yasser, 187
Aristophanes, 46
Arnold, Matthew, 22, 158
Auden, W.H., 60, 161

Baader, Andreas, 99, 196
Ball, John, 37
Balzac, Honoré de, 5
Barber, Michael, 6, 11, 24, 81, 139
Beach, Thomas, 3
Begin, Menachem, 187, 192
Behan, Brendan, 114
Behr, Edward, 7
Bell, Julian, 122
Ben-Gurion, David, 205
Bettaney, Michael, 61
Bevin, Ernest, 102
Black September, 196
Blake, George, 62
Blunt, Anthony, 61–62, 119, 120, 121, 122
Bonhoeffer, Dietrich, 108
Booker, Christopher, 174
Boyle, Andrew, 120
Bragg, Melvyn, 4, 7, 11, 24, 64, 94, 117, 118, 119, 181, 182, 184, 187, 191
Brecht, Bertolt, 20
Brooke, Rupert, 83, 171
Browning, Robert, 192
Buchan, John, 10, 15, 143
Buñuel, Luis, 158
Burgess, Guy, 61, 120, 122, 129
Burton, Richard, 68
Byron, George Gordon, Lord, 36

Call for the Dead, 1, 2, 6, 7, 10, 14–39, 40, 41, 43, 44, 47, 51, 57, 59, 63, 64, 65, 66, 68, 73, 79, 86, 96, 115, 119, 123, 124, 128, 134, 136, 147, 164, 166, 168, 171, 175, 182, 193, 209; film version (*The Deadly Affair*), 39; televised extract, 112
Cameron, James, 1, 2, 7, 12
Carré, Mathilde, 3
Carroll, Lewis, 81, 88
Cary, Joyce, 114
Castro, Fidel, 62
Caute, David, 122
Cavell, Edith, 91
Cawelti, John G., 10
Chamberlain, Neville, 109
Chandler, Raymond (Philip Marlowe), 14, 25, 38, 58, 116
Christie, Agatha (Hercule Poirot), 14, 25, 116
Churchill, Winston, 67
CIA, 19, 62, 119, 141, 191
Cohn-Bendit, Daniel, 183
Cold War politics and intelligence work, 61–63, 67–68, 120–22, 169–70
Collins, Wilkie, 163
Conan Doyle, Arthur (Sherlock Holmes), 2, 14, 25, 29, 79, 115, 164, 172
Conrad, Joseph, 5, 10, 11, 29, 36, 138, 139, 158, 163, 192, 209
Copeland, Miles, 121
Cornford, John, 26
Cornwell, Charlotte, 183, 217
Cornwell, David John Moore, *see* le Carré, John
Cornwell, Olive, 4
Cornwell, Ronnie, 4–5

Cornwell, Tony, 4
Crime Writers' Association Gold Dagger Award, 59, 139
Cuban Missile Crisis, 62, 67, 84
Cumming, Mansfield, 65, 91

Deadly Affair, The, see *Call for the Dead*
Dean, Michael, 16, 78, 182
Defoe, Daniel, 211
Dickens, Charles, 36, 139
Dostoevsky, Fyodor, 10
Dubček, Alexander, 131

Eisenhower, Dwight D., 62
Eliot, T.S., 23, 80
Emerson, Sally, 182
Encounter, 60
Ensslin, Gudrun, 99
Eton College, 6–7, 45, 52, 94, 146
Eustace, Valerie Jane, 8

Faulkner, William, 107
FBI, 61
Fell, Barbara, 62
Fielding, Henry, 16, 100
Fleming Ian (James Bond), 10, 15–16, 17, 20, 29, 38, 60, 63, 67–68, 125, 142, 145, 147
Forster, E.M., 122, 137
Forsyth, Frederick, 80
Fowles, John, 5, 9, 12
Franco, Francisco, 26, 122
Freud, Sigmund, 60
Fuchs, Klaus, 22, 61

Gadney, Reg, 129, 140
Gaskell, Elizabeth, 52
Gazit, Shlomo, 184
Gelber, Alexis, 7
Georg, Stefan, 20
George, Saint, 2, 15, 176
Gilbert, Michael, 8, 14
Goethe, Wolfgang von, 20, 36, 146
Golding, William, 9
Gollancz, Victor, 2
Gouzenko, Igor, 22
Green, Vivian, 5
Greene, Graham, 3, 5, 7, 9, 10, 100, 121, 138, 141, 154, 157, 158, 163
Grella, George, 72, 79, 137
Gross, Miriam, 1, 2, 4, 5, 23, 24, 64, 121
Guinness, Alec, 117–18

Halperin, John, 12, 137
Hammett, Dashiell, 38, 163
Hardy, Thomas, 4, 44–45, 57
Harper, Ralph, 10
Hearst, Patty, 204
Hegel, Wilhelm Friedrich, 93
Hemingway, Ernest, 138
Herder, Johann Gottfried von, 20
Hesse, Hermann, 20, 29, 113
Hitchens, Christopher, 189
Hitler, Adolf, 5, 22, 33, 61, 76, 83, 98, 99, 106, 107, 108, 109, 167
Hollis, Roger, 120
Honourable Schoolboy, The, 1, 2, 3, 14, 113, 115, 118, 119, 129, 136, 138–63, 164, 165–66, 169, 171, 172, 175, 178, 182, 183, 184, 190, 192, 193, 194, 196
Houghton, Harry, 62
Hughes, Richard (Dick), 142, 183

Ivanov, Eugene, 63

James Tait Black Memorial Prize, 139
Jonson, Ben, 49
Joyce, James, 113, 148–49

Keating, H.R.F., 100, 115
Keats, John, 20, 115
Keeler, Christine, 63
Kennaway, James, 113–14
Kennaway, Susan, 113
Kennedy, John F., 62
Keynes, John Maynard, 122
KGB, 63, 121
Khrushchev, Nikita, 62
Kipling, Rudyard, 145

Kleist, Heinrich von, 20
Knight, Maxwell, 7
Knight, Stephen, 10
Knightley, Phillip, 81, 121

Lawrence, D.H., 188
Lawrence, T.E., 132
le Caron, Henri, 3
le Carré, John (individual novels and the trilogy listed separately under titles)
"At Last, It's Smiley," 39, 118
"The Betrayal," 187–88
biographical information, 4–8, 113–14
characterization through speech idiom, 129–30, 139–40
on his childhood, 4
classical detective formula, 14–15, 24–25, 44, 46, 58, 128
critical reputation, 8–13, 162–63
cryptonyms, 178
"Dare I Weep, Dare I Mourn?", 111
drawings for Knight's *Talking Birds*, 7
The End of the Line, 112
on English conservatism, 94
essays, 8, 60, 76, 77, 78, 81, 121, 133
"Exiles in the White Hotel," 187
expansive approach to narration, 115, 119, 126–27, 128–30, 138–39, 141–42, 179
film versions of novels, 39, 68, 81
on George Smiley, 23–24, 117–18
"Hughes of Hong Kong," 142
on Ian Fleming (James Bond), 16, 60
The Incongruous Spy, 59
"Introduction to McCullin's *Hearts of Darkness*, 8
"Introduction" to Page, Leitch, and Knightley's *Philby*, 8, 81, 121, 133
journalism, 8, 39, 118, 142, 186–88
Le Carré Omnibus, The, 59
literary influences, 5–6, 79
on *The Little Drummer Girl*, 181, 204
on *The Looking Glass War*, 78
"Memories of a Vanished Land," 186–87
morality vs. expediency, 71–72, 74–77, 93, 108–10, 150, 159–62, 177–78, 191, 209–10
on *The Naive and Sentimental Lover*, 114
naming of characters, 2
narrative methods, 16–17, 35, 40, 69, 72, 100–1, 125–28, 141–45, 165–66, 189–90
on the Palestinian problem, 184–85, 186–88
pen name, 1–3
on Philby, 121, 133
on plausibility in fiction, 64
on politics and intelligence work, 24, 60, 77, 81
on public schools and social class, 6–7, 52
on *The Quest for Karla*, 118
romance and myth (including Arthurian legends), 115, 117, 136–37, 148–49, 171–75, 178–80, 197–99
satire (caricature, irony), 6, 22–23, 27, 30, 46–51, 68, 79, 104–5, 127, 154–55
short stories, 111–12
on *Smiley's People*, 165
social class, 51–55, 102–4
on spy fiction, 10–12
spy slang, 119
on television adaptations of his fiction, 117–18
television writing, 112
on *Tinker, Tailor, Soldier, Spy*, 116

"To Russia, with Greetings," 60, 76, 77, 78
transformation of spy fiction, 15–17, 19, 20, 22, 26–27, 29, 37–38, 67–68, 80, 94–95
"Unlicensed to Quote," 213
"World Service," 60
Le Queux, William, 15
Leitch, David, 81, 121
Lippmann, Walter, 61
Literary Gazette (Moscow), 7, 60, 78
Literary Review, 189
Little Drummer Girl, The, 4, 6, 7, 8, 112, 113, 115, 116, 117, 118, 181–212, 217
Lonsdale, Gordon, 62, 63
Looking Glass War, The, 6, 7, 60, 62, 63, 78–95, 96, 97, 101, 108, 109, 113, 115, 136, 141, 143, 145, 147, 166, 169, 171, 178; film version, 81
Lumet, Sidney, 39

McCormick, Donald, 8, 9
McCullin, Don, 8
McIlvanney, Hugh, 204
Maclean, Donald, 22, 61, 120
Macmillan, Harold, 63
Malraux, André, 138
Marcuse, Herbert, 99
Marlowe, Christopher, 36
Marx, Karl, 93, 109, 119
Mason, James, 39
Maugham, W. Somerset, 7, 10, 138
May, Alan Nunn, 61
Meinhof, Ulrike, 99, 196, 201
Meir, Golda, 170
Melville, Herman, 172
Merry Bruce, 10, 80, 133
MI5 (British Security Service), 7, 61, 62, 63, 79, 119, 120
MI6 (British Secret Intelligence Service), 7, 19, 61, 62, 63, 65, 79, 90, 91, 95, 121, 155
Molody, Konon, 62
Monagham, David, 12
Moore, G.E., 122
Mosley, Oswald, 98
Mossad, 191
Murder of Quality, A, 6–7, 19, 40–58, 59, 63, 68, 73, 96, 103, 119, 123, 127, 128, 147, 217
Mystery Writers of America's Edgar Allan Poe Award, 59

Naive and Sentimental Lover, The, 6, 9, 12, 96, 112, 113–15, 118, 138, 181, 182, 209
Newsweek, 7, 24, 181, 188

Oakes, Philip, 3, 118
Oates, L.E.G., 143
Observer, The, 186
Oldfield, Maurice, 137, 213
Opitz, Martin, 168
Orwell, George, 61, 70
OSS, 155

Page, Bruce, 81, 121
Palestinian Liberation Organization (PLO), 186–87
Palmer, Jerry, 10, 38, 57
Paul, Saint, 26
Paulin, Tom, 117, 137
Petrarch, 175
Penkovsky, Oleg, 63
Philby, Harold (Kim), 8, 19, 61, 62, 63, 81, 85, 120, 121, 122, 129, 132, 133, 137, 214
Picasso, Pablo, 189
Pierson, Frank, 81
Pincher, Chapman, 120–21
Pontecorvo, Bruno, 61
Pope, Alexander, 189
Portland Spy Ring, 62, 63
Poujade, Pierre, 98
Powell, Anthony, 162
Powers, Gary, 62
Prawer, S.S., 210
Prescott, Peter S., 198
Profumo, John, 63
Proust, Marcel, 183
Pryce-Jones, David, 188